Springer Series on PSYCHIATRY

Carl Eisdorfer, PhD, MD, Series Editor

1
Stress and Human Health
Analysis and Implications of Research

> **Glen R. Elliott, PhD, MD, and**
> **Carl Eisdorfer, PhD, MD**
> Editors

2
Treatment of Psychopathology
in the Aging

> **Carl Eisdorfer, PhD, MD, and**
> **William E. Fann, MD**
> Editors

3
Geropsychiatric Diagnostics
and Treatment
Multidimensional Approaches

> **Manfred Bergener, MD**
> Editor

4
The Psychobiology
of Obsessive–Compulsive Disorder

> **Joseph Zohar, MD,**
> **Thomas Insel, MD, and**
> **Steven Rasmussen, MD**
> Editors

Joseph Zohar, MD, is currently an Associate Professor of Psychiatry in Ben-Gurion University, Deputy Director of Beer-Sheva Mental Health Center, and Director, Obsessive-Compulsive Clinic. He graduated from Tel-Aviv University Sackler School of Medicine in 1973, trained in psychiatry at the University of Washington, Seattle and at Jerusalem Mental Health Center, Israel where he was the director of the Treatment Resistant Unit. In 1974 Dr. Zohar won the Fogarty International Research Fellowship Award and joined the laboratory of Dr. Dennis Murphy at the National Institute of Mental Health, Bethesda, Maryland where he was acting director of the Obsessive-Compulsive Clinic. Dr. Zohar along with Dr. Thomas Insel are the recipients of the A. E. Bennet Award for their work entitled "Obsessive–Compulsive Disorder: Psychobiological Approaches to Diagnosis, Treatment and Pathophysiology." Dr. Zohar served as chairperson on the panel for obsessive–compulsive disorder of the American Psychiatric Association Task Force on Treatments of Psychiatric Disorder and as a member of the DSM-IV Obsessive–Compulsive Disorder subcommittee. He is the author of more than 75 scientific papers and edited three books, the latest of which is entitled *Current Treatments of Obsessive–Compulsive Disorder.*

Thomas Insel, MD, is currently a senior staff fellow in the Section on Comparative Studies of Brain and Behavior at the National Institute of Mental Health in Bethesda, Maryland. He graduated from Boston University School of Medicine in 1974, trained in psychiatry at the University of California, San Francisco, and joined the NIMH in 1979. He began studying obsessive–compulsive disorder in his first year at NIMH by focusing on a wide range of questions from pharmacologic response to family systems in OCD patients. Along with Dr. Dennis Murphy, he completed the first controlled pharmacologic study of OCD patients in the U.S. and has contributed much to the increased focus on OCD in biological psychiatry. In addition, Dr. Insel is a leader in research on the neurobiology of attatchment behavior in rodents and nonhuman primates. His laboratory work includes studies of maternal behavior, sex behavior, and the response of infants to maternal separation. He is the author of more than 125 scientific articles in both psychiatric and neuroscientific journals.

Steven Rasmussen, MD, is currently an Associate Professor of Psychiatry and Human Behavior at Brown University and the Associate Medical Director at Butler Hospital in Providence, Rhode Island. He also directs the Obsessive Disorders Clinic at Butler. He graduated from Brown University Program in Medicine in 1977 and completed his psychiatric residency at Yale University, where he was a Biologic Science Training Fellow. After two years in the Public Health Service as Director of the North Kingdom Mental Health Center in Vermont, he joined the faculty at Brown, where he has been since 1983. Dr Rasmussen is a member of the DSM–IV subcommittee on OCD and is on the Scientific Advisory Board of the OCD Foundation. His research has centered on the phenomenology and treatment of OCD.

THE
PSYCHOBIOLOGY OF
OBSESSIVE–COMPULSIVE
DISORDER

Joseph Zohar, MD
Thomas Insel, MD
Steven Rasmussen, MD
Editors

SPRINGER PUBLISHING COMPANY
NEW YORK

Copyright © 1991 by Springer Publishing Company, Inc.

Springer Publishing Company, Inc.
536 Broadway
New York, NY 10012-3955

91 92 93 94 95 / 5 4 3 2 1

Library of Congress Cataloging-in-Publication Data

The Psychobiology of obsessive–compulsive disorder / Joseph Zohar,
    Thomas R. Insel, Steven A. Rasmussen, editors.
      p. cm. — (Springer series on psychiatry ; 4)
    Includes bibliographical references and index.
    ISBN 0-8261-7520-1
    1. Obsessive–compulsive disorder. 2. Biological psychiatry.
I. Zohar, Joseph. II. Insel, Thomas R., 1951– . III. Rasmussen,
Steven A. IV. Series.
    [DNLM: 1. Obsessive–Compulsive Disorder. W1 SP685SEM v. 4 / WM
176 P9735]
RC533.P75 1991
616.85'227—dc20
DNLM/DLC
for Library of Congress   91-4606
                                                  CIP

Printed in the United States of America

Contents

Preface

Ten years ago this volume would have been nearly inconceivable. Obsessive–compulsive disorder, at that time, connoted a rare, treatment–resistant neurosis for which there was scarcely an experimental literature, let alone a psychobiological one. Two developments in the past decade have been responsible for transforming how we see this disorder. First, a spate of well-controlled studies demonstrated that many obsessive–compulsive disorder patients responded to specific behavioral and pharmacologic treatments. These selective antiobsessional treatments have not only provided a new therapeutic optimism, they have helped to clarify the boundaries of this syndrome. A second major development has been the emerging epidemiologic evidence that obsessive–compulsive disorder is far more common than previously thought. Indeed, the most frequently quoted prevalence estimates in the United States are above 2.0%, perhaps 40–50 times more common than traditional estimates cited in psychiatric textbooks. Obsessive–compulsive disorder has not actually become more prevalent, but perhaps our ability to recognize the disorder even when it is obscured by secretiveness or comorbid diagnoses has improved severalfold.

The advent of effective antiobsessional treatments, along with the increased recognition of the disorder have led to a surge in research on various facets of obsessive–compulsive disorder, with at least a 300% increase in the monthly number of scientific publications in the past decade. Although there have been several recent books on obsessive–compulsive disorder, this is the first devoted to critically reviewing the psychobiologic research. The need for such a book is suggested by several important questions generated by the first generation of psychobiologic studies. For instance, family history studies have pointed to a genetic component—could this be an abnormality of a single gene locus and, if so, what other disorders might be affected by this same gene? Imaging data has suggested that frontal-striatal-thalamic circuits are involved in obsessive–compulsive disorder—are these metabolic abnormalities associated features or could they represent causative aspects of this disorder? Serotonin has been implicated in the antiobsessional pharmacologic response—is serotonin involved in the pathophysiology of obsessive–compulsive disorder? Is this essentially a neurologic illness with obsessions representing psychological tics and compulsions complex stereotypies or is this mostly a learned behavior with no discrete localizing lesion? Is this disorder heterogeneous with multiple etiologies?

These are a few of the questions addressed in the present volume. Each author was asked to provide not only a detailed summary of the research methods and results in a specific area, but also to evaluate current problems and potential future directions. As in any area that is changing rapidly, some of these summaries will be outdated by the time this volume goes to press. Hopefully, the conceptual approaches described and the critical appraisal of current problems will prove useful throughout the next generation of studies in this area.

The first three chapters of the book are introductory. Chapter 1 provides an historical overview linking psychodynamic, phenomenologic, neurobiological, and behavioral approaches to obsessive–compulsive disorder. Chapter 2 reviews clinical and epidemiologic aspects with an emphasis on subtypes. Developing a taxonomy for obsessive–compulsive disorder remains one of the most important clinical tasks that will guide psychobiologic research. In Chapter 3, the major rating scales for obsessive–compulsive disorder research are described, including their virtues and shortcomings (an appendix provides the various scales).

The different psychobiological approaches are then described in Chapters 4 through 8. In Chapter 4, a review of the genetic approaches examines the possibility that obsessive–compulsive disorder and Tourette's syndrome may share a common genotype. Chapter 5 describes results of brain imaging studies with obsessive–compulsive disorder patients and proposes a functional neuropathology for the syndrome. Chapter 6 reviews a range of neurologic studies in obsessive–compulsive disorder, from electrophysiologic responses to soft signs, in search of some common evidence for a neurologic lesion. In Chapter 7, various biologic markers are examined in obsessive–compulsive disorder patients, with the goal of relating this disorder to other forms of psychopathology. Finally, Chapter 8 describes the various pharmacologic challenge studies that have been tried, with particular reference to the effects of serotonergic agents in obsessive–compulsive disorder.

We have included three additional chapters which we believe will prove useful for the clinician, the clinical researcher, and the basic researcher interested in animal models of obsessive–compulsive disorder. Chapter 9 critically reviews the pharmacologic approaches to treatment, including practical guidelines for the use of antiobsessional compounds. Chapter 10 has a more theoretical bent—examining the neurobiology of displacement behavior and aggression as possible analogues of compulsive rituals. Chapter 11 is a grand synthesis—an attempt to integrate the biochemical, neuropsychological, psychoanalytic, behavioral, and neuroanatomic findings with our growing understanding of the subtypes of obsessive–compulsive disorder.

At this stage, the research described does not provide any definitive answers—it refines questions and it suggests new ways of understanding the experience of obsessive–compulsive disorder. Edison once described his life's work as "a splash of insight and an ocean of hard work." We believe this book demonstrates that the obsessive–compulsive disorder field has had a few splashes of insight, but several oceans of work will now be required to link these very preliminary psychobiological results with clinical phenomena. To the extent that this volume helps new researchers to follow this path, it will be a success.

JOSEPH ZOHAR
THOMAS INSEL
STEVEN RASMUSSEN

Contributors

Lewis R. Baxter, Jr., MD, Department of Psychiatry and Biobehavioral Sciences and UCLA School of Medicine, Los Angeles, CA.

Dennis S. Charney, MD, Department of Psychiatry, Yale University School of Medicine and West Haven Veterans Administration Hospital, West Haven, CT.

Joseph DeVaugh-Geiss, MD, Director of Clinical Neuropharmacology, Glaxo, Inc., Research Triangle Park, NC.

Jane L. Eisen, MD, Brown University, Butler Hospital, Providence, RI.

Wayne K. Goodman, MD, Department of Psychiatry, Yale University School of Medicine and the Connecticut Mental Health Center, New Haven, CT.

Barry H. Guze, MD, Department of Psychiatry and Biobehavioral Sciences and UCLA School of Medicine, Los Angeles, CA.

Michael R. Liebowitz, MD, N.Y.S. Psychiatric Institute, College of Physicians and Surgeons of Columbia University, New York, NY.

Eric Hollander, MD, N.Y.S. Psychiatric Institute, College of Physicians and Surgeons of Columbia University, New York, NY.

Carlos N. Pato, Department of Psychiatry and Behavioral Science, State University of New York at Stony Brook, Stony Brook. NY.

Michele T. Pato, Department of Psychiatry and Behavioral Science, State University of New York at Stony Brook, Stony Brook. NY.

David L. Pauls, PhD, The Child Study Center and Department of Human Genetics, Yale University School of Medicine, New Haven, CT.

Roger K. Pitman, MD, Research Service, Veterans Administration Medical Center, Manchester, NH, and Harvard Medical School, Boston, MA.

Lawrence H. Price, MD, Department of Psychiatry, Yale University School of Medicine and the Connecticut Mental Health Center, New Haven, CT.

Cindy L. Raymond, BA, The Child Study Center, Yale University School of Medicine, New Haven, CT.

Mary Robertson, MD, Middlesex Hospital, University of London, London, England.

Wilma G. Rosen, MD, N.Y.S. Psychiatric Institute, College of Physicians and Surgeons of Columbia University, New York, NY.

Jeffrey M. Schwartz, MD, Department of Psychiatry and Biobehavioral Sciences and UCLA School of Medicine, Los Angeles, CA.

Abraham Weizman, MD, Geha Psychiatric Hospital, Belinson Medical Center, Petah Tikva, Israel.

James T. Winslow, PhD, Laboratory of Clinical Sciences, National Institute of Mental Health, Poolesville, MD.

Scott W. Woods, Department of Psychiatry, Yale University School of Medicine and Connecticut Mental Health Center, New Haven, CT.

1

Historical Considerations

Roger K. Pitman

Biology is truly a land of unlimited possibilities. We may expect it to give us the most surprising information and we cannot guess what answers it will return in a few dozen years to the questions we have put to it. They may be of a kind which will blow away the whole of our artificial structure of hypotheses.

SIGMUND FREUD (1920/1955)

MECHANISM AND VITALISM IN THE NINETEENTH CENTURY

The integrative term, psychobiology, implies that mental or psychic phenomena, such as obsessions and compulsions, are approachable from the standpoint of the basic biological sciences, including physics and chemistry. Psychobiology may, therefore, be considered to have its origin in the ascendance of the scientific philosophy of Mechanism over that of Vitalism during the middle and latter portions of the nineteenth century. While detailed written descriptions of what is now recognizable as obsessive–compulsive disorder (OCD) appeared centuries earlier (Hunter & MacAlpine, 1963), these were interpreted as resulting not from physical causes but from spiritual ones, such as demonic possession, and have little to do with psychobiology.

Vitalism held that there exists in living organisms a vital principle that is distinct from physical forces, and that life is self-determining. Mechanism held that no forces other than the common physical–chemical ones are active within the organism. "Organisms . . . are all phenomena of the physical world; systems of atoms, moved by forces, according to the principle of the conservation of energy . . ." (Brücke, 1874, cited in Jones, 1953, p. 41.)

1

A PSYCHODYNAMIC PSYCHOBIOLOGIST

Sigmund Freud regarded Brücke as his most influential mentor and attempted throughout his career to incorporate mechanistic principles into his psychoanalytic psychology. Central to Freud's psychobiological theory is the concept of libidinal energy, which provides the driving force behind the psychological processes that it happens to "cathect." Freud hypothesized the existence of oral, anal, and genital erogenous zones, which, in that order, are supplied with libidinal energy in the normal course of human development.

Freud (1913/1924) hypothesized that the predisposition to obsessional neurosis resulted from a preponderant "sadistic-anal-erotic sexual organization." In the individual patient, this could arise from fixation at the anal level during development, or more commonly, from regression to it as a consequence of frustration of functioning at the higher genital level. The most frequent reason for genital-level frustration, Freud suggested, is internal conflict, especially the Oedipal conflict. However, external frustration due to lack of opportunity for genital outlet may also suffice. In the case of either internal conflict or external frustration, Freud proposed that libidinal energy could be diverted from the genital organization to the anal-sadisitic organization, through the process of regression: ". . . it is easy to observe a certain indifference as to the path along which the discharge takes place, so long as it takes place somehow" (Freud, 1923/1955, p. 45). Once charged with energy, the anal-sadistic organization produces impulses and wishes alien to the sufferer's ego: impulses to dominate, control, hurt, and soil. In an effort to avoid the anxiety created by these negative impulses, the patient employs characteristic defenses, including reaction formation, isolation, and undoing. These impulses and the defenses against them in turn produce obsessive–compulsive symptoms.

ANOTHER PSYCHODYNAMIC PSYCHOBIOLOGIST

The Freudian psychobiological theory of obsessional neurosis is no doubt familiar to readers of this volume, given the tendency for psychoanalysis to dominate American psychiatry until only the very recent decades. At the same time that Freud was constructing his theory in Vienna, a contemporary physician and psychologist, less famous but of equal stature, was pursuing a similar goal in Paris. The works of Pierre Janet are less familiar to the American reader, in part because of a lack of English translations (Pitman, 1984, 1987a). Janet considered that obsessions and compulsions constituted the most advanced manifestation of a condition he termed psychasthenia, a synthesis that also included tics, phobias, and depersonalization. Janet was strongly influenced by his mentor, Théodule Ribot, who had borrowed from Claude Bernard the idea that disease is an experience instituted by nature (Ellenberger, 1970). Janet faithfully applied this notion: "Whatever interpretation one assigns to their mental state, one must remember that psychasthenics are before everything else sick people" (Janet 1903/1976, p. 398). Through Ribot, Janet was influenced by Jackson's conception of the evolutionary hierarchical organization of the nervous system, and its downward dissolution in pathological conditions (Jackson, 1884/1932).

In his theory of psychasthenia, Janet, like Freud, endeavored to take a mechanistic approach and to apply concepts borrowed from the physics of the time to the psychological phenomena that he described. On the basis of his work with psychasthenic patients, Janet conceptualized a hierarchy of psychological functions. The highest level is the reality function, which includes the capacity to fully relate to the present ("presentification"), to perform real actions that require high effort such as social adjustment and adaptation to novel circumstances, and to experience emotions adapted to present reality. Janet suggested that psychasthenics have the most difficulty in these areas. Below the reality function, Janet described the disinterested mental activities and habitual actions, followed by imagination and abstract reason, visceral emotional reactions, and useless muscle movements, in descending order.

If libidinal energy was the basis of Freud's psychobiology, the basis of Janet's was "psychological tension." According to Janet, the degree of each individual's psychological tension determines the most elevated level in the psychological hierarchy that he can attain. Janet considered that psychological tension corresponded to some physiological tension in the central nervous system. He proposed an analogy with electricity: a voltage of 90v may be able to run a motor, but 115v may be needed to light a lamp. Janet used the term "psycholepsy" to describe precipitous drops in psychological tension, in an analogy with epilepsy. He considered that the essential problem in psychasthenia was deficit in psychological tension, sometimes acute, but more often of a chronic, degenerative, and ultimately inherited origin.

Janet also postulated the existence of psychic energy, which he considered to flow in the nerves in the manner that blood flowed in the circulation. He proposed that the diversion of this energy accounted for the appearance of obsessions and compulsions, as well as rumination, tics, phobias, and anxiety (all of which he termed forced agitations). According to Janet, forced agitations tend to arise when the psychasthenic patient wishes to initiate an action or make a decision, a high-level psychological operation. Inability to complete the high-level operation, due to low psychological tension, leads to the appearance of lower-level phenomena, as the mental energy intended for the higher operations becomes diverted into the lower one(s). "When a force originally destined to be expended on the production of a certain phenomenon remains unutilized because the phenomenon has become impossible, then it creates diversions, that is, the force expends itself in producing other phenomena that are both unanticipated and unnecessary" (Janet 1903/1976, p. 555). Because higher-level phenomena require more energy than lower ones, the resulting symptomatic agitations may be quantitatively disproportionate. While Janet acknowledged that it was sometimes true, as proposed by Freud, that genital excitation may be the source of the diverted energy, he asserted that energy from other uncompleted emotions such as grief and fear, as well as energy from failed efforts of attention or belief, was often involved.

A PROBLEM FOR BOTH THEORIES

Janet disputed Freud's belief in the universal importance of sexuality in the etiology of obsessional and other neuroses. Janet considered sexual dissatisfaction to be a result, not a cause, of the illness, deriving from psychasthenic patients' psychological incompleteness. Janet's psychology was from the beginning what would today be viewed as an ego psychology, while Freud arrived at his ego psychology after his formulation of the concept of libidinal energy, essentially an id phenomenon. On the other hand, Janet did not afford to intrapsychic conflict the same recognition as did Freud, nor carry its development as far.

Thus did these two rivals' psychological theories differ in many important respects. On the other hand, their psychobiological theories show striking similarities which include: (a) hierarchical organization of the mental apparatus assumed to be on an underlying physical basis, (b) functional regression from a higher hierarchical level to a lower one, and (c) diversion of mental energy into lower-level functions, resulting in symptom formation. Similar in construction in these respects, both theories have been equally vulnerable to subsequent scientific developments. Their viability ultimately depended on the successful identification of the biological equivalent of libidinal energy in Freud's case, or of psychological tension in Janet's. No such equivalents have been forthcoming, and no modern neuroscientific investigator would any longer consider it worthwhile to pursue the search. Scientific history has pronounced the "general, deserved destruction of simplistic energy models" of behavior (Dawkins, 1976, p. 8). This point will be taken up again later.

SUPPORT FROM AN UNEXPECTED QUARTER

The demise of the energy models has not necessarily meant that Freud's and Janet's theories have lost all psychobiological relevance. Support was to emerge from a very different area of behavioral biology. About a half decade after Freud and Janet formulated their theories, ethologists described what are now referred to as "displacement activities" (Tinbergen, 1949). Observed in a wide variety of animal species, displacement activities involve out-of-context actions that occur when motivated behaviors are thwarted. For example, a stickleback fish engaged in a border dispute with a rival of the same species may be observed to suddenly engage in vigorous nest-building activity. This behavior is presumably brought about by the conflict of aggressive and escape motivations. Ethologists have observed that displacement activities appear to involve the activation of biologically innate motor behaviors, or fixed action patterns. The most typically observed classes of displacement activities are grooming or cleaning, feeding, and nest building.

The similarity between ethologists' observations of displacement activities in animals and Janet's characterization of forced agitations in humans is remarkable. Nearly all the elements of displacement activities, as well as the purported mechanism behind their formation, had been described by Janet in his observations of the so-called "diversions" of human obsessive–compulsive patients a half century earlier. The one important element missing from Janet's formulation of the forced agitations was a precipitating role for motivational conflict. However, this was supplied by Freud, who assigned a central role to conflict in the genesis of obsessive–compulsive symptoms.

DISPLACEMENT ACTIVITY AS A MODEL FOR OCD

Holland (1974) explicitly proposed that displacement activity might serve as a useful animal model for obsessive compulsive disorder, although he does not appear to have been aware of Janet's contribution. The points of similarity between displacement activities in animals and forced agitations in obsessive compulsive humans may be enumerated as follows: occurrence in situations of conflict, absence of consummation of antecedent motivated behavior, inappropriateness to environmental context, stereotyped quality, and possibly even biological innateness. The same compulsive rituals, namely cleaning and checking, tend to appear across cultures in studies of OCD. These behaviors potentially confer adaptation, such as reducing the risk of infectious disease in the case of cleaning rituals (Heisel, unpublished), or reducing exposure to danger in the case of checking. The combination of cross-cultural consistency and adaptive value suggest that compulsive behaviors may represent response tendencies of the human species that have been selected during evolution and become activated out of context in OCD in an analogous manner to the displacement activities observed in lower species. A similar argument has been advanced for the universality and potential evolutionary adaptiveness of phobias (Seligman, 1971), which Janet included among the forced agitations.

EARLY NEUROLOGICAL CONCEPTIONS

An even earlier student of the disorder we now know as OCD was the German neurologist Carl Westphal (1878). Writing several decades before Freud and Janet, Westphal suggested that the essential feature of the disorder was pathological compulsive ideas, without any necessary underlying emotive basis. He considered associated affective or emotional disturbances to be secondary. Westphal believed that the most common etiology lay in a hereditary predisposition to neurosis, but he observed that in isolated cases compulsive ideas could occur in connection with epilepsy. Westphal described the case of a 14-year-old girl with compulsive thoughts who displayed twitching movements, vocalizations, coughing tics, and motor explosiveness alternating with immobility. He commented that "essentially a mental process was involved in all these . . . spasm-like acts." In passing, Westphal mentioned that the referring diagnosis had been St. Vitus' dance, "excusable . . . after a superficial examination." Westphal did not pursue the possibility that a neurological condition such as St. Vitus' dance (also known as Sydenham's chorea) might underlie both a compulsive mental process and motor pathology.

A few years later in France, Georges Gilles de la Tourette (1885) described the neurological syndrome of multiple tics, vocalizations, and coprolalia that was to bear his name. Although he himself described obsessional qualities to the coprolalia of one patient, a dissociation of motor from mental symptoms appeared early in the Tourette syndrome literature and persisted until only very recently (Shapiro, Shapiro, Bruun, & Sweet, 1978). The connection between obsessions, compulsions, and tics was not lost, however, on the French neurologists Meige and Feindel (1902/1907), who proposed that the frequency with which obsessions and tics were associated could not be simple coincidence. Much later, in an apparent vindication of Janet's psychasthenic synthesis, a common genetic basis was to be demonstrated for Tourette syndrome, and at least some forms of OCD (Pauls & Leckman, 1986) and agoraphobia (Comings & Comings, 1987).

FURTHER NEUROLOGICAL CONTRIBUTIONS

The 1915–1926 pandemic of von Economo's disease (encephalitis lethargica) strengthened the neurological link between pathological mental and motor phenomena by providing a population of patients with Parkinsonian symptoms who also suffered from compulsive thoughts and behaviors, together with choreic and tic-like movements (Bromberg, 1930). These patients' symptoms ranged from simple automatisms, through compulsive and instinctive behaviors, to classical affect-laden obsessive thinking. Most interesting were the mental phenomena that accompanied their oculogyric crises (Jelliffe, 1932). Brickner, Rosen, and Munro (1940) described several patients who at the time of oculogyric attacks displayed typical obsessions and compulsions, such as worrying about having insulted somebody, worrying whether the door was properly closed, anxious rumination about killing one's father and/or raping one's mother, handwashing, and other cleaning behaviors. These were held to result from the activation of underlying "neurointellectual neuronal beds." Wexberg (1937) emphasized the organic unity of the mental and somatic phenomena involved in oculogyric crises, postulating that the two were linked by an intimate connection of meaning that he called a "pattern." Schilder (1938) observed that cases of compulsion neuroses accompanied by neurological signs tended to be characterized by repetition, counting, and a special relation to symmetry and asymmetry. Grimshaw (1964) found that the incidence of neurological illness in obsessive compulsive patients (19.4%) was more than twice that of controls (7.6%). Leading Grimshaw's tally of presumably predisposing conditions was Sydenham's chorea.

It may be seen that the trend of neurological data accumulated over the past century has pointed toward the basal ganglia as a likely site of disturbance in OCD. This brain area serves as a neuroanatomic common denominator to Tourette syndrome, Parkinsonism, and chorea. It is of historical interest that early neurologists who took an interest in obsessive–compulsive phenomena were also students of basal ganglia disorders. Carl Westphal described an early case of hepatolenticular degeneration, while the English translator of Meige's and Feindel's treatise on tics, SAK Wilson, definitively described this condition, which came to be known as Wilson's disease. Meige first described the ex-trapyramidal syndrome that bears his name and involves blepharos-pasm and oromandibular dystonia, along with occasional psychiatric manifestations.

In the Jacksonian tradition, MacLean (1977) recently proposed a neuroethological hierarchy of the brain. He placed the basal ganglia at the lowest "protoreptilian" level, the limbic system at the middle "paleomammalian" level, and the cortex at the highest "neomamma-lian" level. The protoreptilian level was proposed to be the site of expression of many species-typical fixed action patterns (MacLean, 1978). Interestingly, displacement behavior in the rat depends on the integrity of the "protoreptilian" nucleus accumbens (Robbins & Koob, 1980).

CONDITIONING THEORY

In contrast to Freud and Janet, who made detailed studies of clinical phenomena and speculated about their underlying psychobiology, the Russian psychophysiologist Ivan Pavlov made direct laboratory studies of psychobiological phenomena and speculated about their applicability to clinical conditions. As the discoverer of the conditioned reflex, Pavlov (1926/1927) founded the conception of the brain as mediator between causal stimulus and resultant response. This experimentally based, eminently mechanistic theory of human behavior was ultimately more influential than the theories of the psychodynamicists. Although he was not intimately familiar with OCD, Pavlov did express some psy-chobiological views about it. He regarded the disorder as involving an excess of excitatory over inhibitory cortical processes, with resulting "pathological inertness" manifest in stereotypy and perseveration (Beech, 1974). However, Pavlov's major impact on OCD was indirect, inasmuch as his conditioning theory set the stage for the emergence in America of behaviorism.

So much has been written regarding the behaviorist theory of OCD (Foa, Steketee, & Ozarow, 1985; Rachman & Hodgson, 1980) that it is hardly necessary to repeat it here. The most important contribution appears to have been Mowrer's (1939) two-stage theory of fear and avoidance. In the first stage, a fear response to a stimulus is acquired by means of classical (Pavlovian) conditioning. In the second stage, avoid-ance of the stimulus is negatively reinforced by means of operant con-ditioning. This approach is useful for explaining compulsions but less so for obsessions.

THE RETURN OF VITALISM

No mechanistic behavioral science has been able to reliably predict behavior. Freud (1920/1924) acknowledged this failure for psychoanalysis, but the situation is no better for behaviorism. The difficulty is summarized in the often replicated observation that "Under conditions of constant pressure, volume, and temperature, the behaving organism will do exactly as it damn well pleases." Stimulus is inadequate to predict response because it does not take into account what the organism pleases at the time of the stimulus. In order to predict response, not one but two quantities must be known: stimulus and goal. Given access to a water tap, an OCD patient may be observed on one occasion to compulsively wash his hands, but on another occasion he may be observed to take a drink. The water tap stimulus is insufficient to determine the response, because the response also depends of the goal, which may be in one instant to relieve a feeling of contamination, but in another to relieve thirst.

The notion that goal plays an essential role in determining behavior, necessary as it appears at present, would have been rejected in horror by Freud's scientific contemporaries as vitalistic teleology. But mechanistic as he tried to be, Freud could not help but let the concept of goal into his psychobiology. Its influence is clear, or example, in his recognition of the components of instinct as including not only source, impetus, and object, but also aim (Freud, 1915/1924). Goals and purposes are what set living things apart from inanimate objects and what make up their vitality. Human obsessive–compulsive behavior is purposeful; indeed it is a caricature of purpose. A science that does not allow for purpose cannot grasp it.

CYBERNETICS AND OCD

The foundation of a behavioral science that recognizes the purposefulness of human activity, and affords to goal a role equal to stimulus and response, was laid by two Americans, the mathematician Norbert Wiener (1948), and the engineer William Powers (1973). The title of Powers' book, *Behavior: The Control of Perception*, summarizes his theory. Powers postulated that the behaving organism constitutes a complex control system that attempts to control not its behavioral output, as one might naively assume, but rather its input or perception, through a negative feedback process. The core of the control system is its "comparator" mechanism. This functions to compare a "perceptual" signal with an

internal "reference" signal and to generate an "error" signal representing the difference between the reference and perceptual signals, that is,
the amount of "mismatch." Powers argued that perceptual, reference,
and error signals all represent information quantified in the nervous
system. The error signal generates behavioral output designed to bring
the perceptual signal closer to the reference signal, that is, to reduce
mismatch. Behavior continues until perceptual signal matches reference
signal and error is zero. In the language of behaviorism, the perceptual
signal may be considered to represent the stimulus, and the error or
output signal the response. The novel element, that is, the reference
signal, represents the goal.

Gray (1982) was the first to propose a control system model of OCD.
He postulated that the septo-hippocampal system of the brain (and
associated limbic areas) functions as a comparator. Gray suggested that
this system compares predicted to actual sensory events and activates a
behavioral inhibition system when mismatch is detected. According to
Gray, obsessions and compulsions represent checking activities within
the behavioral inhibition system. However, Gray conceives that perceptions are matched to predictions or expectations, rather than to goals
or intentions. To this extent, his contribution falls short of a model of
purposeful obsessive–compulsive behavior.

Such a model was outlined by Pitman (1987b), who proposed that
obsessive–compulsive symptoms result from an exaggerated, un-
successful attempt to match a perceptual signal to an internal reference
signal, or goal for the perception. According to Pitman, the core problem
in OCD is the persistence of high error signals, or mismatch, that cannot
be reduced to zero through behavioral output. Mismatch find its subjective manifestation in the pervasive incompleteness and doubt that
characterize the disorder. Obsessive–compulsive behavior is repetitive
and stereotyped because behavioral programs are re- and re-executed in
a vain effort to reduce error signals.

CONCLUDING COMMENTS

This historical trail ends here. The writer had tended to follow the
developments he finds most interesting, and such important elements
as the relationship between OCD and depression, or the disorder's
genetics, have not been tracked. However, enough has been covered to
indicate the formidable task that awaits anyone endeavoring to formu-
late a psychobiological theory of OCD that is truly integrative. This task
will require tying together important threads from several different

biological disciplines. To the extent that any is omitted, the fabric will be imperfect.

REFERENCES

Beech, H. R. (1974). Approaches to understanding obsessional illness. In H. R. Beech (Ed.), *Obsessional states* (pp. 3–17). London: Methuen.

Brickner, R. M., Rosen, A. A., & Munro, R. (1940). Physiological aspects of the obsessive state. *Psychosomatic Medicine, 2,* 369–383.

Bromberg, W. (1930). Mental symptoms in chronic encephalitis. *Psychiatric Quarterly, 4,* 537–566.

Comings, D. E., & Comings, B. G. (1987). Hereditary agoraphobia and obsessive–compulsive behaviour in relatives of patients with Gilles de la Tourette's syndrome. *British Journal of Psychiatry, 151,* 195–199.

Dawkins, R. (1976). Hierarchical organization: A candidate principle for ethology. In P. P. G. Bateson & R. A. Hinde (Eds.), *Growing points in ethology* (pp. 7–54). New York: Cambridge University Press.

Ellenberger, R. (1970). *The discovery of the unconscious: The history and evolution of dynamic psychiatry.* New York: Basic Books.

Foa, E. B., Steketee, G. S., & Ozarow, B. J. (1985). Behavior therapy with obsessive-compulsives: From theory to treatment. In M. Mavissakalian, S. M. Turner, & L. Michelson (Eds.), *Obsessive-compulsive disorder: Psychological and pharmacological treatment* (pp. 49–129). New York: Plenum.

Freud, S. (1913/1924). The predisposition to obsessional neurosis. *Collected papers 2,* 122–132. London: Hogarth Press Ltd.

Freud, S. (1915/1924). Instincts and their vicissitudes. *Collected papers 4,* 60–83. London: Hogarth Press Ltd.

Freud, S. (1920/1924). The psychogenesis of a case of homosexuality in a woman. *Collected papers 2,* 202–231. London: Hogarth Press Ltd.

Freud, S. (1920/1955). *Beyond the pleasure principle: Standard edition 18,* 7–64. London: Hogarth Press Ltd. and the Institute of Psycho-Analysis.

Freud, S. (1923/1955). *The ego and the id. Standard edition 19,* 3–66. London: Hogarth Press Ltd. and the Institute of Psycho-Analysis.

Gilles de la Tourette, G. (1885). Étude sur une affection nerveuse caracterisée par de l'incoordination motrice accompagnée de echolalie et de coprolalie. *Archives de Neurologie, 9,* 19–42, 158–200.

Gray, J. A. (1982). *The neuropsychology of anxiety: An enquiry into the functions of the septo-hippocampal system.* Oxford: Oxford University Press.

Grimshaw, L. (1964). Obsessional disorder and neurological illness. *Journal of Neurology, Neurosurgery, and Psychiatry, 27,* 229–231.

Holland, H. C. (1974). Displacement activity as a form of abnormal behavior in animals. In H. R. Beech (Ed.), *Obsessional states* (pp. 161–173). London: Methuen.

Hunter, R., & MacAlpine, I. (1963). *Three hundred years of psychiatry.* London: Oxford University Press.

Jackson, J. H. (1884/1932). Evolution and dissolution of the nervous system. In J. Taylor (Ed.), *Selected writings of John Hughlings Jackson* (pp. 45–75). London: Hodder & Stroughton.

Janet, P. (1903/1976). *Les obsessions et la psychasthénie*, Vol. 1. Paris: Alcan. (Reprinted in New York: Arno, 1976).

Jelliffe, S. E. (1932). *Psychopathology of forced movements in oculogyric crises*. Washington: Nervous and Mental Disease Publishing Co.

Jones, E. (1953). *The life and work of Sigmund Freud*, Vol. 1. New York: Basic Books.

MacLean, P. D. (1977). On the evolution of three mentalities. In S. Arieti, & G. Chrzanowshi (Eds.), *New dimensions in psychiatry: A world view*, Vol. 3 (pp. 305–328). New York: Wiley.

MacLean, P. D. (1978). Effects of lesions of globus pallidus on species-typical display behavior of squirrel monkeys. *Brain Research, 149*, 175–196.

Meige, H., & Feindel, E. (1902/1907). *Tics and their treatment*. New York: William Wood & Co.

Mowrer, O. H. (1939). A stimulus–response theory of anxiety. *Psychological Review, 46*, 553–565.

Pauls, D. L., & Leckman, J. F. (1986). The inheritance of Gilles de la Tourette's syndrome and associated behaviors: Evidence for autosomal dominant transmission. *New England Journal of Medicine, 315*, 993–997.

Pavlov, I. P. (1926/1927). *Conditioned reflex*. Oxford: Clarendon Press.

Pitman, R. K. (1984). Janet's *Obsessions and Psychasthenia*: A synopsis. *Psychiatric Quarterly, 56*, 291–314.

Pitman, R. K. (1987a). Pierre Janet on obsessive–compulsive disorder (1903): Review and commentary. *Archives of General Psychiatry, 44*, 226–232.

Pitman, R. K. (1987b). A cybernetic model of obsessive–compulsive psychopathology. *Comprehensive Psychiatry, 28*, 334–343.

Powers, W. T. (1973). *Behavior: The control of perception*. Chicago: Aldine.

Rachman, S. J., & Hodgson, R. J. (1980). *Obsessions and compulsions*. Englewood Cliffs, NJ: Prentice-Hall.

Robbins, T. W. & Koob, G. F. (1980). Selective disruption of displacement behavior by lesions of the mesolimbic dopamine system. *Nature, 285*, 409–412.

Schilder, P. (1938). The organic background of obsessions and compulsions. *American Journal of Psychiatry, 94*, 1397–1416.

Seligman, M. E. P. (1971). Phobias and preparedness. *Behavior Therapy, 2*, 307–320.

Shapiro, A. K., Shapiro, E. S., Bruun, R. D., & Sweet, R. D. (1978). *Gilles de la Tourette Syndrome*. New York: Raven Press.

Tinbergen, N. (1949). *The social behavior of animals*. London: Methuen & Co.

Westphal, C. (1878). Über Zwangsvorstellungen. *Archive für Psychiatrie und Nervenkrankheiten, 8*, 734–750.

Wexberg, E. (1937). Remarks on the psychopathology of oculogyric crises in epidemic encephalitis. *Journal of Nervous and Mental Diseases, 85*, 56–69.

Wiener, N. (1948). *Cybernetics*. New York: Wiley.

2

Phenomenology of OCD: Clinical Subtypes, Heterogeneity and Coexistence

Steven Rasmussen
Jane L. Eisen

Rapid growth in our understanding of the neurobiology of brain function has led to a radical change in our conceptualization of the etiology of the major psychiatric disorders over the last twenty years. Recent advances in molecular genetics, neuroimaging, and receptor subtyping suggest that the impact of the neurobiologic revolution on the treatment of these disorders has only begun. While these advances have over-shadowed phenomenologic characterization of clinical syndromes, they have not diminished their importance. Clinical observations, made at the turn of the century, have taken on new meaning in the light of our increased understanding of the neurobiology and genetics of obsessive–compulsive disorder (OCD). If Freud and Janet had had access to the wealth of neurobiologic and genetic data available today on OCD and Tourette's syndrome, their hypotheses regarding the etiology of these disorders would most certainly have been radically different. In addition to having this knowledge to help guide our observations and form conclusions, phenomenologists can now take advantage of computerized data bases and improved methodology for classifying and recording clinical observations.

One of the major advantages for researchers working with OCD is its relative homogeneity in comparison to other psychiatric disorders such as schizophrenia and depression. Psychiatric illnesses that are homogeneous tend to have low prevalence rates in the general population. Until recently, OCD was thought to be a rare disorder. Results from the Epidemiology Catchment Area (ECA) Study, published in 1984, found that OCD had a lifetime prevalence of 2.5% (Robins, Helzer,

Weissman, et al., 1984) and a 6-month point prevalence of 1.6% (Myers, Weissman, Tischler, et al., 1984) in the general population. These initial figures were confirmed in a subsequent analysis of the total sample of 18,500 probands (Karno, Golding, Sorenson, & Burnom, 1988). An epidemiologic study that interviewed 3,258 randomly selected residents of Edmonton with the Diagnostic Interview Schedule (DIS) confirmed the U.S. ECA results (Bland, Newman, & Orn, 1988a). The lifetime prevalence of OCD was 3.0% while the six-month-point prevalence was 1.6% (Bland, Newman, & Orn, 1988b). These figures have been criticized on the grounds that the study's use of the DIS and lay interviewers were felt to have led to the overestimation of the prevalence of some disorders, particularly the phobias and OCD. These criticisms were supported by follow-up studies of ECA subjects that utilized interviews that were semistructured and were completed by psychiatrists (Anthony, Folstein, & Romanowski, 1985; Helzer, Robins, & McEvoy, 1985). Both studies found significantly lower prevalence rates of OCD than were reported in the original ECA study. However, these studies have also been subject to criticism due to the small number of subjects interviewed, as well as the fact that the psychiatrists were not focusing on OCD. Unfortunately, no follow-up study of ECA obsessive–compulsive subjects using structured interviews and rating scales has been completed.

A more careful study of the prevalence of OCD in a population of high school students has recently been published by Flament, Whitaker, Rapoport, et al. (1988). They screened 5,000 students with the Leyton Obsessional Inventory. All of these students were interviewed by a psychiatrist who was an expert at childhood OCD. Fifteen, or 0.3% of the total 5,000 students were diagnosed as meeting *Diagnostic and Statistical Manual of Mental Disorders* (3rd ed., revised) (DSM-III-R) (APA, 1987, Washington, D.C.) criteria for OCD. It is worth noting that the average age of this population was 15.4 years while the average age of the onset of the disorder is 19.6. Coupled with the secretiveness of the disorder, this finding suggests that this figure is an underestimate of the true prevalence. Considering all the available data, it appears likely that the lifetime prevalence of OCD in the general population approaches 1 to 2%.

The identification of homogeneous clinical subtypes of OCD has important implications for our understanding of the etiology and prognosis of the disorder. In general, there have been five major approaches to identifying these subtypes within psychiatric illnesses: (1) by clinical symptoms, (2) by course of illness, (3) by family history or genetics, (4) by biologic markers, and (5) by treatment response. Until recently, only the first two approaches had received systematic attention. Recent advances in biological markers, psychopharmacological approaches to treatment, neuropharmacologic challenge studies, and the genetics of OCD are reviewed by Pauls, Raymond, and Robertson, Chapter 3, Weizman, Zohar, and Insel, Chapter 7, Goodman, Price, Woods, and Charney, Chapter 8, and DeVeaugh-Geiss *this volume*. The validity of all of the studies described by these authors is dependent on the careful selection of their patient population. Variability in the data both between and within studies may be due in part to the fact that there were significant differences in the inclusion and exclusion criteria for patients making up the study populations.

The goal of this chapter is to present data that is pertinent to the identification of clinical subtypes of OCD and to discuss its importance for our understanding of the pathogenesis of the syndrome. We have systematically collected such data on 250 patients who have presented to an Obsessive Disorders Clinic over the past five years. In order to accomplish our aim, four major areas are addressed: (1) age of onset and natural history; (2) the frequency and phenomenologic description of clinical subtypes; (3) the comorbidity and overlap of OCD with other psychiatric syndromes; and (4) the developmental antecedents of the disorder and its relationship to compulsive personality. These findings will be discussed with regard to the heterogeneity of the disorder and identification of clinically homogeneous subtypes. Finally, we discuss the core phenomenologic features of the syndrome and how they might relate to the cognitive and emotional factors that are crucial to its pathogenesis. The relevance of these phenomenologic findings for future neurobiologic and genetic studies of OCD will be reviewed.

METHODS

Subjects

Two hundred and fifty subjects were consecutively evaluated at an Obsessive Disorders Clinic that offered a multimodal treatment strategy including behavioral, pharmacologic, and family approaches. All patients included in the study met *DSM-III-R* criteria for OCD. Referrals to the clinic were from a variety of sources including: referral from other mental health professionals, self referrals, and response to media articles or programs. The group was representative of a clinical population found in a typical catchment area in the Northeast of one to two million people. The demographic characteristics of the population are given in Table 2.1.

TABLE 2.1 Demographics of OCD Sample (n = 250)

Sex	Percentage	Race	Percentage	Marital status	Percentage	Religion	Percentage
Male	45	Caucasian	98	Single	43	Catholic	72
Female	55	Non-caucasian	2	Ever Married	52	Protestant	21
				Ever Divorced	5	Jewish	5
						Other	2

Evaluation

On admission, each of the 250 probands was evaluated by one of the principal authors with a semistructured interview lasting approximately 90 minutes. This interview covered demographics, a checklist of obsessive–compulsive symptoms, course of illness, past medical history, a developmental history, past history of treatment response, and family history. Additional developmental history was obtained by interviewing parents and siblings.

In addition we administered the SADS-LA (Fyer & Endicott, 1984) to 70 probands in order to determine current and lifetime histories of other Axis I psychiatric disorders. As the Schizophrenia and Affective Disorders Schedule, Lifetime Anxiety version (SADS-LA) was developed primarily for patients with panic, the instrument was further modified to more reliably determine primary and secondary diagnoses for OCD, depression, and other anxiety disorders.

Approximately 150 out of the 250 patients have been actively followed for treatment in our clinic. Detailed case histories and phenomenologic observations were collected on a subset of 50 of the 150 probands who were prototypic of the clinical subtypes of the disorder and who were particularly capable of carefully observing and articulating their symptoms.

Data was systematically collected and entered into a database management system. Statistical analysis was completed using *t*-test analysis for continuous variables and chi-square or Fisher exact for noncontinuous variables.

Age of Onset

The mean age at onset of obsessive compulsive symptoms for the 200 patients was 19.8 ± 9.6 Standard Deviation (SD) years. The mean age at which treatment was first sought for the disorder was 25.6 + 10.7 years. Two hundred six or 83% of the patients described their onset of clinically significant illness as first appearing between the ages of 10 and 24, confirming previous studies which have shown that for the majority of patients the illness begins in adolescence or early adulthood (Rasmussen & Tsuang, 1984). Men had a mean age of onset of 17.5 ± 8.7 compared with 21.2 ± 9.8 for women (See Figure 2.1). This differential age of onset for males versus females is particularly interesting in light of the possible etiologic role of sex steroids in OCD (Casas, Alvarez, & Duro, 1986).

The frequencies of the most common types of obsessions and compulsions are given in Table 2.2. It is worth noting that most patients presented with multiple obsessions and compulsions on admission and

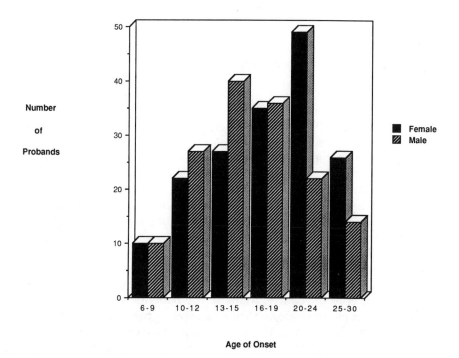

Figure 2.1 Age of onset in obsessive–compulsive disorder in Brown's study.

TABLE 2.2 OC Symptoms on Admission

Obsessions ($n = 200$)	Percentage	Compulsions ($n = 200$)	Percentage
Contamination	45	Checking	63
Pathologic Doubt	42	Washing	50
Somatic	36	Counting	36
Need for Symmetry	31	Need to ask or confess	31
Aggressive	28	Symmetry & Precision	28
Sexual	26	Hoarding	18
Other	13	Multiple Compulsions	48
Multiple Obsessions	60		

Course of illness ($n = 200$)

Age of Onset	Type	Percentage	Pre-cipitant	Percentage
Male 17.5 ± 6.8	Waxing & Waning	72.0	Not Present	88
Female 20.8 ± 8.5	Continuous	16.0	Present	22
	Deteriorative	9.0		
	Episodic	3.0		

that the frequency of patients with only obsessions or compulsions was low.

Natural Course

Each patient's course of illness was determined as falling into one of four categories: episodic, continuous, chronic waxing and waning, or deteriorative. Patients who met criteria for OCD, but whose onset of illness was less than 5 years prior to evaluation, were excluded from this analysis. The remainder of the group had a mean difference between age of onset and age at interview of 7.1 ± 8.9.

Table 2.2 reveals that the overwhelming majority (72%) of patients had a chronic waxing and waning course: 16% had a continuous course, and 9% a chronic deteriorative course. Only 3% of the total were felt to have had an episodic course. Many of the patients with a deteriorative course had given up resisting their obsessive or compulsive symptoms.

The overwhelming majority reported a gradual onset of illness. Only 22% could reliably identify an environmental precipitant that seemed to trigger their illness. Increases in responsibility such as the birth of a child or promotion to a new job, or significant losses such as the death of a family member, or the loss of a job were the most common precipitants

reported. Almost all patients reported that stressful life ev
their obsessive–compulsive (OC) symptoms. Sixty perce
menstruating age reported worsening of their sympt(
menstrual period.

PHENOMENOLOGIC SUBTYPES

Inevitably, the beginning clinician is struck by the diversity of the
clinical presentations of OCD. However, this initial impression is soon
replaced by the realization that the number of types of obsessions and
compulsions are remarkably limited and stereotypic. The basic types
and frequencies of OC symptoms have been found to be consistent
across cultures and time (Rasmussen & Tsuang, 1986; Ahktar, Wing, &
Varma, 1975; Okasha, Kamel, & Hassen, 1968). Why these particular
symptom patterns develop remain a mystery; a mystery whose solution
could provide important clues to ultimately unraveling the disorder's
pathogenesis. A list of obsessions and compulsions that arose from our
clinical experience with our first 200 patients was used to generate the
symptom checklist for the Yale Brown Obsessive Compulsive Scale (see
Table 2.3) (Goodman, Price, & Rasmussen, et al., 1989).

In the following paragraphs we have attempted to capture the essence
of the phenomenologic presentation of the most common of the OC
subgroups.

Contamination Obsessions

Obsessive fear of contamination coupled with handwashing compulsions is the most common phenomenologic presentation of OCD.
Out of all the obsessive subtypes, their fear structure is most closely
linked to the phobias. The most frequently identified contaminant is dirt
or germs, but a wide variety of substances such as toxic chemicals,
poisons, radiation, or heavy metals can serve as the contaminant.
Although these patients are usually obsessed with external cues or
objects that are contaminated, some become morbidly preoccupied with
cognitive rather than external cues. For example, a 65-year-old woman
became obsessed with feeling contaminated by anyone or anything
that had come into contact with the bread taken at Holy Commu-
nion. A 27-year-old woman developed a contamination fear about
anything her mother touched. Generalization from fear of a specific
object to fear of a more abstract category of objects is frequently seen. A
27-year-old nurse became obsessed with coming into contact with blood

TABLE 2.3 (YBOCS) Yale-Brown Obsessive–Compulsive Symptom Checklist

Aggressive obsessions
  Fear might harm others
  Fear might harm self
  Violent or horrific images
  Fear of blurting out obsessions or
    insults
  Fear of doing something
    embarrassing
  Fear will act on other impulses
    (e.g. rob a bank, to steal grocer-
    ies, to overeat)
  Fear will be response for things
    going wrong (e.g. others will
    lose their job b/o pt)
  Fear something terrible might hap-
    pen (e.g. fire, burglary)
  Other
Contamination obsessions
  Concerns or disgust with bodily
    waste (e.g. urine, feces, saliva)
  Concern with dirt or germs
  Excessive concern with environ-
    mental contaminants (e.g. asbes-
    tos, radiation, toxic wastes)
  Excessive concern with household
    items (e.g. cleansers, solvents,
    pets)
  Concerned will get ill
  Concerned will get ill (Aggressive)
  Other
Sexual obsessions
  Forbidden or perverse sexual
    thoughts, images, or impulses
  Content involves children
  Content involves animals
  Content involves incest
  Content involves homosexuality
  Sexual behavior toward others
    (Aggressive)
  Other
Hoarding/collecting obsessions
Religious obsessions

Obsession with need for symmetry
  or exactness
Miscellaneous obsessions
  Need to know or remember
  Fear of saying certain things
  Fear of not saying things just right
  Intrusive (neutral) images
  Intrusive nonsense sounds, words,
    or music
  Other
Somatic obsession/compulsion
Cleaning/washing compulsions
  Excessive or ritualized handwash-
    ing
  Excessive or ritualized showering,
    bathing, toothbrushing or
    grooming doing
  Involves cleaning of household
    items or inanimate objects
  Other measures to prevent contact
    with contaminants
Counting compulsions
Checking compulsions
  Checking that did not/will not
    harm other
  Checking that did not/will not
    harm self
  Checking that nothing terrible did/
    will happen
  Checking for contaminants
  Other
Repeating rituals
Ordering/arranging compulsions
Miscellaneous compulsions
  Mental rituals (other than
    checking/counting)
  Need to tell, ask, or confess
  Need to touch
  Measures to prevent:
    harm to self
    harm to others
    terrible consequences
    Other

of an AIDS patient. Although she was initially only frightened by direct contact with people that were at high risk for AIDS, she quickly began avoiding any sort of object that was red and that might have been contaminated with blood.

The vast majority of contamination obsessives report anxiety as the dominant emotion but the presence of disgust and shame are also commonly seen (Straus, 1948). Shame and disgust are usually linked to embarassment or guilt. A 28-year-old male developed contamination obsessions about his semen. It was of particular interest that he was able to tolerate contact with semen produced during intercourse but had severe fears about semen produced during masturbation. He reported an overwhelming feeling of guilt and disgust when forced to come into contact with semen following masturbation. Unlike other phobic patients, contamination obsessives often report that they are more concerned that significant others might become ill because of them, rather than their getting ill themselves. Why many contamination phobics are not terrified by AIDS is an interesting question. If contamination phobics were simply frightened by potentially dangerous germs, one would expect that 100% of these patients would be terrified by AIDS. The fact that the majority are not, argues for the presence of some sensitizing influence that creates a limited fear network around a particular object or concept. Another striking but characteristic phenomenon of contamination obsessives is that in their minds contamination is "magically transmitted" from a dirty object to a clean object merely by coming into contact with it. Because objects in the environment are classified as either clean or dirty, objects removed from the source of contamination are often viewed with as much trepidation or disgust as the original contaminant. Although handwashing is the most common compulsion seen in contamination phobics they will also preferentially utilize avoidance of contaminated objects over ritualized handwashing or checking if given the opportunity.

Somatic Obsessions

The irrational persistent fear of developing a serious life-threatening illness can be seen across several diagnostic entities including hypochondriasis, major depression with somatic features, panic disorder, and obsessive–compulsive disorder. We have found in our clinical experience that somatic obsessions with checking compulsions are frequently seen in obsessive–compulsive patients at the time of evaluation.

BZ was a 28-year-old accountant who had multiple severe checking rituals associated with pathologic responsibility for 15 years. He had had numerous episodes of somatic obsessions with checking rituals in the past related to fears of melanoma and a brain tumor. On initial evaluation at our clinic he reported that he was fearful that he had developed epiglottal cancer. Because he had no means of visualizing the epiglottal area he had taken to copulsively palpating his epiglottis, by sticking his fingers down his throat each morning; a procedure that took 45 minutes and resulted in uncontrollable retching as well as substantial pain.

SA was a 27-year-old nurse who developed a severe fear of contracting AIDS during her second pregnancy. She had had a premorbid history of mild checking and arranging compulsions since the age of 13, but did not consider them bothersome enough to seek clinical attention. During the acute exacerbation of symptoms she reported that she developed checking and handwashing rituals as well as extensive avoidance. Her fears would be set off by contact with any object that could have been touched by someone who might have AIDS or that might have some contact with blood from any source.

MV was a 32-year-old surgeon who reported that he was obsessed with the fear that he would develop an incarcerated hernia and die. He had a past history of checking and arranging compulsions as well as marked traits of a compulsive personality. He was compelled to check his inguinal region hundreds of times daily, to the point that he ulcerated the area. He described that at times, the urge to check was so overwhelming; that we would have to break scrub during the middle of an operation to check his inguinal canal.

Many of our patients with somatic obsessions are indistinguishable from hypochondriacs with the exception that they will have multiple other obsessions and compulsions. There is usually no difficulty in distinguishing these patients from those with somatization disorder. Somatic obsessions are most commonly linked to checking and the need for reassurance rituals. However, unlike many OCD patients, those with primary somatic obsessions are primarily concerned with their dying rather than being responsible for harm befalling others. While until recently, cancer, heart attacks, and venereal disease have been the most common fears, patients with obsessions about AIDS are appearing in rapidly increasing numbers.

Related disorders such as dysmorphophobia (Thomas, 1984) or

monosymptomatic hypochondriacal delusional disorder (Munro & Chimara, 1982) are also commonly associated with OCD.

Sexual and Aggressive Obsessions

These patients suffer from recurrent abhorrent thoughts that they have or may have committed an unacceptable sexual or aggressive thought/act towards others. The obsessions tend to focus on a dimension of the self that the patient values most highly. Similarly, Janet noted that these types of obsessions and compulsions often involved thought or actions that were the most objectionable imaginable to the patient and that caused him the most horror (Pitman, 1987).

A very religious man in our clinic was compelled to link the word damn to God everytime he saw, heard, or spoke the word "God." A 26-year-old mother was compelled to get rid of all the knives in her house because of the fear she would stab her baby. A 30-year-old stewardess was obsessed with intrusive sexual thoughts and images of lesbianism and child molestation. A 42-year-old church secretary began having intrusive sexual images of the Virgin Mary whenever she crossed the threshold of the church.

Guilt and anxiety are the dominant affective symptoms. The patient may think she should be jailed for her thoughts; partially as a means of protecting her from what she thinks she might do and partially because she feels she should be punished.

The compulsion to ask or confess is frequently present. The patient is forever telling therapist, spouse, or close friend some terrible thought or deed that he feels he has committed as a way of seeking reassurance that he is really not capable of doing what he is worried about. He will frequently leave the therapist's office after having sought reassurance for the whole hour, only to call back later in the evening to add some additional meaningless detail that he worried about having omitted confessing. The patient frequently checks over and over that he has not committed some terrible crime.

An example is the 28-year-old secretary who became obsessed with the thought that she was the murderer of a six-year-old boy after reading about the crime in the newspaper. In addition to asking family members over and over whether or not she was capable of the crime she was compelled to check newspaper articles and TV programs as well as to go to the scene of the crime each day. Patients may go to extreme lengths to diminish the anxiety that is secondary to their thoughts. A 32-year-old college librarian worried that he was a mass murderer and that unbeknownst to his family he woke up in the middle of the night in a fugue or dissociative state, committed his heinous crimes and conveniently forgot them before slipping back into bed in the early hours of the morning. For the two years prior to admission he had taken to tying himself to the bed with a rope so that if he woke up he would trip on the rope and come to his senses. Even this was not enough to prevent the anxiety associated with his thoughts.

In most cases distinguishing these patients from paraphiliacs and those with true homicidal impulses is not difficult. Most have had past histories that follow the typical course of OCD and have had other types of obsessions and compulsions during their course of illness. Although these patients may worry that they want to do these things, the clinical impression is that they really do spend their time worrying about it; while for paraphiliacs one is more impressed with the guilt attendant with the thoughts and the anxiety secondary to the guilt. However, at times, particularly in patients with Tourette's syndrome and OCD, the distinction can blur. One such patient had the impulse to reach out and touch women's breasts; he subsequently got into significant problems when he couldn't control the impulse while riding on the bus to work. It is important to stress that these impulsive compulsives are a minority of this subtype.

We have been impressed with the number of patients who have had a strict religious upbringing with sexual or aggressive obsessions. Analysis of our large sample has shown that these patients are significantly more likely to have aggressive and sexual obsessions than OC patients with nonstrict upbringings. These patients usually report that since childhood they have felt guilty about small things that most people do not think twice about.

Patients with this subtype of obsessions were instrumental in the development of Freud's theories about conflict, defense, and the structural theory of the ego (Mahl, 1971). According to analytic theory, conflict between aggressive and sexual drives and the moral prohibitions of the superego leads to intolerable anxiety that can overwhelm psychological defense mechanisms and result in neurotic symptom formation. While it is easy to see how the theory grew out of his careful phenomenologic observations of these patients, it remains unclear if the data justified his conclusions about the pathogenesis of the disorder. Our clinical experience has been that premature and, at times, any interpretation of the obsessions as unconscious wishes on the part of the patient usually result in clinical deterioration.

Instead, we favor a more direct explanation based on the phenomenology. It is the patients reaction to the thought or impulse "Oh my God how could I think that" that leads to the obsessive characteristic of the thought. All of us experience unacceptable sexual or aggressive thoughts, but most of us are able to quickly dismiss them. For this group of patients, the thought becomes labeled with intense negative affect and anxiety and is therefore more likely to be conditionally linked to other neutral stimuli, stored, and subsequently replayed with increasing intrusiveness and frequency. Attempts to actively dismiss the thought without dissociation of affect often leads to increasing preoccupation and anxiety.

NEED FOR SYMMETRY AND PRECISION

The phenomenologic presentation of this subgroup of patients is among the most fascinating in all of psychiatry. The clinical picture is dominated by an obsession to have objects or events in a certain order or position, to do and undo certain motor actions in an exact fashion, or to have things exactly symmetrical or "evened up."

In our experience these patients can usually be divided into two groups; those with primary obsessive slowness, and those with primary magical thinking.

A 22-year-old male felt compelled to walk exactly through the center of a doorway. If he thought he had entered the door slightly to the left or right of center, he felt it necessary to enter and reenter until he felt he had succeeded in going right through the middle. This would often involve up to 50 repetitions before he could sit down. On entering my office, he felt compelled to line up his chair at a parallel angle to the radiator on the opposite side of the office. His waking day was totally filled with adjusting the angular relationship of himself or one object to another. His parents reported that his obsession with symmetry and angles had begun as early as age two. They vividly described a toddler who sorted everything by color and size and who would spend hours sorting and lining up crayons in a box, or lining up Legos® or Tinkertoys®. As he grew older he became increasingly preoccupied with whether his books were in alphabetical order and lined up precisely, whether the toes of his shoes in his closet were exactly parallel, and whether his hair was parted just so. He became severely impaired at age 14 and had a prolonged hospitalization. Although he had a partial remission at age 16; he relapsed at age 19, and remained severely impaired until admission to our clinic.

Another example is J., a 26-year-old woman whose initiation of complex motor acts became totally dependent on the reception of sensory signals that fit exact criteria. She reported that on awakening she would feel compelled to search for a threadball on her sheet that was perfectly spherical. She was unable to swing her legs over the side of her bed until she was satisfied that she had found one that met her criteria for perfect roundness. After swinging her legs over the side of the bed, she needed to have the balls and heels of her feet meet the floor simultaneously before she could walk over to her bureau to get dressed. Visual, auditory, and tactile perceptions that were "just so" were needed before initiating most motor patterns. Calling J. could be particularly exasperating. She was unable to pick up the phone until she had heard a ring that started out at exactly the right pitch. This often required 30 to 40 rings.

It was particularly striking that both of these patients reported minimal anxiety associated with their compulsions except for that due to time pressure. Their greatest fears were that something would not be done right and that they would have to start the entire sequence over again from the beginning.

These patients take an inordinate amount of time to complete even the simplest of tasks. They fall into the group that Rachman (1980) has labeled primary obsessional slowness. Unlike most OC patients, they do not experience their symptoms as ego dystonic. Instead, they seem to have lost their goal directedness in favor of completing a given subroutine perfectly. MacLean (1978) has found evidence suggesting that the basal ganglia control motor planning and therefore coordinate motor subroutines as well as what he has termed the master routine. It is tempting to speculate that these patients suffer from some interference in fronto-limbic-basal ganglia function that interferes with their goal directedness, and makes them incapable of distinguishing the importance of subroutines versus overall goal-directed behavior.

Another characteristic that separates these patients from other patients with OCD is the subjective feeling they get when things are not lined up just so or perfectly. It is described as being more a feeling of discontent or tension, than fear or anxiety. It is the preoccupation many of us have with a picture hung crookedly, but magnified many times over. In this sense, these patients can be seen as being on the extreme end of the spectrum of compulsive personality in which the need for every detail to be perfect or just so is taken to a maximum. The description of rising tension followed by release after the act is phenomenologically more similar to the subjective sensory experience of Tourette's patients (Pauls, Cohen, Heimbuch, Detlor, & Kidd, 1983) than to the anxiety experienced by other obsessive compulsives.

In contrast to those with primary obsessive slowness, patients with the need for symmetry and precision with magical thinking are distinguished by the fact that their obsessions and rituals are all connected with an attempt to ward off an imagined disaster that they think is out of their control. These patients are usually beset with a bewildering variety of doing and undoing rituals, lucky and unlucky numbers, and counting rituals. Often they are described by their parents as superstitious during childhood. An extreme example is a 26-year-old male who presented as catatonic and mute. He had been diagnosed as schizophrenic at age 18 and had had multiple hospitalizations. While hospitalized and on neuroleptic medication it was noted that he had had a history of OC symptoms dating back to age 14. He gradually improved over a 6-week hospitalization. As he became more verbal, he reported that over the week prior to admission his rituals had progressed to the point where he was concerned that if he moved or spoke he would potentially be responsible for someone's death. His catatonic, mute state was replaced by an incredible number of complex and seemingly bizarre rituals that involved the need for symmetry and precision and magical thinking as well as checking rituals. Everything had to be done in threes and nines. The top of his sheet had to be lined up in exactly a straight line. Communication was hindered by doing and undoing rituals in that after every third sentence he had to count under his breath to 33. However, in contrast to patients with primary obsessive slowness, all of his rituals were accompanied by severe anxiety.

In our experience, Tourette's syndrome patients with coexisting OCD suffer more from the need for symmetry and precision than OC patients without Tourette's syndrome.

R. developed multiple motor and vocal tics at age 7. Shortly after the onset of his tics he began to check doors and electrical appliances over and over. He also remembered having to repeat actions a certain number of times to prevent something bad from happening. Around that time he developed a system of good numbers and bad numbers. The need to balance feelings and actions symmetrically on the right side as compared to the left side of his body was a particularly troublesome symptom. For example, if he swallowed three times on the right side of his throat he would feel compelled to balance it by swallowing three times on the left side. If his shoe was tied to a certain tension on the left foot he would feel compelled to tie and retie the right side until it felt exactly the same. The need for symmetry and precision began to affect his tics. If he had a series of three head jerks to the left, he would then feel compelled to balance them by voluntarily jerking his head to the right. R. described clear differences in the way he experienced his tics and compulsions, though both were only under partial voluntary control. He reported that the buildup of tension associated with the ties was more of a physical sensation than one associated with anxiety or fear. The time period for the buildup of tension for the tic was shorter, and there was less voluntary control of the tic compared to the compulsion. There was no apprehension that something terrible was going to happen if the tic was not allowed to surface.

Patients suffering from Tourettes and primary obsessive slowness appear to differ in a fundamental way from other OCs, in that anxiety is not the force motivating the compulsion. Learning theorists would argue that the compulsions are a form of passive avoidance and that their repetition is reinforced by their anxiety reducing properties (Rachman, 1980). Obsessions and fears generated by them are the primary cause of compulsions in their model. There are a minority (<10% in our sample) of patients who present with only compulsions and who have no idea why they are doing them. Learning theorists have a difficult time integrating those rare patients who present with only compulsions and who have no idea why they are doing them.

P. suffered from checking compulsions for the past twenty years. As part of her treatment assessment she was asked to write down some of the things that she did over and over again during the course of a normal day while performing routine tasks. The following is an excerpt from her diary recording what it was like for her to complete the simple task of turning on her TV:

"Before I start to turn it on, I have to wash and dry my hands. Then I go and touch the corner curtain followed by touching the side of the TV two times. Then I have to go back and wash my hands. When I am finished with that I will look behind the lamp 2 times, go back and wash my hands, come back, move the lamp to the left and look behind it, move the lamp two times to the right and look behind it, go back, wash my hands, and then look in back of the TV on the left 4 times, washing my hands in between each one. Then I look in back of the TV on the right 8 times, wash my hands, and put the TV on channel 6. Then I turn the knob from channel 6 to 7, 4 times, and from channel 6 to channel 8, 4 times. Then finally I turn it on. The whole thing probably takes around half an hour." She had no idea what motivated her ritualistic behavior.

In addition to the rare patient with pure compulsions, a minority of patients report that they do not know why they have to do their compulsions. These patients raise the interesting possibility that, at least for some individuals, the compulsions are primary and that cognitions are attached to them as a way of justifying a reason for doing them.

HOARDING

About one-fifth of the OCD patients in our clinic are hoarders. However, while the symptom is common, it is relatively rare that it dominates the clinical presentation. A visit to the home of anyone of these true hoarders is not easily forgotten. It is often difficult to find any free space with the exception of a narrow passageway through which one maneuvers, praying that you will not bump into the piles of accumulated junk that threaten to topple down on your head at any instant. Most of the house is in incredible disarray and in no seeming order. Isolated islands of very neatly stacked and sorted items such as shopping bags or cat food cans are surrounded by chaos. The reason given for this is always that the person would like to keep the entire house extremely orderly. However, they have long ago given up any hope of this Herculean task and instead have taken to preserving their need for order by concentrating on the one small segment that they feel they have some control over. Twenty-year-old magazines are stacked six feet high because "they might have an article I should read and I can't bear to throw it out before I do." Scores of unworn sportcoats and shirts are strewn in piles in the basement as "I might just get around to wearing them someday." Piles of garbage are stacked up in the kitchen because it has to be gone through carefully before it is thrown out. The only reason most patients come to treatment is because of the complaints of family or friends or the fact that the person becomes isolated and lonely, because of being embarrassed to invite anyone over to the house. These patients often feel compelled to check their possessions over and over to make certain nothing is missing, or to check their garbage to make certain that they have not inadvertently thrown something valuable out. The ego syntonic nature of their symptoms makes one wonder if the syndrome should not be seen as part of a compulsive personality instead of OCD. However, the checking rituals and anxiety attendant with the potential loss of their valued possessions makes it seem more reasonable to classify these patients as suffering from true OCD.

There is a little known animal literature on hoarding and its relationship to the cingulate gyrus, a brain structure that is often implicated in the pathophysiology of OCD (MacLean 1985; Stamm, 1953). Also the need to prepare for a rainy day "just in case" makes for a neuroethologic explanation for hoarding that is consistent with the abnormal risk assessment or need to be on the safe side seen with other OCD subtypes.

PATHOLOGIC RESPONSIBILITY OR DOUBT

This group of patients is characterized by incessant worrisome thoughts that something bad will happen because they have failed to check something thoroughly or completely.

> S. is a 28-year-old fireman. Every night, before going to bed, he has a well-developed checking routine that takes approximately two hours to complete and that includes checking such things as doors, windows, gas, electrical appliances, faucets, medications, etc. He is beset with making "absolutely certain" that doors are "completely" shut and locked, and appliances are "totally" off or unplugged. He is continually obsessed about the possibility that something terrible will happen even though he recognizes that the possibility is an extremely remote one. He knows the door is locked but feels compelled by some overwhelming force to check it over and over because "what if" it was not completely locked.

The experience of pathologic doubt is present across phenomenologic subtypes, but is seen in its purest form in this subgroup of patients. An interesting question that one can ask of these patients is "when are you satisfied that the door is really locked or the faucet is really off?" Many say that if it was not for the fact that they would lose their job or family, they would check all day. One of several strategies is usually adopted in the interest of reducing the time spent checking so the individual can maintain functioning. The most common is to limit the number of checks by counting. Often these patients also develop counting rituals with a system of good and bad numbers. Another is the application of physical force, leading to the snapped off window handles, broken locks, and stripped washers that are often found in the homes of these patients. Some patients report what they describe as the "click phenomena." In the words of one of our checkers, "I will be checking something over and over and the feeling that it's not totally shut is there until suddenly for no rhyme or reason the feeling will no longer be there. It is like clicking a light switch off."

These patients are frequently perfectionists. As Rachman (1980) has noted, they often report having had overly meticulous or overly critical parents. Usually the fear is centered around making certain that nothing terrible will happen, for example, a fire or their children being poisoned by medication left unopened in the medicine cabinet. However, this is not always the case. At times these patients are plagued by constant doubts about things that really do not matter; such as, is the refrigerator door totally shut? is the car window totally shut? Although rationally they will tell you that they would always rather have the thing that they fear happening actually happen to them, rather than have to put up with the incessant checking rituals and obsessive thoughts, they are truly incapable of exacting cognitive and motor control over their behavior.

RELIGIOUS OBSESSIONS

About one in ten patients in our clinic suffer from religious obsessions. It is interesting to note from the perspective of choice of type of OC symptoms, that the frequency of religious OC symptoms appears to be culturally bound. Areas of the world that have religions with strict moral codes are more likely to have higher frequencies of patients with religious obsessions (Akhtar et al., 1975; Okasha, Kamel, & Hassan, 1968; Greenberg, 1984). Also the incidence of religious OC symptoms in OC patients, well-described in the literature on scrupulosity, appears to be on the decline in the United States, concurrent with the liberalization of church laws and procedures. We agree with Greenberg (1984) who hypothesized that patients who develop OC symptoms have a preexisting genotype, and that the development of religious obsessions and compulsions are dependent on that genotype. They obsess over the meaning between mortal and venial sins or whether or not they have followed the letter of the religious law. They tend to be overly serious and hypermoral. Examples are the 37-year-old wife of a Jewish rabbi who spent her entire waking day preparing perfectly Kosher food for her family, or the 26-year-old priest who was continually obsessed with whether or not he had remembered to totally explain all of his sins to God. These patients commonly suffer from the need to confess.

COMORBIDITY OF OCD WITH OTHER AXIS I DISORDERS

Biologic marker and neuropharmacologic challenge studies are dependent on the selection of homogeneous clinical populations that will reduce the variance. In studying a disorder like OCD, comorbidity with other Axis I disorders is a serious obstacle for researchers wishing to

TABLE 2.4 Coexisting Axis I Diagnoses in Primary OCD (n = 100)

Diagnosis	Current Semi-structured percentage	Lifetime	
		Semi-structured percentage	From SADS (n = 60; percentage)
Major depressive disorder	31	67	78
Simple phobia	7	22	28
Separation anxiety disorder	—	2	17
Social phobia	11	18	26
Eating disorder	8	17	8
Alcohol abuse (dependence)	8	14	16
Panic disorder	6	12	15
Tourette's syndrome	5	7	6

obtain homogeneous subgroups. The majority (57%) of OC patients presenting to our clinic had at least one other DSM-III-R diagnosis on admission. To complicate matters further, OCD is a chronic illness; an even higher percentage of our patients have had a history of another lifetime Axis I disorder. Distinguishing primary from secondary diagnoses can be particularly difficult, if not at times impossible.

Almost a third of our patients met criteria for major depressive disorder on admission (see Table 2.4). The next most common secondary diagnoses were simple phobia, social phobia, eating disorders, alcohol abuse, panic disorder, and Tourette's syndrome.

The finding of a high frequency of current and lifetime anxiety disorders suggest that OC patients are vulnerable to virtually all types of anxiety. The high prevalence of anxiety states in these patients may be due to common developmental/temperamental traits whose phenotypic expression are secondary to shared genotypic/psychosocial factors. Of particular interest in this regard is the high lifetime prevalence of separation anxiety in this group of patients, a finding that has also been well-documented in panic disorder (Gittelman & Klein, 1985).

The frequency of coexisting lifetime major depression was 67%, a figure close to that seen for lifetime major depression in panic disorder (Breier, Charney, & Heninger, 1986). Approximately 10% of our patients had psychotic features associated with their primary OCD. This figure corresponds closely to the percentage of psychotic patients that Janet

TABLE 2.5 Common Developmental Antecedents in Adult OCD Probands

Separation anxiety	Perfectionism
Resistance to change or novelty	Hypermorality
Risk aversion	Ambivalence
Submissiveness (compliance)	Excess devotion to work
Sensitivity	

found in his OC clinical population (Pitman, 1987). The group of patients having OCD with psychotic features appears to be heterogeneous (Insel and Akiskal, 1986). Four subtypes have been identified according to clinical symptoms, course of illness, and treatment response (see Table 2.5). Patients with subtypes I and II (schizophrenia and OCD, and schizotypal, marked magical thinking and the need for symmetry plus OCD), appear to have two distinct comorbid disorders. In contrast, patients with subtypes III and IV appear to be suffering from a more severe form of OCD that is similar to nonpsychotic in regard to course of illness and treatment response.

One can look at the coexistence question from a different angle by asking how many patients with other primary diagnoses have significant obsessions or compulsions? Chart review studies of the Chestnut Lodge Followup Study have shown that about 10% of schizophrenics have obsessions and compulsions (Fenton, & McGlasnan, 1986). Several authors have found that a high percentage of Tourette syndrome patients have coexisting OCD (Nee, Caine, Polinsky, & Ebert, 1980; Pauls et al, 1983). Breier and colleagues and Mellman and Uhde, (1987) have reported that 15% of patients with panic disorder also have OCD.

COMORBIDITY OF OCD WITH AXIS II DIAGNOSES

A multicenter collaborative personality study of OCD using structured self-report and obsessions-rated personality inventories has recently been completed. Results have shown that avoidant and dependent personality disorders are the most common among OCD probands (J. Greist, personal communication). Compulsive personality disorders as defined in DSM-III are the next most common. The high incidence of avoidant and dependent personality features in other anxiety disorders further suggests that there is a shared vulnerability between these disorders and OCD. Jenike and colleagues (1986) had found that OCD patients with schizotypal personality have a poor prognosis. Although our initial (Rasmussen & Tsuang, 1986) study found a lower frequency of comorbid schizotypy, there is general agreement among clinicians familiar with OCD that these patients are often treatment resistant.

DEVELOPMENTAL ANTECEDENTS

There has been little systematic study of the developmental antecedents of OCD since Janet's work. In his *Obsessions and Psychasthenia*, Janet outlines how obsessions and compulsions are the most severe stage of an underlying state of psychasthenia. He defined psychasthenia as a syndrome consisting of feelings of incompleteness and imperfection and believed that all patients with obsessions and compulsions at one time passed through a psychasthenic stage. His clinical descriptions of the temperamental features of psychasthenics coincide remarkably well with the childhood traits of our OCD patients and the children of panic patients described by Rosenbaum et al. (1988). His description of the patient who "finds on the stairway, the word that needed to be said in the parlor" is a beautiful clinical description of the independent variable chosen by Kagan, Reznick, and Snidman (1987) to measure behavioral inhibition, that is, speech latency in a novel social situation.

It is important to note that Janet includes four of five elements of DSM-III's compulsive personality disorder in his description of the psychasthenic state: perfectionism, indecisiveness, restricted emotional expression, and timeliness; while the orderly and obstinate aspects of our current definition of compulsive personality derived from Freudian origins (Pitman, 1987). Previous studies have shown that a considerable portion, if not the majority of patients with OCD do not meet DSM-III-R criteria for compulsive personality disorder (Rasmussen & Tsuang, 1984; Rosenberg, 1967). The European diagnostic schema for anakastic personality is more directly related to Janet's original definition of psychasthenia and is consistent with the idea of an obsessive spectrum that ranges from normal obsessional behavior through obsessional personality to OCD.

We have recently conducted a retrospective study of 100 of our OC probands using a semistructured format that was designed to elicit personality traits or temperamental factors commonly found in OCD (unpublished observations). During this study we identified nine factors that were commonly found in our adult OC probands as children (see Table 2.5 and Figure 2.2). These traits tended to be constant throughout development.

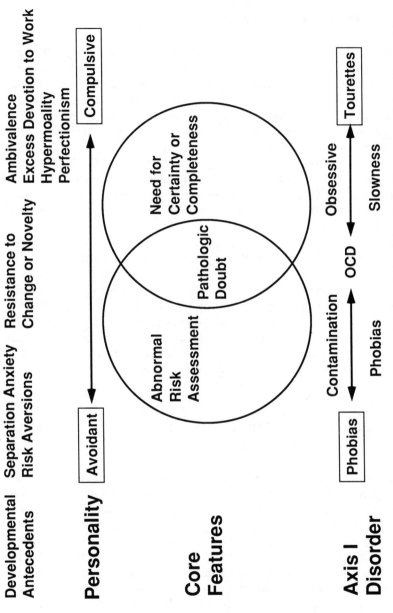

Developmental Antecedents

Separation Anxiety
Risk Aversions

Resistance to
Change or Novelty

Ambivalence
Excess Devotion to Work
Hypermoality
Perfectionism

Personality

Avoidant

Compulsive

Core Features

Abnormal
Risk
Assessment

Pathologic
Doubt

Need for
Certainty or
Completeness

Axis I Disorder

Phobias

Contamination

Phobias

OCD

Obsessive

Slowness

Tourettes

Figure 2.2 Heterogeneity and comorbidity in OCD: Relationship to core features and developmental antecedents.

35

SOME ARGUMENTS FOR HOMOGENEITY ACROSS PHENOMENOLOGIC SUBTYPES

We have conducted an extensive analysis comparing different phenomenologic subgroups across a variety of demographic variables, course of illness, other clinical features, and comorbid diagnoses. To our surprise, there were very few significant differences between subgroups that were identified; suggesting that the disorder is much more homogeneous than its diverse phenomenologic presentations would suggest. Significant differences of interest included more patients with the need for symmetry who had psychotic features ($p < .01$) Tourette's syndrome ($p < .05$), and a continuous or deteriorative course ($p < .01$). Patients with strict religious upbringing were more likely to have religious, sexual, and aggressive obsessions compared to those who had nonstrict upbringings.

Other evidence arguing for relative homogeneity of the disorder includes the following: (a) patients frequently present with multiple obsessions and compulsions; (b) patients usually have several principal obsessions or compulsions over the course of their illness; for example, patients who are primarily troubled by fear of contamination and washing rituals can subsequently develop pathologic doubt with checking and vice versa; and (c) preliminary results from a prospective family study show that in families that have more than one member affected by OCD, the clinical subtype is frequently different.

THE CORE SYNDROME: PHENOMENOLOGIC EVIDENCE FOR HOMOGENEITY

As noted previously, the inexperienced clinician is immediately struck with the diversity of the clinical presentations of OCD. However, although there are many variations in the content of obsessions and compulsions, their underlying form is remarkably consistent: (1) all phenomenologic subgroups with the exception of those who suffer from primary obsessive slowness describe anxiety as the dominant affective symptom; (2) almost all OC patients fear that something terrible will happen to themselves or others for which they will be responsible; and (3) with rare exceptions, compulsions initially serve to reduce anxiety over the short term. It is this anxiety-diminishing property that leads to their reinforcement and maintainence, even in the face of diminished social and occupational function. Although they alleviate anxiety in the short term, they eventually lead to decreased function and adaptive capacity. This is followed by ever-increasing anxiety, feelings of helplessness, and secondary depression.

There is a conflict between rational (cognitive) and irrational (emotional) forces that is present in all subtypes. This conflict in OCD, described by Freud (1916) in his case studies of the Rat Man and Wolf Man led to the formulation of the structural theory of the psyche. It remains to be seen whether or not it will be possible to explain this conflict in explicit neuroanatomical or neurophysiologic terms, regardless of whether or not OCD provides a unique model to study the biologic underpinnings of conflict and defense. MacLean (1985) has pointed out that the primate brain evolved in a hierarchical fashion into a triune brain. He also postulated that rapid evolution of the neomammalian brain may have led to a lack of communication between the new and old brains that could result in neurotic symptoms such as obsessions or compulsions. This hypothesis has taken on new meaning with the demonstration of abnormalities in the orbito medial caudate loop in OCD using PET technology (Baxter et al., 1987).

ABNORMALITIES IN RISK ASSESSMENT: WHAT IF?

OCD is a "what if" illness. Levels of anticipatory anxiety are high across phenomenologic subtypes with the exception of obsessively slow probands. Most OC patients are continually worried about the possibility that something terrible will happen, even if that possibility is a very remote one. If there is a one in a million chance that something terrible will happen, they somehow convince themselves that it will happen to them. There appears to be abnormal risk assessment for possible negative contingencies (see Figure 2.2). "The very fact that it is within the realm of possibility, however unlikely, that I will stab my baby, or poison my child, is enough to terrify me so that I can think of nothing else no matter how hard I try." All of us are faced daily with situations that involve risks. The frontocaudate loop is thought to be involved in the assimilation of tertiary sensory information and its integration with knowledge of past experience as a way of formulating action and selecting motor plans. The orbitomedial frontal areas as well as the caudate and nucleus accumbens, which appear to be abnormal in PET scan studies (Baxter et al., 1987) are thought to integrate limbic or emotional content with other sensory and stored information in the generation of these motor plans. Our brains are designed to make decisions that will optimize security while minimizing risk. Obsessive compulsives tend to be highly conditionable for negatively reinforced events. There is substantial preclinical evidence to suggest that serotonergic neurons are involved in the behavioral punishment system, and that abnormalities in serotonin may result in an animal that is particularly susceptible to negative contingencies in operant conditioning (Gray, 1982). In general, they are willing to trade pleasure to minimize risks. This phenomenon of if there is a one-in-a-million chance it will happen to me, is characteristic of other phobic patients as well as obsessive compulsives. Whereas most of us would have a preconscious mechanism that dismisses a one-in-a-million chance as something to be ignored in planning a motor action, patients with OC are constrained to focus their attention on very unlikely probabilities associated with risk in a given situation, and in focusing their attention on these risks they become obsessed. This may create a response bias that leads to limitations on the range of motor plans that can be selected, which in turn leads to perseveration and compulsivity.

It is likely that this inappropriate focusing of attention on possible negative consequences in the process of decision making and motor planning is at the root of pathologic doubt. From a neuroethological perspective, successful adaptation involves knowing when to take appropriate risks. Studies of primates (Suomi, 1986) have shown that there is a distinct minority of about 20% of individuals making up the gene pool who have been shown to have characteristics of behavioral inhibition that are similar to those found in the behaviorally inhibited children described by Kagan et al. (1987). The overall adaptive advantage for a minority of the gene pool of a given species having a play-it-safe or uptight strategy has been outlined by Suomi (1986). Preliminary evidence indicates that a higher percentage of the offspring of obsessive–compulsive patients are behaviorally inhibited.

We have many patients with OCD who take risks. For example, the 35-year-old female who was afraid of contaminating someone with germs and who had to open doorknobs with paper towels who also loved to parachute. The origin of the specificity and coherence of these patient's fear network is unclear. In explaining the relative stereotypic presentation of OC symptoms, we face the same dilemma found in the simple phobias that Seligman (1971) attempted to explain by his preparedness argument. As noted by Rapoport and Wise (1988), it is possible that obsessions and compulsions are pathologic exaggerations of complex species-specific behaviors stored in the basal ganglia. It remains unclear if the emotional input of the rare but potentially disastrous event is overweighted, or if, as Janet suggested, the compensatory logical mechanisms of cognitive control are deficient or if it is a combination of the two. Stated in clinical terms it remains unclear whether the primary deficit should be linked to excessive anxiety from limbic input, a deficiency in the cognitive factors associated with will or control, or in the mechanism that integrates the two. Understanding in simple neural systems like aplysia how risks are calculated and weighted, and their impact on the formulation of motor plans, may be important in furthering our understanding of the pathophysiology of OCD.

PATHOLOGIC DOUBT: HOW CAN I BE SURE?

Closely linked to this risk assessment abnormality that is found across phenomenologic subgroups is the phenomenon known as pathologic doubt (see Figure 2.2). Although this symptom is most marked in checkers, the need to be absolutely certain is found in all groups. In many ways, pathologic doubt can be seen as a variation of the abnormal risk assessment discussed above. However, one of the criticisms of the concept of risk assessment as being critical to the etiology of OCD is its nonspecificity, i.e., that it is also likely to be important in the etiology of most of the other anxiety disorders. Here then is the opportunity to introduce another concept originally formulated by Janet as being an integral piece of the puzzle of the pathophysiology of OCD, namely the concept of incompleteness (Pitman, 1987). Janet felt that psychasthenics were continually tormented by an inner sense of imperfection. Their actions were never completely achieved and therefore did not produce the sought for satisfaction. It is interesting that the overwhelming majority of our perfectionistic patients report that their parents were not the ones who set impossible standards for them to achieve. Instead they describe an inner drive that is connected to a wish to have things perfect, absolutely certain and under total control. When this perfection is finally achieved, they describe attaining a curious sensation of elation that they can compare to no other feeling. Janet called it "the occasional brief appearance of sublime ecstasy." This absolute certainty or perfection is rarely attained by these patients; and therefore they are usually subject to a feeling of incompleteness. The drive to have the timing just perfect, the sides perfectly balanced, everything in its place, becomes an end in itself and may help explain the perseveration of our patients with obsessive slowness who seem to have gotten preoccupied with the perfection of a given motor subroutine to the exclusion of the overall master routine. This feeling of incompleteness is also found in checkers who want to make absolutely certain the door is totally shut and the faucet is completely off.

When the need for certainty or completeness is applied to the play-it-safe mentality of these patients, pathologic doubt is generated (see Figure 2.2). Beneath this drive for absolute certainty and control lies basic survival instincts. When they are activated it is easier to understand how they might short circuit rationality in a hierarchial Jacksonian model of central nervous system function.

The tendency to overweigh possible negative contingencies as well as the need for certainty are both improved in patients who have a therapeutic response to the serotonin uptake inhibitors. Uncovering the role that serotonin plays in the higher cognitive processes of emotional or limbic input into decision-making processes promises to be an important area for future research.

SOME FUTURE DIRECTIONS

The ongoing characterization of the heterogeneity of OCD and its coexistence with Axis I and II disorders will continue to be important as advances occur in our understanding of the neurobiology, molecular genetics, and treatment of the disorder. Neuropharmacologic and treatment efficacy trials can benefit from the selection of homogenous clinical populations and the exclusion of patients with coexisting disorders. Inclusion of patients with severe depression, psychosis, or personality disorders can create significant differences in results between studies that are otherwise similar in design. However, in genetic studies, strict inclusion criteria may be undesirable, as transmission patterns may be obscured by eliminating coexisting disorders that may have shared genotypic determinants. Data collected over the past five years in our clinic has reaffirmed the brilliant foresight of the clinical observations first made by Pierre Janet almost a century ago. Our ever increasing knowledge in the neurosciences and the advantages of computerized data bases as well as improved methodology for classifying and recoding observations puts us in a position that Janet and Freud could only envy. We can look forward to the analysis of treatment response data according to clinical subtypes and plasma levels from large multicenter pharmacologic trials over the next two years. Completion of ongoing family studies should allow for a more complete analysis of genetic transmission of the disorder, and its relationship to other anxiety disorders, depression and Tourette's syndrome. Data from biologic marker studies can also be correlated with clinical subtype and treatment response data. In the long run, unraveling the relationship between genotypic and psychosocial factors that contribute to the pathogenesis of the disorder is one of its biggest challenges for the next decade. OCD's high prevalence rate and relative homogeneity make it a good candidate for the molecular genetic and family studies that are necessary for this undertaking. Study of the developmental antecedents of the disorder and their relationship to genotypic and environmental factors hold particular promise for clinical researchers. It is very possible that Janet's grouping of phobias, tics, and OC patients under the rubric of psychasthenia will be justified by those studies. Furthering our neurobiologic understanding of the cognitive factors that underlie pathologic doubt, risk assessment and incompleteness is also a major challenge. It is likely that careful phenomenologic observation of patients and neuroethological models of OCD will play an instrumental role in the development and guidance of future studies in this area.

REFERENCES

Akhtar, S., Win, N. N., Varma, V. K., Pershad, D., & Verma, S. K. (1975). A phenomenological analysis of symptoms in obsessive–compulsive neurosis. *British Journal of Psychiatry, 127,* 342–348.

Anthony, J. C., Folstein, M., Romanoski, A. J., Von Korff, M. R., Nestadt, G. R., Chahal, R., Merchant, A., Brown, C. H., Shapiro, S., Karmer, M., & Gruenberg, E. (1985). Comparison of the lay diagnostic interview schedule and a standardized psychiatric diagnosis. *Archives of General Psychiatry, 42,* 667–671.

Baxter, L. R., Phelps, M. E., Mazziotta, J. C., Guze, B. H., Schwartz, J. M., & Selin, C. E. (1987). Local cerebral glucose metabolic rates in obsessive compulsive disorder. *Archives of General Psychiatry, 44,* 211–218.

Bland, R. C., Orn, H., & Newman, S. C. (1988a). Lifetime prevalence of psychiatric disorders in Edmonton. *Acta Psychiatrica Scandinavica, 77*(suppl. 338), 24–32.

Bland, R. C., Newman, S. C., & Orn, H. (1988b). Period prevalence of psychiatric disorders in Edmonton. *Acta Psychiatrica Scandinavica, 77*(suppl. 338), 33–42.

Breier, A., Charney, D. S., & Heninger, G. R. (1986). Agoraphobia with panic attacks. *Archives of General Psychiatry, 43,* 1029–1036.

Casas, M., Alvarez, E., Duro, P., Garcia-Ribera, C., Udina, C., Velat, A., Abella, D., Rodriguez-Espinosa, J., & Slava, F. (1986). Antiandrogenic treatment of obsessive–compulsive neurosis. *Acta Psychiatrica Scandinavica, 73,* 221–222.

Fenton, W. S., & McGlashan, T. H. (1986). The prognostic significance of obsessive–compulsive symptoms in schizophrenia. *American Journal of Psychiatry, 143,* 437–441.

Flament, M. F., Whitaker, A., Rapoport, J. L., Davies, M., ZarembaBerg, C., Kalikow, K., Sceery, W., & Shaffer, D. (1988). Obsessive compulsive disorder in adolescence: An epidemiological study. *Journal of American Academy Child Adolescent Psychiatry, 27,* 764–771.

Freud, S. (1916). Lectures on psycho-analysis. *The Complete Psychological Works of Sigmund Freud, Volume XVI.* London: Hogarth Press.

Fyer, A., & Endicott, J. (1984). The schedule for affective disorders and schizophrenia lifetime version: Modified for study of anxiety disorders. New York State Psychiatric Institute.

Gittelman, R., & Klein, D. F. (1985). Childhood separation anxiety and adult agoraphobia. In A. Y. Tuma & J. D. Maser (Eds.), *Anxiety and the anxiety disorders* (pp. 389–402). Hillsdale, NJ: Erlbaum.

Goodman, W., Price, L. H., Woods, S. W., & Charney, D. S. (1991). Pharmacologic challenges in obsessive–compulsive disorder. In J. Zohar, T. Insel, & S. Rasmussen (Eds.), *The psychobiology of obsessive–compulsive disorder* (pp 162–186). New York: Springer Publishing Company.

Goodman, W. K., Price L. H., Rasmussen, S. A., Mazure, C., Fleishchman, R. L., Hill, C. L., Heninger, G. R., & Charney, D. S. (1989). The Yale-Brown obsessive–compulsive scale. I. Development, use, and reliability. *Archives of General Psychiatry, 46,* 1006–1011.

Gray, J. A. (1984). *The neuropsychology of anxiety: An enquiry into the functions of the septo-hippocampal system.* Oxford: Oxford University Press.

Greenberg, D., & Chir, B. (1984). Are religious compulsions religious or compulsive: A phenomenological study. *American Journal of Psychotherapy, 38,* 524–532.

Helzer, J. E., Robins, L. N., McEvoy, L. T., Spitznagel, E. L., Stoltzman, R. K., Farmer, A., & Brockington, I. F. (1985). A comparison of clinical and diagnostic interview schedule diagnoses. *Archives of General Psychiatry, 42,* 657–666.

Insel, T. R., & Akiskal, H. S. (1986). Obsessive–compulsive disorder with psychotic features: A phenomenologic analysis. *American Journal of Psychiatry, 143,* 1527–1533.

Jenike, M. A., Baer, L., Minichiello, W. E., Schwartz, C. E., & Carey, R. J. (1986). Concomitant obsessive–compulsive disorder and schizotypal personality disorder. *American Journal of Psychiatry, 143,* 530–532.

Kagan, J., Reznick, J. S., & Snidman, N. (1987). The physiology and psychology of behavioral inhibition in children. *Child Development, 58,* 459–473.

Karno, M., Golding, J. M., Sorenson, S. B., & Burnom, A. (1988). The epidemiology of obsessive compulsive disorder in five U.S. communities. *Archives of General Psychiatry, 45,* 1094–1099.

MacLean, P. (1978). Effects of lesions of globus pallidus on species-typical display behavior of squirrel monkeys. *Brain Research, 149,* 175–196.

MacLean, P. D. (1985). Brain evolution relating to family, play, and the separation call. *Archives of General Psychiatry, 42,* 405–417.

Mahl, G. J. (1971). *Psychological conflict and defense.* San Diego, CA: Harcourt, Brace, Jovanivich.

Mellman, T. A., & Uhde, T. W. (1987). Obsessive–compulsive symptoms in panic disorder. *American Journal of Psychiatry, 144,* 167–172.

Munro, A., & Chmara, J. (1982). Monosymptomatic hypochondriacal psychosis: A diagnostic checklist based on 50 cases of the disorder. *Canadian Journal of Psychiatry, 27,* 374–376.

Myers, J. K., Weissman, M. M., Tischler, G. L., Holzer, C. E., Leaf, P. J., Orvaschel, H., Anthony, J. C., Boyd, J. H., Burke, J. D., Kramer, M., & Stoltzman, R. (1984). Six-month prevalence of psychiatric disorders in three sites. *Archives of General Psychiatry, 41,* 959–971.

Nee, L. E., Caine, E. D., Polinsky, R. J., & Ebert, M. H. (1980). Gilles de la tourette syndrome: Clinical and family study of the 50 cases. *Annals of Neurology, 7,* 41–49.

Okasha, A., Kamel, M., & Hassan, A. H. (1968). Preliminary psychiatric observations in Egypt. *American Journal of Psychiatry, 114,* 949–955.

Pauls, D. L., Cohen, D. J., Heimbuch, R., Detlor, J., & Kidd, K. K. (1983). Familial pattern and transmission of Gilles de la tourette syndrome and multiple tics. *Archives of General Psychiatry, 38,* 1091–1093.

Pauls, D. L., Raymond, C. L., & Robertson, M. (1991). The genetics of obsessive–compulsive disorder: A review. In J. Zohar, T. Insel, & S. Rasmussen (Eds.), *The psychobiology of obsessive–compulsive disorder* (pp. 89–100). New York: Springer Publishing Company.

Pitman, R. K. (1987). Pierre Janet on obsessive–compulsive disorder (1903). *Archives of General Psychiatry, 44,* 226–232.

Rachman, S. J., & Hodgson, R. J. (1980). *Obsessions and compulsions.* Englewood Cliffs, NJ: Prentice-Hall, Inc.

Rapoport, J., & Wise, S. P. . Obsessive–compulsive disorder: Is it Basal Ganglia dysfunction? In J. Rapoport (Ed.), *Obsessive–compulsive disorder in children and adolescents* (pp. 327–344). Washington DC: APA Press.

Rasmussen, S. A., & Tsuang, M. (1986). Clinical characteristics and family history in DSM-III obsessive–compulsive disorder. *American Journal of Psychiatry, 143,* 317–322.

Rasmussen, S. A., & Tsuang, M. T. (1984). The epidemiology of obsessive compulsive disorder. *Journal of Clinical Psychiatry, 45,* 450–457.

Robins, L. N., Helzer, J. E., Weissman, M. M., Orvaschel, H., Gruenberg, E., Burke, J. D., & Regier, D. A. (1984). Lifetime prevalence of specific psychiatric disorders in three sites. *Archives of General Psychiatry, 41,* 949–959.

Rosenbaum, J. F., Biederman, J., Gersten, M., Hirshfield, D. R., Meminger, S. R., Herman, J. B., Kagan, J., Reznick, S., & Snidman, N. (1988). Behavioral inhibition in children of parents with panic disorder and agoraphobia. *Archives of General Psychiatry, 45,* 463–470.

Rosenberg, C. M. (1967). Familial aspects of obsessional neurosis. *British Journal of Psychiatry, 113,* 405–413.

Seligman, M. E. P., & Hager, J. (1971). Phobias and preparedness. *Behavior Therapy, 2,* 307–320.

Stamm, J. S. (1953). Effects of cortical lesions on established hoarding activity in rats. *Journal of Comparative Physiology Psychology, 46,* 299–304.

Straus, E. W. M. (1948). On obsession: A clinical and methodological study. *Nervous and Mental Disease Monographs, 73,* 1–124.

Suomi, S. J. (1986). Anxiety like disorders in young nonhuman primates. In R. Gittelman (Ed.), *Anxiety disorders of childhood* (pp. 1–23). New York: Guilford Press.

Thomas, C. S. (1984). Dysmorphophocbia: A question of definition. *British Journal of Psychiatry, 144,* 513–516.

Weizman, A., Zohar, J., Insel, T. (1991). Biologic markers in obsessive-compulsive disorder. In J. Zohar, T. Insel, & S. Rasmussen (Eds.), *The psychobiology of obsessive–compulsive disorder* (pp. 146–161). New York: Springer Publishing Company.

3

Psychometrics in Obsessive–Compulsive Disorder

Michele Tortora Pato
Carlos N. Pato

The emergence of more effective treatments for obsessive–compulsive disorder (OCD) has lessened the "therapeutic pessimism" (Rack, 1973) of clinicians in the field, and has encouraged the careful definition and quantification of symptoms. This systematic characterization of obsessive–compulsive symptoms is necessary to more objectively assess treatment efficacy. However, at present, many of the rating scales used in research studies of obsessive–compulsive disorder are institution specific. This greatly reduces our ability to objectively compare the results from different research groups. The situation is further complicated by the absence of published data on the reliability and validity for many of the scales in use.

This chapter reviews a representative group of some of the more frequently used scales for obsessive–compulsive symptoms. Throughout this chapter, we will comment on the strengths and weaknesses of each of the scales with respect to their value as clinical and research instruments.

A number of specific issues arise when studying obsessive–compulsive disorder. To objectively assess change in these patients, it is often necessary to include measures of depression and anxiety in the rating batteries, and to attempt to control for change in those symptom clusters that are not directly related to obsessive–compulsive disorder (Philpott, 1975). In addition the severity of the disorder is not simply related to the frequency of symptoms but to the level of interference or avoidance experienced (Orme, 1968). It is common to see patients increase their level of avoidance during an exacerbation of their illness.

This can result in a significant decrease in the frequency of symptoms but a significant increase in the degree of interference (Allen & Tune, 1975; Capstick, 1975).

In assessing the relative worth of the various obsessive–compulsive scales, validity and reliability must be considered. Validity is an assessment of how well a scale measures what it claims to measure (Derogatis, & Cleary 1977; Goodman et al., 1989a). In the broadest terms it is hoped that a rating scale will not only describe the phenomonology of an illness—content validity—but that it will measure the elements of the illness it is designed to measure, construct validity (Goodman et al., 1989b; Murphy, Pickar, & Alterman, 1982).

Reliability is a measure of how consistently a scale performs. There are several types of reliability to consider. Interrater reliability is a measure of the variability of a scale as a function of the rater, that is, rater consistency. Internal consistency is a measure of how representative a particular item is of the rest of the items in a scale that are specific to the disorder (Derogatis et al., 1974). Test–retest reliability is a measure of the consistency or stability of ratings over different administrations. Test–retest reliability is best assessed on items that should not change on different administrations of the scale. In scales designed to measure quantitative changes over time, one can not think of test–retest reliability in the truest sense because the expectation is that items will change over time (Murphy et al., 1982). Nonetheless the general concept remains important as the underlying assumption of any scale that measures change is that if the traits being measured are unchanged between two ratings, the ratings will remain the same as well (see Table 3.1).

Rating scales can be categorized in several ways. Perhaps one of the simplest ways is to divide them into those that are self administered and those that are rater administered. Each has advantages and disadvantages many of which are outlined in the remainder of this chapter.

SELF-RATING SCALES FOR OCD

Self-rating scales provide several significant benefits. These scales give access to the patient's inner state, which can be particularly important in OCD which is often a secretive illness. Self-rating affords a savings of professional time and expense, and in particular no rater training is required, though patients may need some instructions on filling out the scales correctly. In measures of depression self-rating scales have correlated well with other measures of depression. The major limitation of self rating is its dependence on the accuracy of the patient's self perception (Murphy et al., 1982). The problem of inaccurate self perception is

TABLE 3.1 Rating Scales for Obsessive–Compulsive Disorder

Scale	Diag-nostic	Repeated Measure	Itemized	Global	Self Rated	Rater Rated	Validity construct	Reliabil-ity inter-rater	Reliabil-ity (test–retest)
LOI	+	+	+		+		?	NA	?
MOCI	?	+	+		+		+	?	+
YB OCS		+	+			+	+	+	+
CPRS-8		+	+ (factor analysis)			+	?	+	NA
HSCL-OC	+	+	+ (factor analysis)		+		?	+	+
NIMH OC		+	+			+	+	NA	NA
NIMH Global OC		+		+		+	+	+	NA
CGI-OC		+		+	+	+	+	NA	NA

? = conflicting reports; NA = not available; LOI = Leyton Obsessional Inventory; MOCI = Maudsley Obsessive Compulsive Inventory; YB OCS = Yale–Brown Obsessive–Compulsive Scale; CPRS = Comprehensive Psychopathological Rating Scale; HSCL-OC = Hopkins Symptom Checklist–Obsessive Compulsive Subscale; NIMH OC–National Institute of Mental Health Obsessive Compulsive Scale; NIMH Global OC = National Institute of Mental Health Global Obsessive Compulsive Scale; CGI-OC = Clinical Global Impression Scale adapted for Obsessive Compulsive Disorder; + = supporting data available.

of particular relevance in OCD as these patients may have particular problems in assessing their own status. Moreover, in some cases the ratings may become a ritual in themselves (Insel et al., 1983). In addition, patients with obsessional doubt may find it difficult to decide between rating items like moderate, much, and severe. In some patients obsessional slowness or need to check may prevent them from completing the form, or extend the time it takes to do the forms as to make repeated measures in the research setting impractical. Finally, as Insel comments, "Some patients consistent with the rigidity that may be seen in compulsive character disorder, resist changing self-ratings until long after clinical improvement was noted by observers" (Insel et al., 1986, p. 610).

The self-rating scales come in many forms. They can include itemized checklists or inventories, global improvement scales (to be discussed later), and visual analog scales like the Individual Self Rating Scales (ISS), which target specific compulsions and chart their change over time, on an 100 mm line (Thoren, Asberg, Cronholm, Jornestedt, & Trachman, 1980). Visual analog scales have the benefit of not asking the patient to decide between different categories of answers (Murphy et al., 1982), this may be of benefit in OCD where the decision process can be so difficult. This hypothesis, however, has not been formally tested.

Leyton Obsessional Inventory

The Leyton Obsessional Inventory (LOI) was developed in the context of a larger study aimed at assessing in detail the daily interactions and activities of very young children at home. As the study progressed a group of mothers were observed who were described as "house proud" or "perfectionistic in their approach to housework and childrearing" (Cooper, 1970). An inventory, later to become known as the LOI, was developed to explore these obsessional traits and attitudes. Hence, the goal of the LOI was to be sufficiently sensitive to differentiate between normals, house proud housewives, and obsessional patients (Cooper, 1970).

The original inventory consisted of two sets of yes–no questions. There were 46 symptom–related questions and 23 trait–related questions. The symptom questions are structured so that a yes answer signifies an element of distress, complaint or nuisance (Cooper, 1970). In all there are ten categories of symptom questions, these are: unpleasant recurring thoughts, checking, dirt and contamination, dangerous objects, personal cleanliness and tidiness, household cleanliness and tidiness, order and routine, repetition, over conscientiousness and lack of satisfaction, and indecision. The trait questions are divided into eight categories: hoarding, cleanliness, meanness, irritability and nervousness, rigidity, health (bowels), regularity and method, and punctuality (Cooper & Kelleher, 1973). The yes answers are followed by a set of two questions, one on resistance and one of interference, each scored on a 0–3 scale. The inclusion of interference and resistance scores was designed to address the issue of severity of symptoms and allow for a clearer discrimination between high scoring normals and low scoring obsessionals (Cooper, 1970). The rationale for this was that the obsessionals would have high interference and resistance scores because of the ego dystonic nature of their symptoms.

The construct validity of the LOI for differentiating between house proud housewives, obsessionals, and normals was established with a significance of $p < .01$ on difference of the means analysis. In addition, construct validity was also significant when discriminating between high scoring normals (house proud housewives, $n = 16$; and normal women, $n = 6$) and low scoring obsessionals ($n = 6$).

There are some problems with the validity of this scale, however. First, because the scale was designed in the context of house proud women, unpleasant obsessional thoughts like blasphemous, obscene, and violent obsessive thoughts, as well as more florid bizarre symptoms, were excluded (Phillpott, 1975) to guard against making this scale offensive to the housewives to whom it was administered (Cooper, 1970). However, leaving out these items compromises the scale's content validity since these potentially important symptoms in OCD patients are missing. In the same vein, many of the questions are oriented toward the home, cleaning and tidiness, and females in general; this makes it less valid for male OCD patients and to patients not involved in maintaining a household. Though there are modified versions of the scale in which questions vary with the sex of the subject (Allen & Tune, 1975) this does not totally allienate the problem. Finally, convergent validity was not tested as no other good OC measures existed at the time.

Cooper did report on test–retest reliability in 30 pairs of pooled subjects from other studies. Symptom subscales showed a product moment correlation of 0.87 and trait subscales yielded 0.91, but changes in resistance and interference scores were noted (Cooper, 1970). Snowdon, in a study of 50 medical students, found that the inventory total scores, symptom scores, and trait scores were all significantly higher on the first administration compared to the second administration ($p < .01$). In reviewing these findings one is led to the conclusion, as Allen notes, ". . . it seems justifiable to use the mean Leyton score as evidence that a given group of patients falls into the obsessional compulsive clinical category, but not as a sole indicator of severity, nor of improvement in studies designed to compare alternative methods of treatment" (Allen & Rack, 1975, p. 43).

Maudsley Obsessive Compulsive Inventory

The Maudsley Obsessive Compulsive Inventory (MOCI, see Appendix 1) was initially developed as a questionnaire for "assessing the existence and extent of different obsessional–compulsive complaints" and also as an outcome measure in treatment research but not as a diagnostic instrument for OCD (Hodgson & Rachman, 1977, p. 389) (see Table 3.1). At the time, it was hoped that delineating among the different types of OC symptoms might have some "theoretical and practical implications." Thus, the 30 questions of the MOCI can be scored as a total and as 4 subscales (Rachman & Hodgson 1980).

The MOCI consists of 30 true–false questions balanced for true and false answers to guard against acquiescent response sets. Responses to these 30 questions underwent principal component analysis with oblique rotation. Forty-three percent of the total variance was accounted for by the four components that became the four subscales of the MOCI. These four components were checking, cleaning, slowness, and doubting. A fifth component, obsessional ruminations, was ignored because only two questions were loaded for this component, but it should be noted that pure ruminators had been excluded from the study sample. Thus unlike the LOI, the MOCI, has a component for slowness and places less emphasis on obsessions.

Not surprisingly, individual patients often scored high on more than one of these subscales. Hodgson emphasized that these four subscales refer to types of problems and not to types of patients (Hodgson & Rachman, 1977). He also pointed out that one potential use of the MOCI in a more clinical setting is to assure that most common symptoms of OCD are covered and to reassure the patient that the therapist has an understanding of their obsessional problems.

Validity and reliability were established in several ways. The authors felt that the scale had inherent content validity because it contained many of the common complaints reported by their patients, furthermore, in the case of checking and cleaning, the components were observable in the patients. Because these were observable, convergent validity was assessed by calculating gamma correlations for the MOCI subscales for cleaning and checking, with therapist global ratings of cleaning and checking. The global ratings were a simple dichotomous rating of 1 = slight or no problem and 2 = moderate or severe problem.

The gamma coefficients were 0.7 and as such considered satisfactory. Convergent construct validity was also established comparing the LOI total score with the MOCI total score with a correlation of 0.6, which was considered good.

A final measure of construct validity was done to assess the MOCI as a measure of change. Pre- and post treatment MOCI total scores were compared to global assessment of improvement by both the clinicians and the patients. The global assessment consisted of a simple three-point scale with 1 = not improved, 2 = slight improvement, and 3 = much improvement. Correlations between the two therapists global scores and the MOCI were 0.67 and 0.74. This was higher than the correlation between patient global scores and the MOCI, which was 0.53 (Hodgson & Rachman, 1977; Rachman & Hodgson, 1980). The superior correlation between the clinician's global assessment and the MOCI to the patient's global assessment and the MOCI is significant because it highlights the problem of self-ratings in this patient population.

A significant flaw in the MOCI when it is used as a measure of change is that each question mandates a simple true or false response. Though Hodgson has encouraged the use of the MOCI as a measure of change, there is no way to measure degree of change in any particular item (Hodgson & Rachman, 1977). Similarly, while it is valuable to establish construct validity, the use of such unspecific measures as a clinician or patient global assessment as a source of comparison provides only a simple validation for the specific items of the MOCI scale.

Reliability measures for the MOCI have also been done. Test–retest reliability was done on a random population of 50 night school students, the tests were administered one month apart and resulted in a Kendall's Tau = 0.8 (Hodgson & Rachman, 1977). A measure of internal consistency was good, with alpha coefficients of 0.7 for checking, slowness, and doubt, and 0.8 for cleaning. Thus, the individual subscales appear to be representative of obsessive–compulsive illness.

Because the MOCI is a self-rating scale, interrater reliability is not a usable concept. However, one would hope for a way of assessing the consistency of the patient's responses. In a sense, such an assessment has been built into the MOCI. There are 6 pairs of questions in the questionnaire, 4 pairs (2/8, 3/7, 10/12, 17/21) that should be answered similarly and 2 pairs (6/22, 16/26) that should be answered oppositely. Taken together, a patient who is consistent in his responses should score a six, one point for each pair done correctly. Any score of three or less, is considered an indicator of inconsistency and the rating should be considered suspect (Hodgson & Rachman, 1977).

Probably the biggest disadvantage in using either of these self-rating scales for outcome studies is that they rely on specific symptoms.

Moreover, any symptom that does not appear in the MOCI or the LOI, no matter how severe, is not reflected in the total scores. On both the MOCI and the LOI, it is the number of symptoms that increases the score, whereas in OCD severity of illness is often a matter of degree and related to interference caused by the symptoms. In this sense the LOI is better than the MOCI because one can use interference and resistance to grade the intensity of the symptoms. However the reliability and validity of these two subcomponents of the LOI are inconclusive.

Hopkins Symptom Checklist (HSCL)

The Hopkins symptom checklist (HSCL, see Appendix 2) is a self-report measure designed for use as a general measure of psychiatric outpatient symptomatology in research and in clinical settings. (Derogatis, Lipman, & Covi, 1973; Guy, 1976). Its intended uses included; outpatient screenings in psychiatric outpatient settings, obtaining symptom information in nonpsychiatric settings, and use as a repeated measure in treatment studies (Guy, 1976). As a self-report scale, it allows for economy of professional time, and an assessment of the inner state of the subject (Derogatis et al., 1974). However, as such, it has many of the flaws we have already noted for self-report measures.

The HSCL comes in two forms. The original form is a 58-item questionnaire, with five symptom dimensions, usually called the HSCL. However, an expanded version of this scale containing 90 items, and nine symptom dimensions, in total, has gained recent popularity and is called the Symptom Checklist 90 (SCL-90) (Guy, 1976; Murphy et al., 1982). The original HSCL symptom dimensions included; obsessive–compulsive, anxiety, depression, somatization, and interpersonal sensitivity. The four added dimensions in the SCL-90 are hostility, phobic anxiety, paranoid ideation, and psychoticism (Derogatis et al., 1973; Guy, 1976). Each item is rated on a 0–4 scale of distress where 0 = not at all, 4 = extreme distress in frequency and/or intensity. These symptom dimensions were constructed by combining two methods of analysis. An empirical factor analysis, similar to that used for the CPRS; and a "clinical rational clustering" (Derogatis et al., 1973). This "clinical rational clustering" was done by asking skilled clinicians to assign items of the HSCL to homogeneous clinical clusters, based on their clinical experience. These two methods were compared and showed good agreement implying some measure of construct validity (Derogatis et al., 1973).

The OC dimension is present on both the original 58-item HSCL and the 90-item SCL-90 scales. On the HSCL it includes 8 items; trouble remembering things, worried about sloppiness or carelessness, feeling blocked or stymied getting things done, having to do things very slowly in order to be sure you are doing them right, having to check and double check what you do, difficulty making decisions, your mind going blank, and trouble concentrating. The SCL-90 contains an additional two items for the OC scale; unwanted thoughts that won't leave your mind and having to repeat the same actions (Steketee & Coppelt, 1986) (see Appendix 2). Thus the focus of the OC scale is on thoughts, impulses, and actions, experienced as unremitting and irresistible, egodystonic and unwanted (Guy, 1976). These items fit well with the clinical syndrome and DSM-III-R diagnosis. Of the ten items the two that are least specific for OCD are "your mind going blank" and "trouble concentrating."

There exists some reliability and validity data for those Hopkins scales, more for the 58-item scale that has been in use longer. The HSCL showed good internal consistency in neurotics with alpha coefficients between .84 and .87, $n = 1435$ test–retest reliability was also high, between .75 and .84, $n = 1425$. Interrater reliability was measured using Interclass Correlations (ICC) and was high between the two raters $r = .64$ to .80, $n = 15$. In OC patients test–retest reliability was lower, $.28 \leq r \leq .56$, $p < .05$, but significant (Steketee & Doppelt 1986). Further analysis revealed that the majority of the change between sessions in OCD patients could be attributed to a change in the depression dimension, $p < .05$.

But Steketee and Doppelt (1986) found poor discriminant and convergent validity when comparing scores on the HSCL for outpatients with OCD and a mixed group of psychiatric disorders. They tried to find a cutoff level able to discriminate between OCD patients and anxious neurotic patients, but even with a score of sixteen, only two-thirds of these patients would be diagnosed correctly. This was felt to represent poor discriminant validity. This poor discriminant validity is further illustrated by moderate correlations between the OC dimension and depression as measured by the Beck Depression Scale ($r = .48$, $p < .05$) and anxiety as measured by the Self-analysis Inventory ($r = .52$, $p < .05$). Convergent validity for OCD showed a mixed picture in Steketee and Doppelt study. At baseline, during a placebo wash-out period, no significant correlation was found between the HSCL 8-item dimension and the other two measures for OC, the MOCI and the Global assessor ratings of OCD. However, these same measurements done post-treatment showed a moderate to high correlation ($r = .36$, $p < .05$ for the Global assessor ratings, and $r = .65$, $p < .001$ for the MOCI). In this study, the HSCL–OC did not show significant change between pre- and post-treatment. Thus, it would appear that the HSCL–OC has some inconsistent construct validity for measuring change. It should be noted that there are two more items in the OC subscale of the SCL-90, and that they may improve validity (Steketee & Doppelt, 1986).

Factor analysed scales like the SCL-90 and the CPRS (to be discussed later) present an additional problem with validity. As Steketee and Doppelt (1986) point out, simple coherence, or co-occurrence, of items in a long check list of symptoms does not mean that those symptoms encompass a single conceptual entity. Because depression and anxiety often co-exist with OCD, it is not surprising that items related to these disorders show up on the OC subscales; but they probably compromise the validity of these scales.

RATER-ADMINISTERED SCALES

Yale–Brown Obsessive–Compulsive Rating Scale

The Yale–Brown Obsessive–Compulsive Rating Scale (Y-BOCS, see Appendix 3) was developed specifically to provide a measure of the severity of symptoms of OCD, but not as a diagnostic measure. It is assumed in administering this scale that the diagnosis of OCD according to DSM-III-R has already been established. (Goodman et al., in 1984a, b). It was hoped that being sensitive to severity, rather than type of symptoms, this scale would provide a better measure of change in OC symptoms, especially for the study of treatment efficacy. This focus on severity irrespective of type and number of symptoms is unique and valuable. It addresses the major flaw of both the MOCI and the LOI, namely the implication that number of symptoms and severity are directly related. Furthermore, unlike these other scales, it is a rater-administered scale, rather than a self-rated scale, which eliminates the reliability issues inherent in self-rating scales in OC patients.

The Y-BOCS is a 16-item scale, but the core of the scale is comprised of the first 10 items (1–10). The sum of these ten items is reported as the total Y-BOCS score. The reliability and validity studies done to date are for these 10 items. The other 6 items (11–16) are considered associated features and their clinical usefulness is still under investigation. These six items include insight, avoidance, indecisiveness, sense of responsibility, slowness, and pathologic doubt (see Appendix 3).

The 10 core items are divided into two balanced sets, five for obsessions and five for compulsions. The first question of each set assesses the time spent on obsessions and the time spent on compulsions. Then the obsessions as a whole and the compulsions as a whole are each rated for interference, distress, resistance, and control. Each of the 10 items is rated on a 0–4 scale, where 0 corresponds to no symptoms and 4 to extreme symptoms. All items are structured so that the higher the score the more severe the symptoms. Thus the maximum score one can attain is 40, a four on each of the 10 items. Scores in the 20s are typical for untreated OCD outpatients.

A good clinical interview is essential for a valid score on the Y-BOCS. While the scale does not record types of OC symptoms in order to make an accurate clinical assessment of the time spent on obsessions and compulsions, and the interference they cause, an understanding of the features of the illness in the particular OCD subject being rated is important. One of the greatest assets of this scale is that it allows for severity comparison between subjects, regardless of the form of their obsessions or compulsions. The Y-BOCS was specifically designed to rate adult OCD patients and the data presented below is based on the adult form of the scale. However, a child form of the Y-BOCS (CY-BOCS), with simpler language, is available.

One more fundamental construct of this scale should be considered, resistance. Other scales besides the Y-BOCS have noted the importance of resistance. Resistance is the urge or effort made to willfully stop an obsessive thought or compulsive act. Both the LOI and the NIMH global OC scale (to be discussed later) contain aspects of resistance. However, in these two scales, the more effort made to resist the more severe the patient's illness. In the LOI a patient receives a 3 if the response is, "I try very hard to stop," in the NIMH Global OC he receives a severe score in the 10–12 range if he responds, "may spend full time resisting symptoms" (see Appendix 4). The Y-BOCS reverses this concept and equates less effort to resist with more severe illness. The rationale behind this bears some explanation, but appears sound. In the LOI and the NIMH Global OC the assumption is made that the urge to resist is intensified with the severity of the illness because resistance is related to the severity of the distress and the lack of control the patient feels over his symptoms. However, distress, control, and resistance need not be of the same intensity. Therefore, the Y-BOCS separately assesses these three items: distress, resistance, and control. This results in a different, more sensitive scoring measure.

For example, some patients who have had severe time-consuming OCD symptoms for years, make little attempt to resist their symptoms. They have learned through experience that they are unable to stop them, despite their anxiety at performing the compulsion or having the obsession. On the LOI or the NIMH Global OC they would score low on resistance; however, on the Y-BOCS they would score high on distress, control, and resistance. In an attempt to validate this conceptualization of resistance, Goodman examined internal consistency for these two resistance items, one for obsessions and one for compulsions. In baseline ratings of 42 OCD outpatients, these items showed a strong correlation $r = .64$, $p < .0001$ for compulsions and a weaker, but significant, correlation $r = .36$, $p < .05$ for obsessions. This would seem to support the premise that severe OC symptoms are associated with less effort to resist symptoms (Goodman et al., in 1984a).

Establishing construct validity is particularly difficult in OCD because all available scales have deficits. However, attempts at establishing convergent and discriminant validity were made. To establish convergent validity the Y-BOCS was compared to the inventory scale MOCI, and to two global rating scales, the Clinical Global Impression Scale, adapted for OCD (CGI-OC) (Guy, 1976), and the NIMH Global OC scale (NIMH-GOC) (Insel et al., 1983; Murphy et al., 1982). The CGI-OC showed consistently significant, high correlation in OCD patients when compared to the Y-BOCS. The NIMH-GOC was compared to the Y-BOCS in a limited group of OCD patients and showed good correlation. On the other hand, the MOCI showed inconsistent correlation with the Y-BOCS. In a small sample ($n = 10$) where both the CGI-OC and the NIMH-GOC were compared to the MOCI, both failed to show significant correlation with the MOCI. Attempts at establishing discriminant validity between OC, depression, and anxiety remain difficult to interpret (Goodman et al., 1989 a, b).

Goodman and colleagues set out to establish some validity for the Y-BOCS as a measure of change in OC symptoms over time, especially in the context of clinical trials (Goodman et al., 1989b). Individual t-tests of mean scores were done on each of the 10 Y-BOCS items pre- and post-treatment with fluvoxamine. The mean scores on all 10 items showed a downward trend, and in 7 of the 10 items (interference due to obsessions, distress due to obsessions, and distress from compulsions, excluded) these decreases were significant at $p < .05$–$p < .001$, $n = 20$. This finding suggests that all 10 items of the Y-BOCS are sensitive to change in OC symptoms.

In addition, Y-BOCS scores pre- and post-fluvoxamine treatment were compared to MOCI and CGI-OC scores pre- and post-treatment. Both total Y-BOCS and CGI-OC showed significant change between pre- and post-treatment measures as determined by point biserial correlation coefficients; $r = .65$, $p < .01$, $n = 21$ and $r = .77$, $p < .001$, $n = 21$, respectively. The MOCI did not show any significant change pre- and post-treatment. In addition, the Y-BOCS and the CGI-OC scores post-treatment were strongly correlated $r = .89$, $p < .0001$, $n = 21$, but the MOCI was not correlated with either the Y-BOCS or the CGI-OC post-treatment. This illustrates one of the problems with the true and false format of the MOCI, namely that it is insensitive to change in OC symptoms while even a global rating like the CGI-OC, is sensitive to change despite lacking the specificity of the Y-BOCS.

Reliability was also tested in several ways using four raters and 40 OCD patients. For the total 10 item Y-BOCS, interrater reliability was assessed by both Pearson product moment correlation coefficients (between $r = .974$ and $r = .982$, $p < .0001$) and Interclass correlation coefficients (ICC) ($r = .98$, $p < .0001$) indicating a high potential for good interrater reliability (Goodman et al., 1989a). This was better than previous reports with six raters and eight patients, ICC = .92, $p < .05$, $r = .72$ to .98, $p < .05$) (Goodman, Rasmussen, Mazure, & Charney, 1987). Internal consistency between the 10 items was also very high and significant as measured by Cronbach's alpha coefficient, $\alpha = .89$, $p < .001$. Finally, test–retest reliability was assessed by comparing baseline scores six to eight weeks apart during the placebo phase of the study, no significant change in scores was noted.

With all this data on reliability and validity, it seems that at the present time the Y-BOCS is the best rating scale available to measure change in OC symptoms over time, thus making it particularly useful for studies of efficacy of treatment.

Comprehensive Psychopathological Rating Scale

Similar to the Y-BOCS, the Comprehensive Psychopathological Rating Scale (CPRS, see Appendix 4) sets out to "measure change in the severity of psychiatric illness" using a clinical interview (Asberg, Montgomery, Perris, Schalling, & Sedvall, 1978; Thoren et al., 1980). The CPRS, however, is a factor-analyzed scale and as such is much greater in scope than the Y-BOCS, because its intent is to cover a wide range of psychiatric signs and symptoms in its 65 subscales.

The OCD subscale of the CPRS is an eight-item scale. It was derived by administering the full CPRS to 13 OCD patients during a placebo washout period. The items in the scale were then rank ordered according to incidence and magnitude of the scores. These summed ranks were again rank ordered and the eight highest ranks became the CPRS-OC (Thoren et al., 1980). The eight items of the CPRS-OC are rituals, inner tension, compulsive thoughts, concentration difficulties, worry over trifles, sadness, lassitude, and indecision. Each item is scored on a 0 to 3 scale where 0 = no symptoms, 1 = occasional, 2 = frequent, and 3 = extreme. Interrater reliability analysis was done individually on each item with r values between .62 ($p < .05$) and .93 ($p < .001$) with analysis of summed items resulting in a $r = .97$ ($p < .001$). The one item that did not reach significance in this analysis was lassitude with $r = .3$, but it was retained on the scale anyway. The interrater reliability with this subscale is comparable to that seen in the 17-item CPRS subscale for depression ($.71 > r < .99$, $p < .001$) (Montgomery et al., 1978).

There are, however, several weaknesses in the CPRS-OC. In light of the factor analysis technique used in constructing the scale, it is not surprising that four of the eight items on the scale are also found on the subscale for depression (inner tension, concentration difficulties, sadness, and lassitude). This can be easily attributed to the frequency with which depression and OCD coexist. This inclusion probably compromises the discriminant validity of the scale, however, formal analysis of discriminant validity is not available. Likewise, no other reliability measures, other than interrater reliability, are available.

Finally, while the items of rituals and compulsive thoughts show good summed interrater reliability, $r = .87$ ($p < .001$), the narrow 0 to 3 scale for severity makes it difficult to sensitively rate patients. These shortcomings make the CPRS-OC a less powerful instrument for its intended purpose of measuring change in OC symptoms.

NIHM Obsessive–Compulsive Scale

The National Institute of Mental Health Obsessive–Compulsive scale (NIMH–OC, see Appendix 5), is an eight-item scale that, similarly to the Y-BOCS, is designed to measure change, and is not a diagnostic scale. It contains mostly items that are commonly seen in OCD. Namely, it includes items to rate obsessions, rituals, impairment, and resistance like the Y-BOCS. But unlike the Y-BOCS it does not rate these separate for obsessions and compulsions, instead it asks for an assessment of impairment and resistance for obsessions and compulsions together. The NIMH-OC does contain two items, slowness and avoidance, that are not stressed in other scales though they are part of OCD symptomatology. These items are particularly important because they can both effect overall obsessions and compulsions. For instance, a person who avoids touching anything because of her compulsive washing may report only moderate compulsions, one hour of washing a day since she avoided touching things, while in fact if she did use her hands freely she might have spent 6 to 8 hours a day in washing rituals. As the symptoms improve and she becomes less avoidant, her time spent on rituals may increase. In most of the scales this would result in a score indicating a worsening of symptoms, while in fact this reflects improvement because there is less avoidance. In such a case the NIMH-OC would more likely show improvement as the avoidance score would go down, while compulsion scores might rise slightly. Reliability and validity data are only now being collected on this scale. The NIMH-OC has shown good correlation with the CPRS-OC, $r = 0.9$ (personal communication, Thomas Insel, 1989).

GLOBAL SCALES—SELF- AND RATER ADMINISTERED

Global assessment ratings by either the subject or clinician have shown good sensitivity to treatment effect (McNair, 1974). Sensitivity is improved by including seven or more categories from which to make the assessment (McNair, 1974). The deficit of global scales is that they lack specificity. Moreover, the general assumption made in these scales is that they are based on adequate objective clinical assessment, on the part of the rater or the subject who is doing the rating. As has already been discussed in the case of self-ratings in OCD patients, this objectivity is suspect.

There are two basic types of global assessment. One type of global assessment is broad, and as such simply asks the subject or clinician to assess whether the subject "feels better" or if there was an "overall therapeutic effect." Such nonspecificity of response makes it difficult to assess whether a drug has had a specific antiobsessive-compulsive effect, or whether its antidepressant or anxiolytic effects were responsible for the improvement. The second type focuses on specific symptoms in OCD and again asks for a global assessment, encompassing severity of symptoms, interference, and resistance. These scales can provide an additional way of measuring change, are easy and quick to administer, and when given as part of a full battery of OC measures can be useful.

NIMH Global Obsessive–Compulsive Scale

The NIMH Global Obsessive Compulsive Scale (NIMH-GOC, see Appendix 6) is a good example of a global scale. Following the model of global subscales in depression (Murphy et al., 1982; Insel et al., 1983), the NIMH-OC global is a 1 to 15 rater-administered point scale rating subjects only in regard to their OC symptoms. The scale is split into five broad groups: 1 to 3: minimal; within normal; 4 to 6: subclinical OC behavior; 7 to 9: clinical OC behavior; 10 to 12: severe OC behavior; 13 to 15: very severe OC behavior. Within each of the five subdivisions there is a description of the interference and resistance aspects of OC for that level of severity, therefore, as in the LOI, it is on the basis of interference and resistance that the assessment is made. As noted earlier, the greater the resistance the worse the OC symptoms are considered, in contrast to the position taken in the Y-BOCS (Goodman et al., 1984a, b).

Clinical Global Improvement

The Clinical Global Improvement scales (CGI, see Appendix 7) come in many varieties and are examples of the broad global-assessment scales. They usually involve either the rater or the patient assessing their overall sense of improvement either on a scale of numbers like 1 to 7 in which 4 indicates no change, 1 is severely worse, and 7 markedly improved or else recording a similar kind of data on a 100 mm line, analog scale. The CGI-OC is as such a broad scale in which the rater or patient is specifically asked to assess his change in OC symptoms in this general way (Guy, 1976). As noted in the presentation of the YBOCS earlier in this chapter, the CGI-OC has shown good convergent validity with other OC measures like the YBOCS and the NIMH-GOC. (Goodman et al., 1989a, b).

Individual Self-Rating Scale

Though not traditionally thought of as a global assessment, the Individual Self-rating Scales (ISS) (Thoren et al., 1980), which are commonly used in behavioral studies in which certain symptoms are targeted (Marks, Stern, Mawson, Cobb, & McDonald, 1980), are a type of global assessment. They reflect change as a general construct, and not along specific dimensions like time spent, interference, resistance, distress, or avoidance, as in the Y-BOCS or the LOI. Change is expressed as a single number, or line length in the case of visual analogue scales. Thus, as in other global scales, it lacks specificity, but is able to measure change. An additional deficit of the ISS, however, is that because it targets specific symptoms, it may miss change that has taken place in other areas. This is especially true in its use for behavioral therapy where easily observable symptoms like handwashing, or checking, are monitored and obsessions are not. Global scales can provide a quick general nonspecific sense of change and, as noted, have shown some interrater reliability with some measures of depression (Beck et al., 1975).

OTHER OC SCALES

There are several other scales that bear mention, most are institution specific and have not gained wide use.

Lynfield Obsessional Compulsive Questionnaire

The Lynfield Obsessional Compulsive Questionnaire (Allen & Tune, 1975), is a shortened, 20 question version of the Leyton. Similar to the LOI, each question has a resistance and an interference question as well. It was felt that this shortened version focused on obsessional symptoms, regardless of diagnosis and so would be better as a quickly administered pencil and paper version of the LOI for measure of change rather than diagnosis.

Shapiro Card Sort

The Shapiro Card Sort (Capstick, 1975) is also a measure of change that was individualized for each patient and for specific target symptoms. For each symptom the patient would target half to full improvement and rate, on each occasion, which he was closest to; no improvement, half improvement, or full improvement. A cumbersome and time-consuming measure it had the advantage, similar to the Individual self-rating scales (ISS), of being individualized to each patient.

The New Rating Scale for Obsessional and Phobic States

Most intriguing of these little known scales is one devised by Beaumont (1975) that hoped to measure change in OC symptoms for a drug trial in the early 1970s. It contained many of the items included in the better scales already mentioned, including measures of obsessions and compulsions on the dimensions of anxiety, resistance, and interference, and measures of related symptoms like depression. Interestingly it also included assessment of whether performance of the ritual increased or decreased anxiety, an intriguing concept in the context of behavioral treatment and one that has not been included in other OC rating scales.

Challenge Scales

This chapter has focused on diagnostic measures and measures of change in treatment trials of DSM-III-R Axis I Obsessive–Compulsive Disorder. Those scales most sensitive to change like the Y-BOCS, were designed to be given at weekly intervals (Goodman, 1989a, 1989b). This leaves a real gap for studies that try to measure change over a very short period of time as in pharmacologic challenge studies. Because of the short time interval between repeated measures, scales need to be quick and easy to complete and very sensitive to change. In addition, in the case of OCD patients many of the rituals are performed in secret, or only in specific situations that may not be present in the exam room at the time of the study, acute improvement or worsening of symptoms is particularly hard to assess. To date, researchers have tried to address these problem by using a combination of global assessments, both self-rated and rater rated (Charney et al., 1988; Zohar, Mueller, Insel, Zohar-Kadouch, & Murphy, 1987; Zohar, Insel, Zohar-Kadouch, Hill, & Murphy, 1988). For self-ratings, visual analogs scales seem to be an option for this purpose because they are easier to complete for OC patients, and because of the sensitivity to change of such global ratings (McNair, 1974). Zohar and colleagues used a modified version of the CPRS 8, called the CPRS 5 that excludes the items of sadness, inner tension, and worrying about trifles, as a repeated measure in a challenge study (Zohar et al., 1987, 1988). Their results seemed to show that the CPRS 5 was sensitive to change in this challenge setting. A challenge scale version of the Yale Brown Obsessive Compulsive Scale (Goodman, W., personal communication 1989) has also been devised. (see Appendix 4) The validity and reliability of these measures in this context have not been studied.

CONCLUSIONS

As in rating any group of patients, one tries to obtain a reliable and valid scale for what one chooses to measure. In the case of OCD ratings, the problem of reliability and validity is compounded by the ritualistic and secretive nature of the illness, and its poorly demarcated interface with both depression and anxiety disorders.

For measuring change in symptoms over time and with repeated measures, the Y-BOCS is probably the most sensitive measure available. The MOCI is less sensitive to change because of its true–false format, and the HSCL-OC symptom dimension has questionable validity, (Steketee & Doppelt, 1986) and the limits of a self-report measure. The CPRS-OC, though a rater administered measure of change, might lack specificity, as half of its items are also included in depression, and might lack some sensitivity because severity is rated on a 0 to 3 rather than a 0 to 4 scale. In addition there is little formal data on the reliability and validity of the CPRS-OC. The LOI was not designed as a measure of change (Allen & Rack, 1975), and has problems on test–retest reliability (Snowdon, 1980).

Despite their lack of specificity, a global rating like the CGI-OC or

NIMH global OC are easy to administer and have shown sensitivity to change (McNair, 1974). Finally, in an assessment of OC the issue of avoidance and its relation to symptom severity should not be over-looked, both in the baseline measures and over time.

For a diagnostic assessment MOCI can be of some additional help to a good clinical interview in initial assessment by identifying specific symptom types in a quick self-administered manner. If a more extensive diagnostic test is desired the LOI can be given as well.

Any time one is assessing OC symptoms it is impossible to avoid symptoms of depression and anxiety. Therefore, full assessment of OCD at baseline or over time should include some measure of anxiety and depression as well, though they are not formally part of an OC measure. This way the covariance of these symptoms with OC symptoms can be studied and a fuller picture of what is, and is not, changing over time can be assessed.

REFERENCES

Allen, J., & Rack, P. (1975). Changes in obsessive-compulsive patients as mea-sured by the Leyton inventory before and after treatment with clomipra-mine. *Scottish Medical Journal, 20,* 41.

Allen, J., & Tune, G. (1975). The Lynfield obsessional compulsive question-naires. *Scottish Medical Journal, 20,* 21.

Asberg, M., Montgomery, S., Perris, C., Schalling, D., & Sedvall, G. (1978). A comprehensive psychopathological rating scale. *Acta Psychiatrica Scandinavi-ca, 271* (suppl.), 5.

Beaumont, G. (1975). A new rating scale for obsessional and phobic states. *Scottish Medical Journal, 20,* 25.

Beck, P., Gram, L., Deim, E., Jacobsen, O., Vitger, J., & Bolwig, T. (1975). Quantitative rating of depressive states. *Acta Psychiatrica Scandinavica, 51,* 161.

Capstick, N. (1975). The Shapiro Cards Scale as a method of assessment of obsessional symptoms in clomipramine therapy. *Scottish Medical Journal, 20,* 17.

Charney, D., Goodman, W., Price, L., Woods, S., Rasmussen, S., & Heninger, G., (1988). Serotonin function in obsessive–compulsive disorder. *Archives of General Psychiatry, 45,* 177–185.

Cooper, J. (1970). The Leyton obsessional inventory. *Psychiatric Medicine, 1,* 48.

Cooper, J., & Kelleher, M. (1973). The Leyton obsessional inventory: A principal component analysis on normal subjects. *Psychiatric Medicine, 3,* 204.

Derogatis, L., Lipman, R., & Covi, L. (1973). The SCL-90: An outpatient psy-chiatric rating scale. *Psychopharmacology Bulletin, 9,* 13.

Derogatis, L., Lipman, R., Rickels, K., Wilemhuth, E., & Covi, L. (1974). The

Hopkins symptom checklist (HSCL): A self-report symptom inventory. *Behavioral Science, 19,* 1.

Derogatis, L., & Cleary, P. (1977). Confirmation of the dimensional structure of the SCL-90: A study in construct validation. *Journal of Clinical Psychology, 33,* 981–989.

Dinning, W., & Evan, R. (1977). Discriminant and convergent validity of the SCL-90 in psychiatric inpatients. *Journal of Personality Assessment, 41,* 304–310.

Goodman, W., Price, L., Rasmussen, S., Mazure, C., Leischmann, R., Hill, C., Heninger, G., & Charney, D. (1989a). The Yale-Brown obsessive compulsive scale (Y-BOCS): Part I. Development, use and reliability. *Archives of General Psychiatry, 46,* 1006–1011.

Goodman, W., Price, L., Rasmussen, S., Mazure, C., Leischmann, R., Hill, C., Heninger, G., & Charney, D. (1989b). The Yale-Brown obsessive compulsive scale (Y-BOCS): Part II, Validity. *Archives of General Psychiatry, 46,* 1012–1016.

Goodman, W., Rasmussen, S., Mazure, C., & Charney, D. (1987). Measurement of treatment response in OCD: Use and validation of the Yale-Brown obsessive compulsive scale. *Abstract ACNP.*

Guy, W. (1976). ECDEU assessment manual for psychopharmacology. Publication 76-338. U.S. Department of Health, Education, and Welfare. Washington, DC: U.S. Government Printing Office.

Hodgson, R., & Rachman, S. (1977). Obsessional compulsive complaints. *Behaviour Research Therapy, 15,* 384.

Insel, T., Murphy, D., Cohen, R., Atterman, I., Kilts, C., & Linnoila, M. (1983). Obsessive compulsive disorder: A double-blind trial of clomipramine and dorgyline. *Archives of General Psychiatry, 40,* 605.

Marks, I., Stern, R., Mawson, D., Cobb, J., & McDonald, R. (1980). Clomipramine and exposure for obsessive compulsive rituals. *British Journal of Psychiatry, 136,* 1.

McNair, D. (1974). Original investigations self-evaluations of antidepressants. *Psychopharmacology, 37,* 281.

Montgomery, S., Asberg, M., Jornestedt, L., Thoren, P., Traskman, L., McAulet, R., Montgomery, D. & Shaw, P. (1978). Reliability of the clinical psychopathological rating scale between the disciplines of psychiatry, general practice, nursing, and psychology in depressed patients. *Acta Psychiatrica Scandinavica, 271* (suppl.), 29.

Murphy, D., Pickar, D., & Alterman, J. (1982). Methods for the quantitative assessment of depression and manic behavior. In E. Burdock, A. Sudilovsky, & S. Gershon (Eds.), *The behavior of psychiatric patients: Quantitative techniques for evaluation* (pp. 355–392.) New York: Marcel Dekker.

Orme, J. (1968). Are obsessionals neurotic or are neurotics obsessional? *British Journal of Medical Psychology, 41,* 415.

Philpott, R. (1975). Recent advances in the behavioral measurement of obsessional illness: Difficulties common to these and other measures. *Scottish Medical Journal, 20,* 33.

Rachman, S., & Hodgson, R. (1980). Obsessions and compulsions. New York: Prentice Hall.

Rack, P. (1973). Clomipramine (anafranil) in the treatment of obsessional states with special reference to the Leyton obsessional inventory. *Journal of International Medical Research, 1,* 397.

Snowdon, J. (1980). A comparison of written and post box forms of the Leyton obsessional inventory. *Psychological Medicine, 10,* 165.

Steketee, G. & Doppelt, H. (1986). Measurement of obsessive–compulsive Symptomalogy: Utility of the Hopkins symptom checklist. *Psychiatry Research, 19,* 135–145.

Thoren, P., Asberg, M., Cronholm, P., Jornestedt, L., & Trachman, L. (1980). Clomipramine treatment of obsessive compulsive disorder. A controlled clinical trial. *Archives of General Psychology, 37,* 1281.

Zohar, J., Mueller, E., Insel, T., Zohar-Kadouch, R., & Murphy, D. (1987). Serotonergic responsivity in obsessive-compulsive disorder: Comparison of patients and healthy controls. *Archives of General Psychology, 44,* 946–951.

Zohar, J., Insel, T., Zohar-Kadouch, R., Hill, J., & Murphy, D. (1988). Serotonergic responsivity in obsessive–compulsive disorder: Effects of chronic clomipramine treatment. *Archives of General Psychology, 45,* 167–172.

Appendix 1: The Maudsley Obsessional–Compulsive Inventory (MOC)

Instructions: Please answer each question by putting a circle around the "TRUE" or the "FALSE" following the question. There are no right or wrong answers, and no trick questions. Work quickly and do not think too long about the exact meaning of the question.

1. I avoid using public telephones because of possible contamination.   TRUE   FALSE
2. I frequently get nasty thoughts and have difficulty in getting rid of them.   TRUE   FALSE
3. I am more concerned than most people about honesty.   TRUE   FALSE
4. I am often late because I can't seem to get through everything on time.   TRUE   FALSE
5. I don't worry unduly about contamination if I touch an animal.   TRUE   FALSE
6. I frequently have to check things (e.g., gas or water taps, doors, etc.) several times.   TRUE   FALSE
7. I have a very strict conscience.   TRUE   FALSE
8. I find that almost every day I am upset by unpleasant thoughts that come into my mind against my will.   TRUE   FALSE
9. I do not worry unduly if I accidentally bump into somebody.   TRUE   FALSE
10. I usually have serious doubts about the simple everyday things I do.   TRUE   FALSE
11. Neither of my parents was very strict during my childhood.   TRUE   FALSE
12. I tend to get behind in my work because I repeat things over and over again.   TRUE   FALSE
13. I use only an average amount of soap.   TRUE   FALSE
14. Some numbers are extremely unlucky.   TRUE   FALSE
15. I do not check letters over and over again before mailing them.   TRUE   FALSE
16. I do not take a long time to dress in the morning.   TRUE   FALSE
17. I am not excessively concerned about cleanliness.   TRUE   FALSE
18. One of my major problems is that I pay too much attention to detail.   TRUE   FALSE
19. I can use well-kept toilets without any hesitation.   TRUE   FALSE
20. My major problem is repeated checking.   TRUE   FALSE
21. I am not unduly concerned about germs and diseases.   TRUE   FALSE
22. I do not tend to check things more than once.   TRUE   FALSE
23. I do not stick to a very strict routine when doing ordinary things.   TRUE   FALSE
24. My hands do not feel dirty after touching money.   TRUE   FALSE
25. I do not usually count when doing a routine task.   TRUE   FALSE

26.	I take rather a long time to complete my washing in the morning.	TRUE	FALSE
27.	I do not use a great deal of antiseptics.	TRUE	FALSE
28.	I spend a lot of time every day checking things over and over again.	TRUE	FALSE
29.	Hanging and folding my clothes at night does not take up a lot of time.	TRUE	FALSE
30.	Even when I do something very carefully I often feel that it is not quite right.	TRUE	FALSE

Scoring Key for the Maudsley Obsessional–Compulsive Inventory

Instructions: Score 1 when a response matches that of this key and 0 when it does not; maximum scores for the five scales are, therefore, respectively 30, 9, 11, 7, 7. Factor 5 (i.e., ruminations) has not been scored, since only Q2 and Q8 loaded on it. A "TRUE" response to these two items is possibly a sign of ruminations. Only the checking, washing, and total obsessional scores have been validated; the "slowness–repetition" and doubting–conscientious" factors need replication and validation.

	Total Obsessional Score	Checking	Washing	Slowness Repetition	Doubting Conscientious
Q1	True	—	True	—	—
Q2	True	True	—	False	—
Q3	True	—	—	—	True
Q4	True	—	True	True	—
Q5	False	—	False	—	—
Q6	True	True	—	—	—
Q7	True	—	—	—	True
Q8	True	True	—	False	—
Q9	False	—	False	—	—
Q10	True	—	—	—	True
Q11	False	—	—	—	False
Q12	True	—	—	—	True
Q13	False	—	False	—	—
Q14	True	True	—	—	—
Q15	False	False	—	—	—
Q16	False	—	—	False	—
Q17	False	—	False	—	—
Q18	True	—	—	—	True
Q19	False	—	False	—	—
Q20	True	True	—	—	—
Q21	False	—	False	—	—
Q22	False	False	—	—	—
Q23	False	—	—	False	—
Q24	False	—	False	—	—
Q25	False	—	—	False	—
Q26	True	True	True	—	—
Q27	False	—	False	—	—
Q28	True	True	—	—	—
Q29	False	—	—	False	—
Q30	True	—	—	—	True

Appendix 2: Hopkins Symptom Checklist (SCL = 90)

NAME _____
LOCATION _____ DATE _____

RATER _____ TECH. _____ S. NO. _____
REMARKS _____
_____

INSTRUCTIONS

Below is a list of problems and complaints that people sometimes have. Please read each one carefully. After you have done so, please fill in one of the numbered spaces to the right that best describes HOW MUCH THAT PROBLEM HAS BOTHERED OR DISTRESSED YOU DURING THE PAST   IN-CLUDING TODAY. Mark only one numbered space for each problem and do not skip any items. Make your marks carefully using a No. 2 pencil. DO NOT USE A BALLPOINT PEN. If you change your mind, erase your first mark completely. Please do not make any extra marks on the sheet. Please read the example below before beginning.

EXAMPLE

HOW MUCH WERE YOU
BOTHERED BY

	Not at all	A little bit	Moderately	Quite a bit	Extremely / Backaches
Backaches	⓪	①	②	③	④

HOW MUCH WERE YOU
                    BOTHERED BY

	Not at all	A little bit	Moderately	Quite a bit	Extremely
1. Headaches	⓪	①	②	③	④
2. Nervousness or shakiness inside	⓪	①	②	③	④
3. Unwanted thoughts words or ideas that won't leave your mind	⓪	①	②	③	④
4. Faintness or dizziness	⓪	①	②	③	④

5. Loss of sexual interest or pleasure   ⓪   ①   ②   ③   ④
6. Feeling critical of others   ⓪   ①   ②   ③   ④
7. The idea that someone else can control your
   thoughts   ⓪   ①   ②   ③   ④
8. Feeling others are to blame for most of your
   troubles   ⓪   ①   ②   ③   ④
9. Trouble remembering things   ⓪   ①   ②   ③   ④
10. Worried about sloppiness or carelessness   ⓪   ①   ②   ③   ④
11. Feeling easily annoyed or irritated   ⓪   ①   ②   ③   ④
12. Pains in heart or chest   ⓪   ①   ②   ③   ④
13. Feeling afraid in open spaces or on the streets ⓪ ① ② ③ ④
14. Feeling low in energy or slowed down   ⓪   ①   ②   ③   ④
15. Thoughts of ending your life   ⓪   ①   ②   ③   ④
16. Hearing voices that other people do not hear ⓪ ①   ②   ③   ④
17. Trembling   ⓪   ①   ②   ③   ④
18. Feeling that most people cannot be trusted ⓪   ①   ②   ③   ④
19. Poor appetite   ⓪   ①   ②   ③   ④
20. Crying easily   ⓪   ①   ②   ③   ④
21. Feeling shy or uneasy with the opposite sex ⓪   ①   ②   ③   ④
22. Feeling of being trapped or caught   ⓪   ①   ②   ③   ④
23. Suddenly scared for no reason   ⓪   ①   ②   ③   ④
24. Temper outbursts that you could not control ⓪   ①   ②   ③   ④
25. Feeling afraid to go out of your house alone ⓪ ①   ②   ③   ④
26. Blaming yourself for things   ⓪   ①   ②   ③   ④
27. Pains in lower back   ⓪   ①   ②   ③   ④
28. Feeling blocked in getting things done   ⓪   ①   ②   ③   ④
29. Feeling lonely   ⓪   ①   ②   ③   ④
30. Feeling blue   ⓪   ①   ②   ③   ④
31. Worrying too much about things   ⓪   ①   ②   ③   ④
32. Feeling no interest in things   ⓪   ①   ②   ③   ④
33. Feeling fearful   ⓪   ①   ②   ③   ④
34. Your feelings being easily hurt   ⓪   ①   ②   ③   ④
35. Other people being aware of your private
    thoughts   ⓪   ①   ②   ③   ④
36. Feeling others do not understand you or are
    unsympathetic   ⓪   ①   ②   ③   ④
37. Feeling that people are unfriendly or dislike
    you   ⓪   ①   ②   ③   ④
38. Having to do things very slowly to insure
    correctness   ⓪   ①   ②   ③   ④
39. Heart pounding or racing   ⓪   ①   ②   ③   ④
40. Nausea or upset stomach   ⓪   ①   ②   ③   ④
41. Feeling inferior to others   ⓪   ①   ②   ③   ④
42. Soreness of your muscles   ⓪   ①   ②   ③   ④
43. Feeling that you are watched or talked about
    by others   ⓪   ①   ②   ③   ④
44. Trouble falling asleep   ⓪   ①   ②   ③   ④
45. Having to check and double-check what you
    do   ⓪   ①   ②   ③   ④
46. Difficulty making decisions   ⓪   ①   ②   ③   ④
47. Feeling afraid to travel on buses, subways or
    trains   ⓪   ①   ②   ③   ④

48. Trouble getting your breath   ⓪ ① ② ③ ④
49. Hot or cold spells   ⓪ ① ② ③ ④
50. Having to avoid certain things, places, or activities because they frighten you   ⓪ ① ② ③ ④
51. Your mind going blank   ⓪ ① ② ③ ④
52. Numbness or tingling in parts of your body   ⓪ ① ② ③ ④
53. A lump in your throat   ⓪ ① ② ③ ④
54. Feeling hopeless about the future   ⓪ ① ② ③ ④
55. Trouble concentrating   ⓪ ① ② ③ ④
56. Feeling weak in parts of your body   ⓪ ① ② ③ ④
57. Feeling tense or keyed up   ⓪ ① ② ③ ④
58. Heavy feelings in your arms or legs   ⓪ ① ② ③ ④
59. Thoughts of death or dying   ⓪ ① ② ③ ④
60. Overeating   ⓪ ① ② ③ ④
61. Feeling uneasy when people are watching or talking about you   ⓪ ① ② ③ ④
62. Having thoughts that are not your own   ⓪ ① ② ③ ④
63. Having urges to beat, injure, or harm someone   ⓪ ① ② ③ ④
64. Awakening in the early morning   ⓪ ① ② ③ ④
65. Having to repeat the same actions such as touching, counting, washing   ⓪ ① ② ③ ④
66. Sleep that is restless or disturbed   ⓪ ① ② ③ ④
67. Having urges to break or smash things   ⓪ ① ② ③ ④
68. Having ideas or beliefs that others do not share   ⓪ ① ② ③ ④
69. Feeling very self-conscious with others   ⓪ ① ② ③ ④
70. Feeling uneasy in crowds, such as shopping or at a movie   ⓪ ① ② ③ ④
71. Feeling everything is an effort   ⓪ ① ② ③ ④
72. Spells of terror or panic   ⓪ ① ② ③ ④
73. Feeling uncomfortable about eating or drinking in public   ⓪ ① ② ③ ④
74. Getting into frequent arguments   ⓪ ① ② ③ ④
75. Feeling nervous when you are left alone   ⓪ ① ② ③ ④
76. Others not giving you proper credit for your achievements   ⓪ ① ② ③ ④
77. Feeling lonely even when you are with people   ⓪ ① ② ③ ④
78. Feeling so restless you couldn't sit still   ⓪ ① ② ③ ④
79. Feelings of worthlessness   ⓪ ① ② ③ ④
80. Feeling that familiar things are strange or unreal   ⓪ ① ② ③ ④
81. Shouting or throwing things   ⓪ ① ② ③ ④
82. Feeling afraid you will faint in public   ⓪ ① ② ③ ④
83. Feeling that people will take advantage of you if you let them   ⓪ ① ② ③ ④
84. Having thoughts about sex that bother you a lot   ⓪ ① ② ③ ④
85. The idea that you should be punished for your sins   ⓪ ① ② ③ ④
86. Feeling pushed to get things done   ⓪ ① ② ③ ④

87. The idea that something serious is wrong with
your body   ⓪   ①   ②   ③   ④
88. Never feeling close to another person   ⓪   ①   ②   ③   ④
89. Feelings of guilt   ⓪   ①   ②   ③   ④
90. The idea that something is wrong with your
mind   ⓪   ①   ②   ③   ④

SCL-90—Factorial Composition

I. Somatization ($N = 12$)

Item No.	Item
42	Soreness of muscles
52	Numbness or tingling in parts of your body
58	Heavy feelings in your arms or legs
56	Weakness in parts of your body
12	Pains in heart or chest
49	Hot or cold spells
27	Pains in lower back
48	Trouble getting your breath
4	Faintness or dizziness
53	A lump in your throat
1	Headaches
40	Nausea or upset stomach

II. Obsessive–Compulsive ($N = 10$)

45	Having to check and double-check what you do
38	Having to do things very slowly to insure correctness
51	Your mind going blank
9	Trouble remembering things
46	Difficulty making decision
55	Trouble concentrating
10	Worried about sloppiness or carelessness
28	Feeling blocked in getting things done
65	Having to repeat the same actions, *i.e.*, counting, washing
3	Unwanted thoughts, etc., that won't leave your mind

III. Interpersonal Sensitivity ($N = 9$)

6	Feeling critical of others
21	Feeling shy or uneasy with the opposite sex
34	Your feelings being easily hurt
36	Feeling others do not understand you or are unsympathetic
37	Feeling that people are unfriendly or dislike you
41	Feeling inferior to others
61	Feeling uneasy when people are watching or talking about you
69	Feeling very self-conscious with others
73	Feeling uncomfortable about eating or drinking in public

IV. Depression (*N* = 13)

5	Loss of sexual interest or pleasure
14	Feeling low in energy or slowed down
15	Thoughts of ending your life
20	Crying easily
22	Feeling of being trapped or caught
26	Blaming yourself for things
29	Feeling lonely
30	Feeling blue
31	Worrying too much about things
32	Feeling no interest in things
54	Feeling hopeless about the future
71	Feeling everything is an effort
79	Feelings of worthlessness

V. Anxiety (*N* = 10)

2	Nervousness or shakiness inside
17	Trembling
23	Suddenly scared for no reason
33	Feeling fearful
39	Heart pounding or racing
57	Feeling tense or keyed up
72	Spells of terror and panic
78	Feeling so restless you can't sit still
80	Feeling that familiar things are strange or unreal
86	Feeling pushed to get things done

VI. Anger-Hostility (*N* = 6)

11	Feeling easily annoyed or irritated
24	Temper outbursts you can not control
63	Having urges to beat, injure, or harm someone
67	Having urges to break or smash things
74	Getting into frequent arguments
81	Shouting or throwing things

VII. Phobic Anxiety (*N* = 7)

13	Feeling afraid in open spaces or on the streets
25	Feeling afraid to go out of your house alone
47	Feeling afraid to travel on buses, subways, or trains
70	Feeling uneasy in crowds, such as shopping or at a movie
75	Feeling nervous when you are left alone
82	Feeling afraid you will faint in public
50	Having to avoid certain things, etc., because they frighten you

VIII. Paranoid Ideation (*N* = 6)

8	Feeling others are to blame for most of your troubles
18	Feeling that most people cannot be trusted
43	Feeling that you are watched or talked about by others
68	Having ideas or beliefs that others do not share
76	Others not giving you proper credit for your achievements
83	Feeling that people will take advantage of you if you let them

IX. Psychoticism ($N = 10$)
7	The idea that someone else can control your thoughts
16	Hearing voices that other people do not hear
35	Other people being aware of your private thoughts
62	Having thoughts that are not your own
77	Feeling lonely even when you are with people
84	Having thoughts about sex that bother you a lot
85	The idea that you should be punished for your sins
87	The idea that something serious is wrong with your body
88	Never feeling close to another person
90	The idea that something is wrong with your mind

SCL-90 Additional Scales
19	Poor appetite
60	Overeating
44	Trouble falling asleep
64	Awakening in the early morning
66	Sleep that is restless or disturbed
59	Thoughts of death or dying
89	Feelings of guilt

Appendix 3: Yale-Brown Obsessive Compulsive Scale (Y-BOCS)

"I am now going to ask several questions about your obsessive thoughts." [Make specific reference to the patient's target obsessions.]

1. Time Occupied by Obsessive Thoughts
   Q: How much of your time is occupied by obsessive thoughts? [When obsessions occur as brief, intermittent intrusions, it may be difficult to assess time occupied by them in terms of total hours. In such cases, estimate time by determining how frequently they occur. Consider both the number of times the intrusions occur and how many hours of the day are affected. Ask:] How frequently do the obsessive thoughts occur? [Be sure to exclude ruminations and preoccupations which, unlike obsessions, are ego-syntonic and rational (but exaggerated).]
      0 = None
      1 = Mild, less than 1 hr/day or occasional intrusion
      2 = Moderate, 1 to 3 hrs/day or frequent intrusion
      3 = Severe, greater than 3 or up to 8 hrs/day or very frequent intrusion
      4 = Extreme, greater than 8 hrs/day or near constant intrusion

1b. Obsession-Free Interval (not included in total score)
   Q: On the average, what is the longest number of consecutive waking hours per day that you are completely free of obsessive thoughts? [If necessary, ask:] What is the longest block of time in which obsessive thoughts are absent?
      0 = No symptoms
      1 = Long symptom-free interval, more than 8 consecutive hours/day symptom-free
      2 = Moderately long symptom-free interval, more than 3 and up to 8 consecutive hours/day symptom-free
      3 = Short symptom-free interval, from 1 to 3 consecutive hours/day symptom-free
      4 = Extremely short symptom-free interval, less than 1 consecutive hour/day symptom-free

2. Interference due to Obsessive Thoughts
   Q: How much do your obsessive thoughts interfere with your social or work (or role) functioning? Is there anything that you don't do because of them? [If currently not working determine how much performance would be affected if patient were employed.]
      0 = None
      1 = Mild, slight interference with social or occupational activities, but overall performance not impaired
      2 = Moderate, definite interference with social or occupational performance, but still manageable

       3 = Severe, causes substantial impairment in social or occupation-
          al performance
       4 = Extreme, incapacitating

3. Distress Associated with Obsessive Thoughts
    Q: How much distress do your obsessive thoughts cause you? [In most
        cases, distress is equated with anxiety; however, patients may report
        that their obsessions are "disturbing" but deny "anxiety." Only rate
        anxiety that seems triggered by obsessions, not generalized anxiety or
        anxiety associated with other conditions.]
        0 = None
        1 = Mild, not too disturbing
        2 = Moderate, disturbing, but still manageable
        3 = Severe, very disturbing
        4 = Extreme, near constant and disabling distress

4. Resistance Against Obsessions
    Q: How much of an effort do you make to resist the obsessive thoughts?
        How often do you try to disregard or turn your attention away from
        these thoughts as they enter your mind? [Only rate effort made to
        resist, not success or failure in actually controlling the obsessions. How
        much the patient resists the obsessions may or may not correlate with
        his/her ability to control them. Note that this item does not directly
        measure the severity of the intrusive thoughts; rather it rates a man-
        ifestation of health, i.e., the effort the patient makes to counteract the
        obsessions by means other than avoidance or the performance of com-
        pulsions. Thus, the more the patient tries to resist, the less impaired is
        this aspect of his/her functioning. There are "active" and "passive"
        forms of resistance. Patients in behavioral therapy may be encouraged
        to counteract their obsessive symptoms by not struggling against them
        (e.g., "just let the thoughts come"; passive opposition) or by in-
        tentionally bringing on the disturbing thoughts. For the purposes of
        this item, consider use of these behavioral techniques as forms of
        resistance. If the obsessions are minimal, the patient may not feel the
        need to resist them. In such cases, a rating of "0" should be given.]
        0 = Makes an effort to always resist, or symptoms so minimal
           doesn't need to actively resist
        1 = Tries to resist most of the time
        2 = Makes some effort to resist
        3 = Yields to all obsessions without attempting to control them,
           but does so with some reluctance
        4 = Completely and willingly yields to all obsessions

5. Degree of Control over Obsessive Thoughts
    Q: How much control do you have over your obsessive thoughts? How
        successful are you in stopping or diverting your obsessive thinking?

Can you dismiss them? [In contrast to the preceding item on resistance, the ability of the patient to control his obsessions is more closely related to the severity of the intrusive thoughts.]

    0 = Complete control

    1 = Much control, usually able to stop or divert obsessions with some effort and concentration

    2 = Moderate control, sometimes able to stop or divert obsessions

    3 = Little control, rarely successful in stopping or dismissing obsessions, can only divert attention with difficulty

    4 = No control, experienced as completely involuntary, rarely able to even momentarily alter obsessive thinking

"The next several questions are about your compulsive behaviors." [Make specific reference to the patient's target compulsions.]

6. Time Spent Performing Compulsive Behaviors

    Q: How much time do you spend performing compulsive behaviors? [When rituals involving activities of daily living are chiefly present, ask:] How much longer than most people does it take to complete routine activities because of your rituals? [When compulsions occur as brief, intermittent behaviors, it may be difficult to assess time spent performing them in terms of total hours. In such cases, estimate time by determining how frequently they are performed. Consider both the number of times compulsions are performed and how many hours of the day are affected. Count separate occurrences of compulsive behaviors, not number of repetitions; e.g., a patient who goes into the bathroom 20 different times a day to wash his hands 5 times very quickly, performs compulsions 20 times a day, not 5 or $5 \times 20 = 100$. Ask:] How frequently do you perform compulsions? [In most cases compulsions are observable behaviors (e.g., hand washing), but some compulsions are covert (e.g., silent checking).]

    0 = None

    1 = Mild (spends less than 1 hr/day performing compulsions), or occasional performance of compulsive behaviors

    2 = Moderate (spends from 1 to 3 hrs/day performing compulsions), or frequent performance of compulsive behaviors

    3 = Severe (spends more than 3 and up to 8 hrs/day performing compulsions), or very frequent performance of compulsive behaviors

    4 = Extreme (spends more than 8 hrs/day performing compulsions), or near constant performance of compulsive behaviors (too numerous to count)

6b. Compulsion-Free Interval (not included in total score)

    Q: On the average, what is the longest number of consecutive waking hours per day that you are completely free of compulsive behavior? [If

necessary, ask:] What is the longest block of time in which compulsions
are absent?

   0 = No symptoms
     1 = Long symptom-free interval, more than 8 consecutive
       hours/day symptom-free
     2 = Moderately long symptom-free interval, more than 3 and up
       to 8 consecutive hours/day symptom-free
     3 = Short symptom-free interval, from 1 to 3 consecutive hours/
       day symptom-free
     4 = Extremely short symptom-free interval, less than 1 con-
       secutive hour/day symptom-free

7. Interference due to Compulsive Behaviors
   Q: How much do your compulsive behaviors interfere with your social or
     work (or role) functioning? Is there anything that you don't do because
     of the compulsions? [If currently not working determine how much
     performance would be affected if patient were employed.]
     0 = None
       1 = Mild, slight interference with social or occupational activities,
         but overall performance not impaired
       2 = Moderate, definite interference with social or occupational
         performance, but still manageable
       3 = Severe, causes substantial impairment in social or occupation-
         al performance
       4 = Extreme, incapacitating

8. Distress Associated with Compulsive Behavior
   Q: How would you feel if prevented from performing your compulsion(s)?
     [Pause] How anxious would you become? [Rate degree of distress
     patient would experience if performance of the compulsion were sud-
     denly interrupted without reassurance offered. In most, but not all
     cases, performing compulsions reduces anxiety. If, in the judgement of
     the interviewer, anxiety is actually reduced by preventing compulsions
     in the manner described above, then ask:] How anxious do you get
     while performing compulsions until you are satisfied they are com-
     pleted?
     0 = None
       1 = Mild only slightly anxious if compulsions prevented, or only
         slight anxiety during performance of compulsions
       2 = Moderate, reports that anxiety would mount but remain man-
         ageable if compulsions prevented, or that anxiety increases
         but remains manageable during performance of compulsions
       3 = Severe, prominent and very disturbing increase in anxiety if
         compulsions interrupted, or prominent and very disturbing
         increase in anxiety during performance of compulsions
       4 = Extreme, incapacitating anxiety from any intervention aimed
         at modifying activity, or incapacitating anxiety develops dur-
         ing performance of compulsions

9. Resistance against Compulsions
   Q: How much of an effort do you make to resist the compulsions? [Only rate effort made to resist, not success or failure in actually controlling the compulsions. How much the patient resists the compulsions may or may not correlate with his ability to control them. Note that this item does not directly measure the severity of the compulsions; rather it rates a manifestation of health, i.e., the effort the patient makes to counteract the compulsions. Thus, the more the patient tries to resist, the less impaired is this aspect of his functioning. If the compulsions are minimal, the patient may not feel the need to resist them. In such cases, a rating of "0" should be given.]

   0 = Makes an effort to always resist, or symptoms so minimal doesn't need to actively resist
   1 = Tries to resist most of the time
   2 = Makes some effort to resist
   3 = Yields to almost all compulsions without attempting to control them, but does so with some reluctance
   4 = Completely and willingly yields to all compulsions

10. Degree of Control over Compulsive Behavior
   Q: How strong is the drive to perform the compulsive behavior? [Pause] How much control do you have over the compulsions? [In contrast to the preceding item on resistance, the ability of the patient to control his compulsions is more closely related to the severity of the compulsions.]

   0 = Complete control
   1 = Much control, experiences pressure to perform the behavior but usually able to exercise voluntary control over it
   2 = Moderate control, strong pressure to perform behavior, can control it only with difficulty
   3 = Little control, very strong drive to perform behavior, must be carried to completion, can only delay with difficulty
   4 = No control, drive to perform behavior experienced as completely involuntary and overpowering, rarely able to even momentarily delay activity

"The remaining questions are about both obsessions and compulsions. Some ask about related problems." These are investigational items not included in total Y-BOCS score but may be useful in assessing these symptoms.

11. Insight into Obsessions and Compulsions
   Q: Do you think your concerns or behaviors are reasonable? [Pause] What do you think would happen if you did not perform the compulsion(s)? Are you convinced something would really happen? [Rate patient's insight into the senselessness or excessiveness of his obsession(s) based on beliefs expressed at the time of the interview.]

0 = Excellent insight, fully rational

1 = Good insight; readily acknowledges absurdity or excessiveness of thoughts or behaviors but does not seem completely
convinced that there isn't something besides anxiety to be
concerned about (i.e., has lingering doubts)

2 = air insight; reluctantly admits thoughts or behavior seem
unreasonable or excessive, but wavers; may have some un-
realistic fears, but no fixed convictions

3 = Poor insight; maintains that thoughts or behaviors are not
unreasonable or excessive, but acknowledges validity of contrary evidence (i.e., overvalued ideas present)

4 = Lacks insight, delusional; definitely convinced that concerns
and behavior are reasonable, unresponsive to contrary evidence

12. Avoidance

Q: Have you been avoiding doing anything, going any place, or being
with anyone because of your obsessional thoughts or out of concern
you will perform compulsions? [If yes, then ask:] How much do you
avoid? [Rate degree to which patient deliberately tries to avoid things.
Sometimes compulsions are designed to "avoid" contact with something that the patient fears. For example, clothes washing rituals
would be designated as compulsions, not as avoidant behavior. If the
patient stopped doing the laundry then this would constitute avoidance.]

0 = No deliberate avoidance

1 = Mild, minimal avoidance

2 = Moderate, some avoidance; clearly present

3 = Severe, much avoidance; avoidance prominent

4 = Extreme, very extensive avoidance; patient does almost
everything he/she can to avoid triggering symptoms

13. Degree of Indecisiveness

Q: Do you have trouble making decisions about little things that other
people might not think twice about (e.g., which clothes to put on in
the morning; which brand of cereal to buy)? [Exclude difficulty making
decisions which reflect ruminative thinking. Ambivalence concerning
rationally-based difficult choices should also be excluded.]

0 = None

1 = Mild, some trouble making decisions about minor things

2 = Moderate, freely reports significant trouble making decisions
that others would not think twice about

3 = Severe, continual weighing of pros and cons about nones-
sentials

4 = Extreme, unable to make any decisions; disabling

14. Overvalued Sense of Responsibility
    Q: Do you feel very responsible for the consequences of your actions? Do you blame yourself for the outcome of events not completely in your control? [Distinguish from normal feelings of responsibility, feelings of worthlessness, and pathological guilt. A guilt-ridden person experiences himself or his actions as bad or evil.]
    0 = None
    1 = Mild, only mentioned on questioning, slight sense of over-responsibility
    2 = Moderate, ideas stated spontaneously, clearly present; patient experiences significant sense of over-responsibility for events outside his/her reasonable control
    3 = Severe, ideas prominent and pervasive; deeply concerned he/she is responsible for events clearly outside his control; self-blaming farfetched and nearly irrational
    4 = Extreme, delusional sense of responsibility (e.g., if an earthquake occurs 3,000 miles away patient blames herself because she didn't perform her compulsions)

15. Pervasive Slowness/Disturbance of Inertia
    Q: Do you have difficulty starting or finishing tasks? Do many routine activities take longer than they should? [Distinguish from psychomotor retardation secondary to depression. Rate increased time spent performing routine activities even when specific obsessions cannot be identified.]
    0 = None
    1 = Mild, occasional delay in starting or finishing
    2 = Moderate, frequent prolongation of routine activities but tasks usually completed; frequently late
    3 = Severe, pervasive and marked difficulty initiating and completing routine tasks; usually late
    4 = Extreme, unable to start or complete routine tasks without full assistance

16. Pathological Doubting
    Q: After you complete an activity do you doubt whether you performed it correctly? Do you doubt whether you did it at all? When carrying out routine activities do you find that you don't trust your senses (i.e., what you see, hear, or touch)?
    0 = None
    1 = Mild, only mentioned on questioning, slight pathological doubt; examples given may be within normal range
    2 = Moderate, ideas stated spontaneously, clearly present and apparent in some of patient's behaviors; patient bothered by significant pathological doubt; some effect on performance but still manageable

        3 = Severe, uncertainty about perceptions or memory promi-
            nent; pathological doubt frequently affects performance
        4 = Extreme uncertainty about perceptions constantly present;
            pathological doubt substantially affects almost all activities;
            incapacitating (e.g., patient states "my mind doesn't trust
            what my eyes see")

[Items 17 and 18 refer to global illness severity. The rater is required to consider global function, not just the severity of obsessive–compulsive symptoms.]

17. Global Severity: Interviewer's judgement of the overall severity of the patient's illness. Rated from 0 (no illness) to 6 (most severe patient seen). [Consider the degree of distress reported by the patient, the symptoms observed, and the functional impairment reported. Your judgement is required both in averaging this data as well as weighing the reliability or accuracy of the data obtained. This judgement is based on information obtained during the interview.]
    0 = No illness
    1 = Illness slight, doubtful, transient; no functional impairment
    2 = Mild symptoms, little functional impairment
    3 = Moderate symptoms, functions with effort
    4 = Moderate–severe symptoms, limited functioning
    5 = Severe symptoms, functions mainly with assistance
    6 = Extremely severe symptoms, completely nonfunctional

18. Global Improvement: Rate total overall improvement present SINCE THE INITIAL RATING whether or not, in your judgement, it is due to drug treatment.
    0 = Very much worse
    1 = Much worse
    2 = Minimally worse
    3 = No change
    4 = Minimally improved
    5 = Much improved
    6 = Very much improved

19. Reliability: Rate the overall reliability of the rating scores obtained. Factors that may affect reliability include the patient's cooperativenes and his/her natural ability to communicate. The type and severity of obsessive–compulsive symptoms present may interfere with the patient's concentration, attention, or freedom to speak spontaneously (e.g., the content of some obsessions may cause the patient to choose his words very carefully).
    0 = Excellent, no reason to suspect data unreliable
    1 = Good, factor(s) present that may adversely affect reliability
    2 = Fair, factor(s) present that definitely reduce reliability
    3 = Poor, very low reliability

Items 17 and 18 are adapted from the Clinical Global Impression Scale (Guy W: ECDEU Assessment Manual for Psychopharmacology: Publication 76-388. Washington, D.C., U.S. Department of Health, Education, and Welfare (1976).

Additional information regarding the development, use, and psychometric properties of the Y-BOCS can be found in Goodman WK, Price LH, Rasmussen SA, et al.: The Yale-Brown Obsessive Compulsive Scale (Y-BOCS): Part I. Development, use, and reliability. *Arch Gen Psychiatry* (46:1006–1011, 1989). and Goodman WK, Price, LH, Rasmussen SA, et al.: The Yale-Brown Obsessive Compulsive Scale (Y-BOCS): Part II. Validity. *Arch Gen Psychiatry* (46:1012–1016, 1989).

Copies of a version of the Y-BOCS modified for use in children, the Children's Yale-Brown Obsessive Compulsive Scale (CY-BOCS) (Goodman WK, Rasmussen SA, Price LH, Mazure C, Rapoport JL, Heninger GR, Charney DS), is available from Dr. Goodman on request.

Appendix 4: Comprehensive PsychoPathological Rating Scale (CPRS)

NAME_____ DATE_____ RATER_____

Obsessive–Compulsive Disorder Subscale

Reported Psychopathology

1. Sadness

Representing subjectively experienced mood, regardless of whether it is reflected in appearance or not. Includes depressed mood, low spirits, despondency, and the feeling of being beyond help and without hope. Rate according to intensity, duration, and the extent to which the mood is influenced by events.
Elated mood is scored zero on this item.

   0 Occasional sadness may occur in the circumstances.
   1 Predominant feelings of sadness, but brighter moments occur.
   2 Pervasive feelings of sadness or gloominess. The mood is hardly influenced by external circumstances.
   3 Continuous experience of misery or extreme despondency.

2. Inner tension

Representing feelings of ill-defined discomfort, edginess, inner turmoil, mental tension mounting to panic, dread, and anguish. Rate according to intensity, frequency, duration, and the extent of reassurance called for.
Distinguish from sadness (1) and worrying (3).

   0 Placid. Only fleeting inner tension.
   1 Occasional feelings of edginess and ill-defined discomfort.
   2 Continuous feelings of inner tension, or intermittent panic which the patient can only master with some difficulty.
   3 Unrelenting dread or anguish. Overwhelming panic.

3. Worrying over trifles

Representing apprehension, and undue concern over trifles, which is difficult to stop and out of proportion to the circumstances.
Distinguish from inner tension (2) compulsive thoughts (4) and indecision (6).

   0 No particular worries.
   1 Undue concern, worrying that can be shaken off.
   2 Apprehensive and bothered about trifles or minor daily routines.
   3 Unrelenting and often painful worrying. Reassurance is ineffective.

4. Compulsive thoughts

Representing disturbing or frightening thoughts or doubts which are experienced as silly or irrational, but keep coming back against one's will. Distinguish from worrying (3).

0 No repetitive thoughts.
1 Occasional compulsive thoughts that are not disturbing.
2 Frequent disturbing compulsive thoughts.
3 Incapacitating or obnoxious obsessions, occupying one's entire mind.

5. Rituals

Representing a compulsive repeating of particular acts or rituals that are regarded as unnecessary or absurd and resisted initially but cannot be suppressed without discomfort.
The rating is based on the time spent on rituals and the degree of social incapacity.

0 No compulsive behavior.
1 Slight or occasional compulsive checking.
2 Clearcut compulsive rituals which do not interfere with social performance.
3 Extensive rituals or checking habits that are time-consuming and incapacitating.

6. Indecision

Representing vacillation and difficulty in choosing between simple alternatives. Distinguish from worrying (3) and compulsive thoughts (4).

0 No indecisiveness
1 Some vacillation but can still make a decision when necessary.
2 Indecisiveness or vacillation that restricts or prevents actions, makes it difficult to answer simple questions, or make simple choices.
3 Extreme indecisiveness even in situations where conscious deliberation is not normally required, such as whether to sit or stand, enter or stay outside.

7. Lassitude

Representing a difficulty getting started or slowness in initiating and performing everyday activities.
Distinguish from indecision (6).

0 Hardly any difficulty in getting started. No sluggishness.
1 Difficulties in starting activities.
2 Difficulties in starting simple routine activities that are carried out only with effort.
3 Complete inertia. Unable to start activity without help.

8. Concentration difficulties

Representing difficulties in collecting one's thoughts mounting to incapacitating lack of concentration.
Rate according to intensity, frequency, and degree of incapacity produced.

0 No difficulties in concentrating.
1 Occasional difficulties in collecting one's thoughts.
2 Difficulties in concentrating and sustaining thought that interfere with reading and conversation.
3 Incapacitating lack of concentration.

Appendix 5: NIMH Obsessive–Compulsive Rating

For each item, please indicate the number that best describes the patient.

1. Obsessional thoughts [doubts, urges, images] experienced as silly or irrational, but intrude involuntarily. Exclude recurrent memories of past events (ruminations). ____

0 Absent	1, 2 Occasional preoccupa-tion, but not disturbing thoughts	3, 4 Frequent, in-terfere with concentra-tion	5, 6 Intense pre-occupation almost in-capacitating	7 Incapacitated from thoughts

2. Rituals—acts (e.g. washing, checking, undoing) that are regarded as absurd and are accompanied by resistance. Rate on basis of interference in social or work functioning. Interference should be directly related to rituals and not secondary to depression or character pathology. ____

0 Absent	1, 2 Occasional, does not in-terfere	3, 4 Frequent, some in-terference	5, 6 Intense, ma-jor in-terference	7 Incapacitated

3. Resistance to obsessions or compulsions (experience of internal struggle). ____

0 Absent, no subjective sense of struggle, obsessions and com-pulsions ab-sent	1, 2 Resistance leads to clear reduction of symptoms	3, 4 Resistance mostly in public, mod-erately suc-cessful at reducing symptoms	5, 6 Resistance is not associ-ated with decrease in symptoms	7 Struggle abandoned, over-whelmed by obsession or compulsion

4. Slowness (lateness, inability to complete tasks, extended time for routine chores). ____

0 Absent	1, 2 Occasional delay in starting or finishing	3, 4 Routine ac-tivities twice as long but completed	5, 6 Unable to complete routine chores (takes four times as long)	7 Unable to function

5. Neurotic guilt (blames self for unrelated acts, overvalued sense of responsibility). ____

0	1, 2	3, 4	5, 6	7
Absent	Occasional sense of over-responsibility	Considers self bad or weak but not at fault for unrelated events	Blames self irrationally for unrelated events	Delusions of guilt

6. Impairment (combines 1–5) ____

0	1, 2	3, 4	5, 6	7
Absent, functioning at top level	Generally functioning well, occasional subjective sense of impairment	Moderate impairment both subjectively and objectively	Severe deficits in functioning (e.g., unable to work because of symptoms)	Totally impaired

7. Anxiety (excluding panic attacks) related to obsessions or compulsions; this form of anxiety may occur prior to other OC symptoms as anticipatory anxiety or it may be temporally associated with symptoms. ____

0	1, 2	3, 4	5, 6	7
Absent, normal anxiety unrelated to obsessions or compulsions	Slight anxiety from obsessions, not leading to rituals	Moderate anxiety, entirely relieved by or not leading to rituals	Intense anxiety, related to obsessions and rituals	Overwhelmed by anxiety

8. Avoidant behavior ____

0	1, 2	3, 4	5, 6	7
Absent	Infrequent avoidance	Avoidance leads to difficulty at work or everyday functioning (e.g. driving using subway, etc.)		Avoidance leads to inability to work

Appendix 6: NIMH Global Obsessive–Compulsive Scale

1 to 3 *Minimal within range of normal*, mild symptoms. Person spends little time resisting them. Almost no interference in daily activity.

4 to 6 *Subclinical obsessive–compulsive behavior*, mild symptoms that are noticeable to patient and observer, cause mild interference in patient's life and which he may resist for a minimal period of time. Easily tolerated by others.

7 to 9 *Clinical obsessive–compulsive behavior*. Symptoms that cause significant interference in patients life and which he spends a great deal of conscious energy resisting. Requires some help from others to function in daily activity.

10 to 12 *Severe obsessive–compulsive behavior*. Symptoms that are crippling to the patient, interfering so that daily activity "an active struggle." Patient *may* spend full time resisting symptoms. Requires much help from others to function.

13 to 15 *Very severe obsessive–compulsive behavior*. Symptoms that completely cripple patient so that he requires close staff supervision over eating, sleeping, etc. Very minor decision making or minimal activity require staff support, "worst I've ever seen."

Appendix 7: CLINICAL GLOBAL IMPROVEMENT

Rater Global Evaluation

Overall therapeutic effect since patient started the treatment:

1. Very much improved
2. Much improved
3. Minimally improved
4. Unchanged
5. Minimally worse
6. Much worse
7. Very much worse

Patient Global Impressions

Compared with how I felt before the treatment, I now am:

1. Very much improved
2. Much improved
3. Minimally improved
4. Unchanged
5. Minimally worse
6. Much worse
7. Very much worse

4

The Genetics of Obsessive–Compulsive Disorder: A Review

David L. Pauls
Cindy L. Raymond
Mary Robertson

Obsessive–compulsive disorder (OCD) has become the focus of considerable research interest over the last decade. This renewal of interest has been buoyed by the successful treatment of some patients with new behavioral and pharmacologic strategies (Insel & Murphy, 1981; Marks, 1981; Steketee, Foa, & Grayson, 1982). In addition, recent epidemiological research (Robins et al., 1984) has suggested that OCD is much more prevalent than was originally believed. Most of the recent research has focused on the phenomenology of the illness and the response to treatment. While response to pharmacologic agents and findings that specific regions of the brain may be involved with the observed symptomatology suggest a biologic etiology, little work has been done to examine the possible role of genetic factors. In their 1981 review of the evidence for genetic factors in obsessional disorder, Carey and Gottesman cite Slater and Cowie's 1971 review in which they stated that "all of these investigations [twin and family history studies] are rather old now, and it would be very desirable to have more modern work to refer to." Unfortunately, little has changed since 1971. Aside from Carey and Gottesman's review there have been only a few small studies that have examined the possible role of genetics. The results from several of these studies are difficult to compare because distinct assessment strategies were employed and different criteria were used to assign affected status

Acknowledgment: This work supported in part by a grant from NINCDS (NS-16648) and a Research Scientist Development Award from NIMH (MH-00508).

to relatives. In only two recent studies (Lenane et al., 1988; Pauls et al., 1988) did the investigators attempt to assess personally all first degree relatives of OCD probands. Even with these shortcomings, the results from most of the work on OCD suggests that genetic factors may be important in the etiology of the illness.

Before specifically reviewing the data on OCD, we will briefly summarize the kinds of evidence needed to demonstrate that genetic factors are etiologically important for a given illness. A genetic element for a disorder is assumed if an enzyme or structural protein is abnormal or absent. Certain other biochemical aberrations are presumptive evidence of genetic influence even in the absence of family data. Unfortunately for OCD, the biochemical studies done to date have not yet provided evidence for any genetic abnormality. In the absence of biochemical data, there are at least four other types of evidence that suggest genetic factors are responsible for a disease of unknown etiology: (1) a higher concordance rate among monozygotic (MZ) twins than among dizygotic (DZ) twins; (2) a significant aggregation of the illness within families when compared to the population prevalence; (3) a higher incidence of the trait among biological offspring of affected individuals than among biological offspring of unaffected individuals, when those individuals have been reared in adoptive homes where the parents did not have the trait under investigation; and, (4) genetic linkage of the illness with an identifiable allele at a marker locus.

THE TWIN STUDY METHOD

The twin method consists of comparing the number of MZ twin pairs in which both members are affected (i.e., the pair is concordant) to the number of concordant DZ twin pairs. This method is used primarily to obtain preliminary evidence that genetic factors are important in the disorder being studied. The method can also be used to provide an estimate of the heritability of a particular disorder. Heritability is defined as the proportion of the total phenotypic variance trait that is due to genetic factors.

MZ twins are genetically identical. Thus, if differences between MZ twins occur, they can be due to genetic mutations or to different environmental influences experienced by the two developing individuals. Because genetic mutation of this type is an extremely rare event, the differences are usually assumed to be environmentally induced. DZ twins are no more closely related genetically than two siblings born at different times. Any differences between DZ twins are attributed to both genetic and environmental factors. Presumably, if DZ twins are more alike than two siblings, it could be due to shared environment. It should be emphasized that environmental influences begin at conception so that any environmental differences experienced prenatally could also influence behavior.

Rasmussen and Tsuang (1986) reviewed the OCD literature on twins and found of 51 MZ twin pairs where at least one twin had OCD, that 32 (63%) pairs were concordant for OCD. Questions about diagnostic accuracy and zygosity were raised; there was, however, general agreement about diagnosis and zygosity for 20 pairs. Of those 20 pairs, 13 (65%) were concordant for OCD. This MZ concordance rate for OCD is similar to concordances reported for Gilles de la Tourette's syndrome (Price, Kidd, Cohen, Pauls, & Leckman, 1985), affective disorder (Bertelsen, 1978) and anxiety disorders (Carey & Gottesman, 1981). However, without data from dizygotic OCD twins, it is difficult to interpret the results for OCD. In addition, because the reports for OCD were compiled from the literature and because most reports consisted of very small numbers of twins, these concordances should be interpreted with caution.

Two twin studies not included in the review of Rasmussen and Tsuang are the studies of Carey and Gottesman (1981) and Clifford (1983). Carey and Gottesman reported on a sample of 30 twins (15 MZ and 15 DZ) in which at least one twin had received a diagnosis of OCD. Concordance rates were presented for three different criteria: first whether the co-twin had received treatment for any psychiatric disorder; second if treatment was for an illness that involved obsessional symptoms; and, finally, whether the co-twin had obsessional features regardless of treatment status. In all cases the concordance rates were higher for MZ than for DZ twins. Because this sample was quite small there was little power for statistical analyses. Still the authors reported several interesting trends. The majority (50–60%) of those co-twins who had sought treatment for psychiatric problems had done so because of obsessive–compulsive symptoms. Furthermore, when obsessional features were the basis for concordance, 87% of the MZ twins were concordant compared to 47% of the DZ pairs. Obsessional features were defined as "obsessive . . . phenomena that meet criteria for being symptoms (not traits) but that may or may not involve social incapacitation." Individuals with OC features failed to meet DSM-III-R criteria either because the symptoms were not a significant source of distress or did not interfere with social role functioning. While the concordances obtained for OC features were not statistically significant, they suggest that genetic factors play a role in the etiology of OC behaviors.

Clifford (1983) and Clifford, Murray, and Fulker (1984) reported results of genetic analyses carried out on the response data from 419 pairs

of normal twins who had been given the Eysenck Personality Questionnaire (EPQ) and the 42-item version of the Leyton Obsessional Inventory (LOI). Their findings suggested that genetic and specific (nonshared) environmental factors were important for the manifestation of
obsessive–compulsive behavior. Multivariate analyses demonstrated a
genetic relationship between obsessional behavior and the neuroticism
scale of the EPQ. However, there was not a complete overlap. Clifford
and colleagues reported heritabilities of 44% for obsessional traits (as
defined by the 10 item "Trait Scale" of the Brief Leyton Inventory) and
47% for obsessional symptoms (as defined by the 32 item "Symptom
Scale" of the Brief Leyton Inventory). These results support those of
Carey and Gottesman indicating that genetic factors are important for
the expression of OCD and also suggest that genes influence the development and expression of obsessive compulsive traits. However, it
should be noted that in all twin data reported, the concordance for MZ
twins was less than 1.0, and heritability estimates were consistently less
than 1.0. Thus, while genetic factors are important for the expression of
obsessive–compulsive symptomatology, it is clear that these behaviors
are also influenced by nongenetic factors.

FAMILY STUDY METHOD

Studies of biological families can also yield data suggesting genetic
involvement for any given illness. The family study method consists of
comparing rates of illness in families ascertained through an affected
individual (the proband) with rates in the general population or with
rates in families ascertained through unaffected persons (controls). If the
risk of families ascertained through an affected person is significantly
greater than the risk in the population or in the control families, this
suggests that the trait is familial. However, as with twin studies, if a
major environmental component is important in the etiology of the trait
in question, results drawn from family studies will be unable to prove
the existence of genetic factors.

Data from families can, however, be used to demonstrate that vertical
transmission occurs. Furthermore, these patterns of transmission can be
compared to those expected under a variety of specific genetic hypotheses. In this way, data from families can be used to identify specific
modes of genetic transmission. It is assumed that if the pattern of the
illness within families follows closely a pattern predicted by a classical
Mendelian hypothesis, it is unlikely that environmental factors could be
completely responsible for the transmission of the disorder.

A number of studies have examined the relatives of obsessional

TABLE 4.1 Frequency of Obsessive Compulsive Symptomatology in Parents and Siblings of Obsessive–Compulsive Patients

	Diagnosis			
	Obsessive–Compulsive illness		Obsessive–Compulsive features	
Reference	parents	siblings	parents	siblings
Luxenburger (1930)	0.10	0.06	—	0.08
Lewis (1935)	—	—	0.18	0.10
Brown (1942)	0.08	0.07	—	—
Rudin (1953)	0.05	0.03	0.08	0.06
Kringlen (1965)	—	—	0.10	—
Rosenberg (1967)	—	0.004	—	—
Carey (1978)	0.06	0.03	0.08	0.07
Insel et al. (1983)	0	0	0.15	—
Rasmussen & Tsuang (1986)	0.05	—	0.16	—

patients. Data in Table 4.1 summarize the rates of obsessional illness and/or features in the relatives of patients with obsessive–compulsive illness. As is evident from the entries in the table, the majority of studies suggest that obsessive–compulsive symptomatology clusters within families. When data on parents and siblings were available to diagnose obsessive–compulsive illness, all but two studies (Insel, Hoover, & Murphy, 1983; Rosenberg, 1967) found substantial rates of OC illness among those relatives when compared to the population prevalence estimate of OCD (0.5%) obtained at the time of those studies. Even with current estimates of the prevalence (1–2%) (Robins et al., 1984), the rates of illness in parents represent a 5 to 10 fold increase over the population rates. It should be noted that in none of the early studies were relatives personally interviewed; recurrence rates presented are thus undoubtedly underestimates of the true rates.

When the diagnostic criteria are relaxed somewhat to include relatives who have significant OC features but do not meet criteria for OC illness, the rates increase. However, it is difficult to interpret these rates because population rates of OC features are not available for comparison. As noted by Carey and Gottesman (1981) the rates reported by the various investigators depend on the diagnostic criteria employed. Nevertheless, these family data provide suggestive evidence that obsessive–compulsive symptomatology occurs with greater frequency among relatives of OC patients than would be expected by chance.

In the two studies noted above that did not report increased rates of

OCD, the methodology was sufficiently different from the other studies reported to account for the reduced rates. For example, Rosenberg (1967) used unusually strict criteria, requiring that relatives be hospitalized for OCD in order to be included as affected. In the study of Insel et al. (1983), family history data were collected about parents of 27 OCD patients. In 10 families the parents were given the Leyton Obsessional Inventory and the authors required that there be evidence of ego dystonicity for a diagnosis. They did not find any parents in whom it could be documented that obsessions and compulsions were ego dystonic. They did, however, find obsessional behavior unaccompanied by an internal struggle. Given the fact that not all of the parents were directly interviewed and that OC patients can be quite secretive about their symptomatology, the absence of any documented cases of OCD in the parents is not surprising.

Two recent studies (Lenane et al., 1988; Pauls et al., 1988), in which all first degree relatives were directly assessed, gave further convincing evidence that OCD is familial. Lenane and colleagues reported that 17% of the parents of childhood OCD patients met DSM-III-R criteria for OCD. Pauls et al. reported that the rates of OCD among first degree relatives of adult OCD probands were between 15 to 20%. In both studies, if relatives with OC features were included, the rates increased significantly.

However, both studies need to be interpreted carefully. Neither reported data on a control sample, so it is not possible to determine if the rate is significantly elevated in families of OCD patients compared to families of controls. However, because assessment in these family studies used structured interviews similar to the Diagnostic Inventory Schedule (DIS) (Robins et al., 1984), it is possible to compare the rates obtained in the families to population rates in the Epidemiology Catchment Area study (ECA) (Robins et al., 1984). In both studies the rates among the relatives are significantly greater than the rates obtained in the ECA study. Nevertheless, family studies that include families of controls are needed so that adequate comparisons can be made.

Another line of evidence that indicates that at least some forms of OCD are familial and genetic comes from some recent work on Gilles de la Tourette's Syndrome (TS). Pauls et al. (1986) reported that 23% of first degree relatives of TS probands had OCD. Among those relatives about 40% had OCD without TS or tics, hence approximately 10% of all relatives had OCD without tics.

There have been several studies done which suggest that TS is inherited as an autosomal dominant trait (Comings, Comings, Devor, & Cloninger, 1984; Kidd & Pauls, 1982; Pauls & Leckman, 1986; Price et al., 1988). In fact, in one study (Pauls & Leckman, 1986) the inclusion of relatives with a diagnosis of OCD actually improved the fit of the single gene solution. These results suggested that OCD was part of the spectrum of TS (at least in the families of TS probands). In addition, Pauls and Leckman (1986) reported that female relatives of TS probands more often expressed OCD without tics and male relatives more often expressed TS or tics. Thus, they suggested that there may be a sex-modified expression of TS with female relatives of TS probands being more likely to express OCD in the absence of TS or tics.

The work of Green and Pittman (1986) supported these findings. They examined 16 OCD patients (8 male and 8 female) and inquired about a family history of OCD and tics. They found that 8 of 16 OCD patients had a family history of tics. Of note is that six of those eight patients were female. Thus, it appears that it is more likely for a female OCD patient to have a family history of tics than a male OCD patient.

In summary, family studies of OCD provide some evidence that the disorder is familial, particularly if individuals with OC features are included as affected. Nevertheless, additional well-designed studies using current methodologies to evaluate both families of OCD patients and controls are needed. Only with studies like these will it be possible to examine hypotheses regarding genetic transmission of OCD. At the present time it appears that at least some forms of OCD may have a genetic basis because OCD is significantly elevated in TS patients and their families and as TS is believed to be a genetic disorder. It is unlikely, however, that all individuals with OCD have a disorder etiologically related to TS. It remains to be seen whether the OCD that is not related to TS is also familial and, if so, whether the patterns within these families are also consistent with genetic transmission.

GENETIC LINKAGE METHOD

Two additional methods (adoption studies and genetic linkage studies) were noted earlier as being useful in determining if genetic factors are important in the etiology of a disorder. To date neither method has been used in the study of OCD. Although both can be quite useful approaches, the genetic linkage methodology in particular deserves additional discussion.

Genetic linkage is detectable, at least in theory, if a known genetic marker locus is sufficiently close to a locus segregating for alleles affecting the trait under study so that nonrandom segregation of alleles at the two loci results in an association of phenotypes within a family. Figure 4.1 provides a hypothetical example of linkage. The trait under study is a result of the presence of a dominant susceptibility allele. The marker locus has four alleles M_1, M_2, M_3 and M_4 and the top mating (between

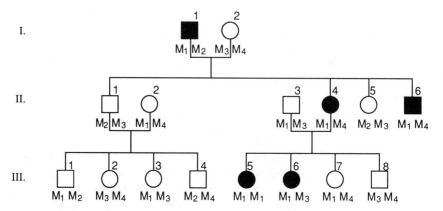

FIGURE 4.1. A pedigree showing linkage of a marker locus to a susceptibility locus with a dominant mode of transmission.

I-1 and I-2) is fully informative because both parents are heterozygous for different marker alleles. As can be seen in Figure 4.1, M_1 is associated with the illness in the father (individual I-1) and all of his affected descendants also carry that same allele because they inherited it from him. Note, however, that there is not a population association between M_1 and the trait because two individuals who married into the family carried the M_1 allele but were unaffected.

Figure 4.1 illustrates that the demonstration of genetic linkage requires studies of multigenerational families in which it can be demonstrated that alleles at two separate loci (the locus for the disease and a marker locus) are physically close on the same chromosome. Family data are used to estimate how frequently the alleles at the two loci are transmitted to a child in combinations different from those in the parents. The degree of linkage is measured as the recombination fraction (the frequency of such new combinations) and can range from zero (complete linkage) to 0.5 (independent assortment). The minimum recombination frequency of zero is found for alleles that are always transmitted in the same combinations from generation to generation. (The family in Figure 4.1 is an example of a situation in which there are no recombinant events.) The maximum recombination frequency of 0.5 is found for alleles (at two separate loci) that have the same likelihood of being transmitted in new combinations as in the same combination from generation to generation. This maximum recombination frequency occurs for alleles at loci far apart on the same chromosome and, of course, for alleles at loci on different chromosomes. Hence, maximum recombination is just another way of phrasing Mendel's second law of independent assortment. Linkage is the violation of that law and occurs because genes are physically very close together on the same chromosome.

Some methodological problems in detecting linkage in human data include small family sizes, the inability to control matings, and the small prior probability that the two loci are linked. Historically, the method has had limited applicability chiefly because of the small number of sufficiently polymorphic genetic markers that were available for humans. This has changed rapidly because of the advance in genetics brought about by recombinant DNA techniques. A new class of polymorphisms has been identified. This class of polymorphisms is referred to as "restriction fragment length polymorphisms" (RFLPs) because they are visualized as inherited variations in the length of defined fragments of DNA when it is digested with specific restriction enzymes.

Using these new polymorphisms as markers, investigators are nearing completion of a genetic map of the entire human genome (Helms et al., 1988). Markers mapped in this way have been extremely useful in mapping other disease loci (e.g., Huntington's disease and Alzheimer's disease). It is expected that this methodology will also be useful in learning more about the underlying genetic factors that may be important for the expression of OCD.

It must be strongly emphasized that the most critical component of any genetic linkage study is diagnostic validity. Without valid and reliable diagnoses, it is impossible to establish with certainty that a linkage relationship exists between the trait (OCD) and some marker locus. It also must be stressed that it is important to establish criteria that can be used to identify individuals with milder variants of the disorder. In particular for OCD, it is important to have valid and reliable diagnostic criteria for the disorder as well as for OC features and traits. Only with data of this sort will it be possible to elucidate the spectrum of behaviors associated with OCD. Furthermore, it is quite likely that it will be possible to establish that linkage exists for OCD only when individuals with milder variants are included in the linkage analyses. Thus, it is critical to begin to establish the spectrum of behaviors associated with OCD. This can be done with family studies, twin studies, and other approaches currently available. For example, in the twin study of Carey and Gottesman (1981), it was demonstrated that the concordance rate increased when co-twins with OC features were included as affected. This suggests that individuals with OC features may be expressing a milder variant of OCD. This relationship can also be examined in family studies in which all family members are interviewed. If there is a significant number of relatives with OC features when compared to a control sample assessed in the same way, then together with the twin data these results would suggest that OC features do represent a milder variant of the genetic factors responsible for the manifestation of OCD.

CONCLUSIONS

Twin and family study data suggest that genetic factors are important in the etiology of obsessive–compulsive behavior. Twin studies have demonstrated that the concordance rate for MZ twins is greater than the concordance for DZ twins. In addition, the concordances increase substantially when co-twins with significant OC features are included in the tabulation. This suggests that the underlying genetic factors may be important for the expression of symptoms as well as for the disorder itself. This notion is supported by the results from normal twins assessed for OC behaviors. Heritability estimates from those twins suggest that about half of the phenotypic variance is due to genetic factors.

Family studies consistently demonstrate that there are a significant number of relatives of OC patients with OCD and/or OC features. These results, together with the twin data, suggest that OC behaviors have a genetic component, though it is not yet understood what the underlying genetic mechanism might be. Additional well-designed studies are needed to allow examination of specific genetic hypotheses. In designing those studies it should be kept in mind that it is quite likely that OCD is etiologically heterogeneous. The data from family studies of Tourette's syndrome suggest that some forms of OCD are related to TS, whereas the data from family history studies of OCD suggest that some but not all OCD patients have relatives with tics. Clearly, more work is needed to understand more completely this relationship between TS, tics, and OCD. Learning how TS, tics, and OCD are related will be helpful for discerning the inheritance of OCD.

It should be emphasized that new genetic methodologies hold promise for eventual understanding of the genetics of OC behaviors. These new methods need to be combined with some careful clinical and epidemiological work in order to elucidate the genetics of OCD. We are confident that these new techniques will be extremely useful in the continued study of the genetic mechanisms involved in the expression of obsessive–compulsive behaviors.

REFERENCES

Bertelsen, A. (1978). A Danish twin study of manic-depressive disorders. In M. Schou & E. Stromgren (Eds.), *Origin, prevention and treatment of affective disorders*. London: Academic Press.

Brown, F. W. (1942). Heredity in the psychoneuroses (summary). *Proceedings of the Royal Society of Medicine, 35,* 785–790.

Carey, G. (1978). *A clinical genetic twin study of obsessive and phobic states.* Doctoral dissenration, University of Minnesota.

Carey G., & Gottesman, I. I. (1981). Twin and family studies of anxiety, phobic and obsessive disorders. In D. F. Klien & J. Rabkin (Eds.), *Anxiety: New research and changing concepts* (pp. 117–136). New York: Raven Press.

Clifford, C. A. (1983). *Twin studies of drinking behavior and obsessionality.* Doctoral dissertation, Institute of Psychiatry, University of London.

Clifford, C. A., Murray, R. M., & Fulker, D. W. (1984). Genetic and environmental influences on obsessional traits and symptoms. *Psychological Medicine, 14,* 791–800.

Comings, D. E., Comings, B. G., Devor, E. J., & Cloninger, C. R. (1984). Detection of a major gene for Gilles de la Tourette syndrome. *American Journal of Human Genetics, 36,* 704–709.

Green, R. C., & Pitman, R. K. (1986). Tourette syndrome and obsessive compulsive disorder. In M. A. Jenike, L. Baer, & W. E. Minicheillo (Eds.), *Obsessive compulsive disorders: Theory and management.* Littleton, MA: PSG Publishing Company, Inc.

Helms, C., Green, P., Weiffenbach, B., Bowden, D., Keith, T., Stephans, K., Smith, D., Akots, G., Bricker, A., Brown, V., Gravius, T., Morgan, D., Muller-Kahle, H., Phipps, P., Rising, M., Ng, S., Rediker, K., Powers, J., Falls, K., Hogan, C., Cannizzaro, L., & Donis-Keller, H. (1988). A human genetic linkage map with 545 genetic loci. *American Journal of Human Genetics, 43*(Supplement), A147.

Insel, T. R., Hoover, C., & Murphy, D. L. (1983). Parents of patients with obsessive compulsive disorder. *Psychological Medicine, 13,* 807–811.

Insel, T., & Murphy, D. L. (1981). The psychopharmacological treatment of obsessive compulsive disorder: A review. *Journal of Clinical Psychopharmacology, 1,* 304–311.

Kringlen, E. (1965). Obsessional neurotics: A long term follow-up. *British Journal of Psychiatry, 111,* 709–722.

Kidd, K. K., & Pauls, D. L. (1982). Genetic hypotheses for Tourette syndrome. In T. N. Chase & A. J. Friedhoff (Eds.), *Gilles de la Tourette syndrome* (pp. 243–249). New York: Raven Press.

Lenane, M. C., Swedo, S. E., Leonard, H., Cheslow, D. L., Rapoport, J. L., & Pauls, D. L. (1988, May). Obsessive compulsive disorder in first degree relatives of obsessive compulsive disorder children. *Proceeedings of the American Psychiatric Association,* Montreal, Canada.

Lewis, A. (1935). Problems of obsessional illness. *Proceedings of the Royal Society of Medicine, 29,* 325–336.

Luxenburger, H. (1930). Hereditat und Familientypus der Zwangsneurotiker. *Archiv fur Psychiatrie, 91,* 590–594.

Marks, I. M. (1981). Review of behavioral psychotherapy, I: Obsessive compulsive disorders. *American Journal of Psychiatry, 138,* 584–592.

Pauls, D. L., & Leckman, J. F. (1986). The inheritance of Gilles de la Tourette's syndrome and associated behaviors: Evidence for autosomal dominant transmission. *New England Journal of Medicine, 315,* 993–997.

Pauls, D. L., Raymond, C. L., Hurst, C. R., Rasmussen, S., Goodman, W., & Leckman, J. F. (1988, May). Transmission of obsessive compulsive disorder and associated behaviors. *Proceedings of the 43rd Annual Meeting of the Society of Biological Psychiatry*, Montreal, Canada.

Pauls, D. L., Towbin, K. E., Leckman, J. F., Zahner, G. E. P., & Cohen, D. J. (1986). Gilles de la Tourette syndrome and obsessive compulsive disorder: Evidence supporting an etiological relationship. *Archives of General Psychiatry, 43*, 1180–1182.

Price, R. A., Kidd, K. K., Cohen, D. J., Pauls, D. L., & Leckman, J. F. (1985). A twin study of Tourette syndrome. *Archives of General Psychiatry, 42*, 815–820.

Price, R. A., Pauls, D. L., Kruger, S. D., & Caine, E. D. (1988). Family data support a dominant major gene for Tourette syndrome. *Psychiatry Research, 24*, 251–261.

Rasmussen, S. A., & Tsuang, M. T. (1986). Clinical characteristics and family history in DSM-III obsessive-compulsive disorder. *American Journal of Psychiatry, 143*, 317–322.

Robins, L. N., Helzer, J. E., Weissman, M. M., Orvaschel, H., Gruenberg, E., Burke, J. D. Jr., & Regier, M. D. (1984). Lifetime prevalence of specific psychiatric disorders in three sites. *Archives of General Psychiatry, 41*, 949–958.

Rosenberg, C. M. (1967). Familial aspects of obsessional neurosis. *British Journal of Psychiatry, 113*, 405–413.

Rudin, E. (1953). Ein beitrag zür frage der zwangskrankhet. *Archive für Psychiatrie Nervenkrankheiten, 191*, 14–54.

Slater, E., & Cowie, V. (1971). *The genetics of mental disorders*. London: Oxford University Press.

Steketee, G., Foa, E., & Grayson, J. (1982). Recent advances in the behavioral treatment of obsessive compulsives. *Archives of General Psychiatry, 39*, 1365–1371.

5

Brain Imaging: Toward a Neuroanatomy of OCD

Lewis R. Baxter, Jr.
Jeffrey M. Schwartz
Barry H. Guze

The development of critical technologies can have an overwhelming influence on our understanding of nature. In no discipline of science has this been demonstrated more consistently than in medicine. Brief reflection on the evolution of our understanding of infectious illnesses—to give but one example—impresses one with the pivotal role played by the techniques of microbiology. Closer to psychiatry, the epilepsies—which were deemed the result of everything from demon possession, to corrupt morals, to psychosocial stressors—became understandable as medical illnesses only with the development of the electroencephalograph earlier in this century (Engel, 1989).

Our understanding of the major psychiatric illnesses—mediated by an organ which, in the functioning state, has been largely inaccessible—is now on the verge of a similar revolutionary, paradigmatic transformation. In the last decade computer-assisted imaging technologies have become available which for the first time allow safe investigations of the human brain in vivo (Andreasen, 1988, 1989).

These computer-assisted brain imaging techniques are conventionally divided into those of brain structure (Xray computed tomography [CT] and magnetic resonance imagery [MRI]) and those of physiological and biochemical function (to date, ^{133}Xenon measured blood flow [Xe-Flow],

This work was supported in part by contract AM03-76-SF00012 from the Department of Energy; grants MH 37916-02, MH37916-06 and MH00752-02 (Research Scientist Development Award, LRB) from the National Institute of Mental Health; donations from the Jennifer Jones Simon Foundation and the Judson Braun Chair in Psychiatry at UCLA.

single photon emission tomography [SPECT], magnetic resonance spectroscopy, and position emission tomography [PET]). This chapter will review the brain imaging studies of obsessive–compulsive disorder (OCD) that have been reported to date—studies that are just the first in what is likely to become an extensive series of investigations into the functional neuroanatomy mediating the complex behaviors of this classical psychiatric illness.

STUDIES OF IN VIVO BRAIN STRUCTURE IN OCD

At the time of this writing (1989), all published work on brain structure in OCD has been done with CT.

Insel, Donnelly, Lalakea, Alterman, and Murphy (1983) studied 18 patients with DSM-III classified OCD, using neuropsychological testing (Wechsler Adult Intelligence Scale and Halstead-Reitan Battery) and electroencephalographic (EEG) recordings. As part of this work they also studied a subgroup of 10 patients with CT. The number of subjects for CT scanning was chosen by a power analysis, based on the degree of difference schizophrenic subjects showed from normal controls in a previous, similar study.

In the original group of eighteen OCD subjects, all had had the illness for over one year, were aged 18 to 65, and did not have psychosis or primary affective disorders (the presence of "secondary" depression was not mentioned). They were all drug-free, although the drug-free interval was not specified. Ten experienced the onset of their illness before age 18. Two were left-handed. All had at least some compulsive rituals at the time of study. Subjects with abnormalities on EEG (two), neuropsychological testing (four), and four others chosen at random, underwent CT scanning. Controls were age and gender matched (six men) subjects without evidence of psychiatric illness or known central nervous system illness, although seven had other known "peripheral illnesses."

All 18 subjects were studied with a General Electric (GE) CT/T 8800 scanner, without contrast. Scans were inspected in random order and evaluated on a number of measures: (1) fixed-arm planimetry, using the cut that gave the largest ventricles, to derive ventricle to brain ratios (VBRs); (2) asymmetry, measured as the width of the left hemisphere minus that of the right; and (3) a visual, global estimate (0–4 scale) of cortical atrophy observed on the highest three tomographic cuts obtained for each subject.

The CT findings in the Insel et al. study were unremarkable. There were no significant differences between OCD subjects and controls on VBRs or the asymmetry measure. No subjects were judged to have marked cortical atrophy by visual inspection.

Another CT study, this time of childhood-onset OCD by Behar et al. (1984), did find significant differences between the VBRs of OCD and normal subjects. The OCD subjects were 14 males and 3 females, 13.7 ± 1.6 [mean ± S.D.] years old, did not have psychosis or primary affective disorder (but could have "secondary" depression, severity not reported), and had I.Q.s over 85. All but two had some type of compulsive ritual. Control subjects were 13 boys and 3 girls whose CT scans were not "questionable clinically" and were not from individuals with changes in consciousness, psychiatric symptoms or "hard" neurological signs. All controls were under some suspicion of having Central Nervous System (CNS) pathology, however, as the clinical reason for the CT study.

A GE CT/T 8800 scanner was used for seven patients and an EMI 5005 for the others. CT studies of controls were apparently done on a variety of machines, at hospitals other than the one at which the OCD patients were studied. Apparently, contrast agents were not employed in any of the CT scanning procedures.

The VBR measurement used by Behar at al. was similar to that of the Insel et al. study. Here VBRs were judged significantly greater in OCD subjects than in controls. The ventricular measures did not show a significant correlation with demographic, disease severity, or prior treatment variables, but it was noted that those with compulsions without obsessions (n = 11) tended to have higher VBRs than those who did have obsessions.

This second research group recently reported results of a second CT study in late adolescents with childhood-onset OCD (Luxenberg et al., 1988). In addition to examining VBRs, the investigators also examined the volumes of the caudate nuclei in this experiment. Subjects were ten young males (age 20.7 ± 2.1; high–low, 17–24), all with the onset of OCD before 18, who had all been ill for at least one year. None were suffering from major depression at the time of study, and all had normal neurological examinations. Controls were ten male subjects in good health, all being part of the National Institute of Aging's Longitudinal Study of Brain Function in Healthy Aging.

Scanning was done with the GE CT/T 8800, without contrast. Subjects' scans were analyzed for the volumes of lateral and third ventricles, the caudate nuclei, and lenticular nuclei. These structures were determined by a rater blind to diagnosis. Volumes were calculated using interpolation between all planes in which a given structure was present. A repeated measures analysis of variance (ANOVA) was used for testing significance. Volumes of the caudate nuclei were found to be significantly smaller in OCD subjects than in controls. All other structures and ventricles were remarkably similar in volume across the two groups, and there were no significant left to right asymmetries.

Presently, there are no published MRI studies of OCD, although several are reported in progress.

CRITIQUE OF STRUCTURAL STUDIES

These studies have several methodological difficulties that make them hard to compare. There are significant differences in the clinical and demographic characteristics of the OCD subjects across studies, but perhaps of more importance, great differences in the controls. Only the Luxenberg et al. study used controls that were without indicators of some physical pathology. The methods of calculating structures and ventricles are somewhat problematic as well, and would be expected to induce varied results in the data from the different centers.

The observation of small caudate volumes in the last study, however, could reconcile differences among the studies on the question of VBRs. The head of the caudate nucleus has a greater influence on ventricle size than its contribution to brain size, as shown in similar work on Huntington's Disease (Stober, Wasso, & Schimrigk, 1984). If individuals with OCD lose caudate volume, but do so in variable locations, this could explain why some studies might show VBR findings and some not, while at the same time all subjects might have caudate masses less than normal. As cited by Luxenberg et al., there is much clinical and experimental evidence implicating the basal ganglia in the pathogenesis of OCD. (See Cummings & Frankel, 1985; also Chapter 6, this volume.) Further, differences in pathology location in the caudate (and other parts of the striatum) might correlate with different clinical symptoms. (See "A Theory of the Functional Neuroanatomy Mediating the Expression of OCD and Related Disorders" below.) It will be critical to try to replicate these findings of caudate nucleus abnormalities with other CT studies, or better still with the higher resolution technique of MRI.

STUDIES OF IN VIVO BRAIN PHYSIOLOGY AND BIOCHEMISTRY IN OCD

No studies of OCD using SPECT or magnetic resonance spectroscopy have been reported at this time.

Xe-Flow

Zohar et al. (1988) have reported the only Xe-Flow study. This technique—in which subjects inhale small quantities of radioactive [133]Xenon gas, which after blood-bourne transport is then measured over the surface of the head with special detectors—has been used as an estimate of blood flow and profusion over the surface convexity of the cerebral cortex. It is a noninvasive method that can be repeated many times in the same subject over relatively short intervals. Its major disadvantages are low resolution and an inability to provide data on deep brain structures.

In the Zohar et al. study 10 subjects, all with washing compulsions and reports of focal stimuli for their obsessions concerning contamination, were studied with Xe-Flow. The accompanying washing compulsions were not secondary to other illnesses, but the presence of other psychiatric diseases, specifically secondary depression, was not detailed. Subjects were six women and four men, aged 36.2 ± 7.7 years, and all were drug-free for at least three weeks. One was left handed. Duration of illness was long—14.7 ± 7.4 years, and over five years in all cases.

Subjects underwent two single-blind "placebo Xe" test runs in an attempt to diminish test–situation anxiety. All studies were done with eyes closed for 16 minutes, with 30 minute intervals in between. The subjects underwent, in sequence, Xe-Flow studies (1) in a relaxation state, (2) during imaginal flooding, and (3) during in vivo exposure to stimuli that, in the past, had tended to induce contamination obsessions and washing rituals. All three stimulus state studies were done during a four-hour time period on the same day. The relaxation stimulus was done with an audiotape of a "relaxation scene" (same for all subjects), while the flooding was done with an audiotape of a situation specific to the subject's individual contamination fears. Exposure in vivo was done with the flooding tape, accompanied by placing the contaminating object in contact with the dorsum of the right hand. In an attempt to gain information as to whether results were biased by the fixed sequence of presentation, three subjects returned, 5 to 10 days later, for testing in which exposure was given before flooding.

Measures were taken to control for the effect of pCO_2 on blood flow. Xe-flow data were analyzed using an ANOVA for repeated measures, with post hoc paired t-tests to determine differences between pairings of test situations. Symptom rating-scale scores for anxiety and OCD symptoms, as well as various physiological measures of anxiety, were performed for all subjects.

Both symptom-rating scale scores and physiological measures gave highest values during in vivo exposure and were lowest during relaxation. In contrast, cerebral blood flow was significantly increased in the imaginal flooding, versus the relaxation state, but only in the temporal cortex, and was significantly *decreased* in virtually all cortical regions (specifically temporal, parietal, posterior and in the cortex as a whole) during exposure in vivo. In all three conditions, flow in the left hemisphere was greater than on the right, and the left prefrontal cortex appeared slightly more reactive than the right in the directions cited above. There did not appear to be an effect of order of presentation in the three subjects in whom this was evaluated.

The authors found the results of this study puzzling. They had predicted that the peripheral physiological measures of anxiety would increase going from relaxation to imaginal flooding to in vivo stimulation, which they did. However, they predicted the same direction of effect on cerebral blood flow as well. Instead, blood flow *decreased* in in vivo stimulation.

A number of speculations were offered that might have accounted for the results. Differences in the sensory modalities of the stimuli (i.e., auditory vs. touch) could have been important. Imaginal flooding might require more active cortical involvement than the passive touch situation, but this explanation was not favored, due to patient reports of the degree of conscious activity in the various situations. Another possible explanation was that, in the highly anxiety provoking in vivo exposure situation, blood was being shunted away from the cortical areas of the brain to other areas, such as the caudate nucleus or orbital gyri (see PET studies, below), which cannot be visualized with the Xe-Flow method. Thus, anxiety states might be associated with a decrease in "higher order processing" (cortical) when "lower" centers take over. Another possibility is that increased cortical activity is here associated with decreased flow—if blood flow and metabolic rate are uncoupled from their usual relationship (Phelps, Mazziotta, & Shelbert, 1986) by increased substrate extraction in high anxiety states. The authors suggested PET blood flow, glucose, and oxygen extraction experiments to examine these last two possibilities.

PET

PET (Phelps & Mazziotta, 1985; Phelps et al., 1986; Andreasen, 1989) is a high resolution imaging technique in which tracer amounts of biochemicals of interest are labeled with unstable atoms that emit positrons, the positively charged anti-matter particles that correspond to the negatively charged electron. Positrons annihilate with electrons to give gamma photons, allowing computer-assisted localization of the tracer. Using the principles of tracer-kinetic modeling, an estimate of the concentration and dynamics of the biochemical being studied can, therefore, be derived. Thus, PET is similar to autoradiography, but unlike that technique, can be performed without sacrificing, or indeed harming the subject in any way. Thus, repeated studies can be done in the same individual. Many interesting physiological substances and drugs have been studied in psychiatric conditions using PET technology, but all PET work in OCD to date has used the tracer ^{18}F-fluorodeoxyglucose (FDG).

FDG-PET is used to measure neuroanatomically localized cerebral glucose metabolic rates. Under nonstarvation conditions, glucose, along with oxygen, is by far the predominant energy substrate in the human brain and has been shown to be a highly sensitive indicator of cerebral function (Phelps & Mazziotta, 1985; Phelps et al., 1986). Although the newest of the brain imaging techniques to be applied to OCD, FDG-PET has, as of this writing, been the most extensively employed, with a total of five studies from three different laboratories.

Our group at UCLA examined a sample of OCD patients ($n = 14$), compared to both normal controls ($n = 14$) and patients with unipolar-type major depression ($n = 14$) (Baxter et al., 1987a). All subjects were matched for age, and OCD and depressed subjects had similar Hamilton Depression Rating Scale and Brief Psychiatric Rating Scale tension and anxiety item scores. Six of the depressed subjects had minor doubting obsessions with limited checking rituals that occurred only in major depression and which were not present before and did not persist after treatment. Thus, they did not meet criteria for primary OCD. Nine of the OCD subjects were in a clear-cut secondary major depression at the time of study. Nine of the OCD subjects were drug-free for at least two weeks, but the other five were on a variety of antidepressants, benzodiazepines, and neuroleptics. The normal and depressed subjects were all drug-free. The normal control group had equal numbers of males and females, while the male:female ratio in the depressed group was 5:9, but was 9:5 for OCD. Normal control females were scanned between days 5 and 15 of the menstrual cycle, while those with psychiatric illnesses were studied without regard to cycle phase.

FDG-PET scanning was done with the Neuro ECAT (in-plane resolution = 11 mm, axial = 12.5 mm) in the eyes and ears open state, without specific stimuli. Arteriolized venous blood was used for the calculation of absolute metabolic rates, and an idealized, calculated (rather than measured) attenuation correction was employed. Neuroanatomical regions were drawn by a technician blind to subject diagnosis, and absolute glucose metabolic rates were determined for the whole cerebral hemispheres, hippocampal-parahippocampal complexes, anterior cingulate gyri, heads of the caudate nuclei, putamen nuclei and thalamic nuclei, as well as various gyri in the prefrontal and temporal cortex. A one-way ANOVA was run among the subject groups for each structure, using the first seven subjects only. For those structures yielding significant results, a second, prospective analysis was run using the second group of seven. A separate analysis was also done excluding OCD subjects on drugs. Neuroanatomical regions of interest had to pass all tests to be considered significant. This approach was chosen to decrease the likelihood of Type I (false positive) statistical error, but greatly increased the likelihood of Type II (false negative) error.

Absolute glucose metabolic rates for the whole cerebral hemispheres, caudate nuclei, and orbital gyri were found to be significantly elevated in OCD, compared to the control groups, by these criteria. Furthermore, metabolic rates in the left orbital gyrus, divided by those of the ipsilateral hemisphere ("normalized" metabolic rates) were significantly higher than those found in normals on the left. There was only a trend for this to be the case in the right hemisphere. However, there was no statistically significant left to right asymmetry on this measure, and values on the right were higher in OCD than in normal controls (NC). Normalized caudate metabolic rates in OCD were not different from normal control values.

Ten of these OCD subjects were also studied after treatment with medication. Those who responded with a clinically significant decrease in OCD symptoms had a significant increase in both left and right normalized caudate metabolic rates (to levels significantly higher than normal controls), compared to those who did not respond to drug treatment. There were no changes in the orbital/hemisphere ratios, however.

The subject groups in this first FDG-PET study had several characteristics that were not optimal: (1) unequal numbers of male and female subjects (Baxter et al., 1987b) across the experimental groups; (2) most of the OCD subjects also had concomitant major depression; (3) some of the OCD subjects were on medications; and (4) handedness was not equal across groups. Therefore, a second FDG-PET study (Baxter et al., 1988) was undertaken to compare a new group of drug-free, nondepressed, right-handed OCD patients to NCs of similar age, scanned under the same conditions as before.

Glucose metabolic rates in the cerebral hemispheres, heads of the caudate nuclei and orbital gyri were examined, using an a priori design, employing one-tailed Student's t-test as the statistic, in an attempt to confirm or refute previous findings. The results obtained in this study were similar to those of the previous study. The OCD subjects had significantly higher glucose metabolic rates for the whole cerebral hemispheres, heads of the caudate nuclei and orbital gyri than those found in NC subjects. The orbital gyrus/hemisphere ratio ("normalized" rate) was also elevated in OCD when compared to NC, but in the second study this finding was bilateral. In the previous study, where significant results had been obtained only on the left, there was a higher percentage of males in the OCD group than in the NC group (male:female OCD = 9:5; NC = 7:7). The data in this second study, when analyzed with a repeated measures ANOVA for variance and covariance, showed that there was a significant effect of sex by hemisphere on this measure (with males showing higher values on the left, while females had higher values on the right). The unbalanced sex ratios between the diagnostic groups that obtained in the first study probably accounted for the observation of statistical significance between OCD and normals for the left orbital gyrus/hemisphere ratio, while there was only a trend toward significance in the right hemisphere. We now believe that there are significant elevations in both left and right orbital gyrus/hemisphere ratios in OCD, compared to normals. (Why both OCD and NC females should have a higher orbital gyrus/hemisphere ratio on the right than the left, while males of both groups show the opposite pattern, is a mystery at this time.)

Based on the results of the first study, interpreted in light of clinical and experimental data on the interactions of the orbital and striatal areas of the brain (see Baxter et al., 1987a for review), and supported by consistent data from the second OCD study, we speculated that an imbalance between the orbital frontal-caudate system might mediate the expression of some of the symptoms of OCD. Originally, pathology in the orbital area was considered primary, and the neuropathological process was conceived as increased activity in the orbital areas having outstripped the ability of the caudate nucleus to maintain its integrative capacity in the execution of complex behaviors (see Baxter et al., 1987a). Successful medication treatment would then be mediated by augmentation of caudate activity, reflected by increased normalized caudate metabolic rates, even though normalized metabolic rates observed for the orbital gyri continued to remain abnormally high.

The work of Luxenberg et al., however, suggests that the primary OCD pathology might be in the caudate, and this could result in a secondary increase in orbital activity—according to our present theoretical beliefs (see below). In such a scenario, a defective caudate may have to increase its activity in the remaining undamaged regions to an unusually high degree in order to compensate (see below.)

At the same time that the second UCLA study was being undertaken, two separate groups at the National Institute of Mental Health were performing similar studies independently.

Nordahl et al. (1989) studied 8 physically healthy, nondepressed OCD subjects, aged 32.8 ± 6.0 years, who were drug-free for at least three weeks. Five were male. These subjects were compared with 30 normal volunteers (18 males, 12 females; age 35.5 ± 11.3 years) with no personal or family history of psychiatric problems.

FDG-PET scanning was done using the Scanditronix PC-1024-7B scanner (6 mm in-plane resolution), with tracer uptake taking place during an auditory continuous performance task, with eyes closed. Arterial blood was used, and attenuation was measured with a transmission scan. Neuroanatomical regions of interest were determined by two independent raters. Sixty regions of interest were examined, with those found significant in the previous UCLA studies examined, a priori, with one-tailed Student's t-test. Calculations of global brain metabolic rates, which were also used to normalize rates, were done with gray matter structures only, rather than all supratentorial brain regions, as in the UCLA work. Absolute metabolic rates for whole brain gray matter were calculated, but only normalized values for individual regions of interest were examined.

This group also found normalized regional brain metabolic rates high in OCD compared to normals in both orbital gyri, and normalized OCD caudate rates similar to normals. This group did not find elevated absolute global brain glucose metabolic rates, however. Two-tailed Student's t-tests, with $p < .05$ considered significant, were done for other regions of interest in an exploratory analysis, with no corrections for the number of tests done. Normalized values in the right parietal and left occipital-parietal regions were higher in normals than in OCD subjects by this criterion.

This group interpreted their findings in the orbital cortex as consistent with those of the UCLA group. They went on to cite other data of theirs showing that normals receiving repeated, painful electric shocks also increase activity in the orbital area, and pointed out that animal work suggests that the orbital area is involved in inhibition, habituation and/ or extinction. (Thus, it might be involved in attempts to repress painful sensations and associated emotions and thoughts.) In this context, they wondered if OCD patients might have abnormalities in using mechanisms such as habituation and extinction in dealing with intolerable internal stimuli.

The other NIMH group (Swedo et al., 1989b) examined 9 men and 9 women (aged 27.8 ± 7.4) with childhood-onset OCD (onset before 15, mean 8.9 ± 2.6), but no concurrent major depression or other anxiety disorders. All were drug-free for at least two weeks and physically healthy. These subjects were compared to age and sex-matched, physically and mentally healthy control subjects.

FDG-PET scanning was done in the eyes and ears closed condition with the Scanditronix PC-1024-7B, with arterial blood sampling and measured attenuation correction. Regions of interest were determined by placing templates, derived from studies of normals, over scan images. Circular regions were then drawn for estimated neuroanatomical structure locations on the slice in which those structures were best seen. The global metabolic rate was here calculated based on the simple mean of cortical gray matter only. This measure was used also for normalizing other regions of interest. Uncorrected, two-way (diagnosis and sex) ANOVAs were used for statistical analyses.

The OCD group showed increased absolute glucose metabolism in left orbital and right sensorimotor regions and, bilaterally, in the anterior cingulate gyri and lateral prefrontal areas. Normalized values were significantly increased in right lateral prefrontal and left anterior cingnulate regions only. These authors, however, did observe a significant correlation between absolute and normalized right orbital glucose metabolic activity and a measure of OCD severity. Further, six of these patients, who failed to respond to a subsequent trial of clomipramine, had significantly higher right anterior cingulate and right orbital metabolism than 11 patients who did respond.

This research group interpreted their findings, in light of other work on OCD, to suggest a dysfunction of a frontal lobe-anterior cingulate-basal ganglia loop (Swedo et al., 1988a). In this context, obsessions and compulsions were thought of as fixed action patterns or programs that are being released inappropriately, without volitional control.

DEPRESSION IN OCD

Yet another FDG-PET study provides information relevant to the phenomenon of secondary, major depression in OCD. In this study (Baxter et al., 1989) drug-free, age and sex-matched, right-handed patients with unipolar depression ($n = 10$), bipolar depression ($n = 10$), OCD with secondary major depression ($n = 10$), OCD without depression ($n = 14$), and normal controls ($n = 12$) were evaluated under the same conditions and with the same machinery as in the other UCLA studies. Six nonsex-matched manic subjects (four males) were also evaluated under conditions that were otherwise the same. Depressed patients in all three groups had similar levels of depression on the Hamilton Depression Rating Scale (HAM-D) and OCD patients with and without depression were of similar severity of OCD symptoms, measured on the NIMH OCD scale.

As predicted a priori, ipsilateral-hemisphere-normalized glucose metabolic rates for the left dorsal antero-lateral prefrontal cortex were similar in the unipolar and bipolar subjects, and significantly lower than values obtained for both normals and OCD subjects without depression. Bipolar depressed patients were significantly lower than manics on this measure. Likewise, OCD with major depression showed significantly decreased glucose metabolic values in this brain region, compared to OCD without depression. Further, there was a significant negative correlation ($r=-.5$) between this brain metabolism measure and scores on the HAM-D.

With medication treatment of depression, normalized left dorsal antero-lateral prefrontal cortex activity increased significantly, and the percentage change in HAM-D scores gave a significant ($r=-.5$) negative correlation with percentage change on the metabolic variable. It was concluded that, despite being different on other measures of cerebral glucose metabolic rates, OCD with major depression, like the other two primary major depressions, is distinguished from the nondepressed (OCD) state by a decrease in normalized left dorsal antero-lateral prefrontal glucose metabolic rates.

CRITIQUE OF FUNCTIONAL STUDIES

The major merit of the Xe-Flow study of Zohar et al. (1988) was the examination of several different stimulation states in the same subjects. Drawbacks included difficulties inherent in blinding and order effects, but the biggest problem was the inherent resolution limitations of Xe-Flow, and the technique's inability to visualize important deep structures. As the authors recognized, future studies of similar design should be done with PET. Also, because the presence of other psychiatric pathology is not detailed, one can only wonder about the effects these states might have had on the results.

The different methods used in the various PET studies reviewed make them difficult to compare. There were marked differences in scanners, stimulus conditions, and perhaps of most importance, in the methods used to determine neuroanatomical regions of interest and to calculate absolute and normalized glucose metabolic rates.

For those not familiar with studies of brain biochemical function in vivo, the reasons for the existence of such variations in methods among the different studies may not be readily apparent. Suffice it to say that each difference in method chosen has certain advantages and disadvantages, and that there is not agreement in the field as to which methods are preferred under which circumstances. In fact, in certain instances, all the methods chosen are at best interim solutions that are only being used at this stage of the technology's development—until more fitting methods can be perfected. An example is neuroanatomical localization—using the metabolic data itself to determine structure is problematic, at best! At the time of all of these studies, however, there were no generally accepted techniques to map structural image data (i.e., from MRI) onto functional images. A full discussion of the relative advantages and disadvantages of methods chosen by these PET research teams is far beyond the scope of this chapter and interested readers are referred to other sources (e.g., Phelps, Mazziotta, & Shelbert, 1986; Andreasen, 1989) for more detailed discussion and further references to other books and articles. Foremost, one must remember that, in small "n" studies in which the data can be expected to have a high degree of variance, two studies with the same significant result reveal much (i.e., low chance of Type I error), but different results reveal little (i.e., there is a high probability of Type II error).

In this context, it is noteworthy that the studies of Baxter et al. (1988) and Nordhal et al. (1988), although admittedly the closest in methods, achieved very similar results for normalized orbital (OCD > normals) and normalized caudate (OCD = normals) metabolic rates in OCD versus normal controls. The major difference between the two reports was in global brain metabolic rates. Although the methods of determination were different (Nordhal et al. looked at specific gray matter only, while Baxter et al. measured whole supratentorial brain) and this could have accounted for the different observations, it should be pointed out that some of the methods of Nordhal et al. (using arterial blood, rather than arteriolized venous blood, and measured attenuation, rather than idealized) tend to be the more accurate in determining absolute metabolic rates.

More studies of subjects in different test–retest paradigms, especially before and after treatment, may be helpful to strengthen the case for the involvement of specific neuroanatomical systems (such as the basal ganglion-prefrontal loops) in the mediation of specific behavioral pathology (symptoms) seen in this disease. For such studies, OCD offers a rare opportunity, in that both drug (Zohar & Insel, 1987; Perse, 1988) and behavioral (Meyer, 1966; Marks, Hodgson, & Rachman, 1975; Foa & Steketee, 1984; Perse, 1988) treatments have been shown to produce significant improvements, although with differential effects on obsessions and compulsions (Foa & Steketee, 1984; Perse, 1988). Clearly, the effects of these overtly different treatment modalities on the brains of OCD subjects should be investigated.

Glucose metabolic rates reflect the nerve cell's needs for all energy-requiring activities, whether it be neuronal excitation, inhibition, protein and neurotransmitter synthesis or the maintenance of structural integrity. In most instances, however, it is thought to reflect the energy requirements of ion pumping, and therefore is related to nerve firing rates (Phelps, Mazziotta, & Shelbert, 1986). At present, the perturbed brain processes that may be reflected by PET-revealed abnormal glucose metabolic rates in OCD are unknown. In this regard, reliable PET studies using various receptor ligands—especially ones for serotonin and dopamine [which are present in significant concentrations in the orbital gyrus-striatum circuits (Emson, 1983)]—would be particularly interesting, when developed, for their ability to localize pathology to particular neurotransmitter systems of interest in OCD.

Whether symptoms specific to OCD relate to primary abnormalities in these neuroanatomical regions is, likewise, not clear. Although obsessions and compulsions are the unique pathological features of this illness, anxiety is always present. It is of interest, however, that PET ^{15}O-water studies for blood flow in panic disorder (Reiman et al., 1984; Reiman et al., 1989b) and anticipatory anxiety in normals (Reiman et al., 1989a) have revealed abnormalities in temporal lobe brain structures, and none are apparent at this time in those regions of the brain that have been associated with OCD in FDG-PET studies (E. M. Reiman, personal communication, 1989). As cited above, blood flow and glucose metabolic rates are usually tightly correlated. Nevertheless, future OCD studies might employ patients with generalized anxiety disorder or simple phobias, with similar anxiety levels as in the OCD subjects, as controls.

The high probability of Type II (false negative) error in all these small "n" functional brain studies also needs to be emphasized yet again. None of the PET data on this subject to date demonstrates which cerebral structures are *not* abnormal in OCD. Structures other than those reported so far may well be involved in the mediation of OCD symptoms.

A THEORY OF THE FUNCTIONAL NEUROANATOMY MEDIATING THE EXPRESSION OF OCD AND RELATED DISORDERS (with hypotheses for future investigations)

May of the investigators cited above have hypothesized the involvement of the basal ganglia, limbic, and prefrontal cortex systems in the generation of the symptoms of OCD. PET study findings—especially when taken together with the structural imaging studies and other data—can now be assembled to support a comprehensive, although at this time speculative, theory for how pathology in the orbital prefrontal cortex-striatal interactive system could mediate the expression of OCD and related syndromes.

In discussing their PET data, Norhahl et al. (1988) remind us that the orbital cortex is implicated in behavioral inhibition and extinction. Swedo et al. (1989a) cite the role of the striatum-limbic cortex system in the smooth execution of fixed, perhaps species-specific (MacLean, 1978, 1985; Rolls, Thorpe, & Maddison, 1983) behavioral action patterns. Baxter et al. (1987a) cite the literature that demonstrates that the striatum may act as a highly developed sensory information gating station, or processor, used in the preparation of appropriate behavioral responses (Rolls et al., 1983) and that, when dysfunctional, the resultant unmodified afferent information may lead to inappropriate behavioral responses (Schneider, 1984)—including adventitious and perseverative behaviors (Alexander, DeLong, & Strick, 1986).

Another key PET observation to add to these in thinking about OCD comes from a study of motor task performance in normals versus patients with early Huntington's Disease (HD) studied before the development of structural degeneration in the striatum on x-ray CT—which is characteristic of this late-onset, genetic illness (Mazziotta, Phelps, & Wapenski, 1985). In this experiment when both groups of subjects were asked to sign their names repeatedly—normally an automatic, overlearned task—PET showed that the normals activated the contralateral primary sensory-motor cortex moderately, while the striatum was highly activated, bilaterally. Normals performed this signature-writing task without effort, in an automatic fashion. Normals doing a novel finger-moving sequence task, however, did so with subjective difficulty and reported having to concentrate intensely. In this latter situation, PET showed that they activated only contralateral sensory-motor cortex, and did so to a high degree. There was no increase in activity in the striatum. The HD patients, on the other hand, had great difficulty and reported having to concentrate when doing signature writing, despite the fact that all reported being able to do this without thinking before the onset of their illness. They also displayed increased adventitious movements while signature writing. These HD patients did not activate the striatum in the signature writing task, but did show a significantly greater activation of contralateral sensory-motor cortex than the normals did while doing the same task.

Thus, the ability of normal subjects to perform the signature writing task *in an effortless and automatic fashion* without distractions may be related to their capacity to integrate neocortical and striatal functions. The HD patients, however, not having a fully functional striatum, needed to concentrate on this usually automatic task and experienced many distracting, nontask-related movements, which are thought to be released in the absence of full striatal function. HD patients activated motor cortex alone.

The important point to grasp here is that a concomitant increase in cortex activity seems to be needed when the striatum is not fully functional, and even so, completing the desired activity is rendered difficult because of the distractions of unwanted behaviors that are normally inhibited through the actions of the striatum operating fully in concert with the cortex. We are not implying that OCD and HD involve the same type of striatal pathology—undoubtedly there are different neurochemical systems involved in each. We are saying that when a behavior is so overlearned as to be done without conscious effort, the striatum is involved in executing it along with the cortex, but *in the absence of a fully functioning striatum, the cortex must function in a way that requires conscious effort and other, unwanted behaviors have a tendency to interfere.*

With all of these observations clearly in mind, we now suggest that the primary pathology in OCD might be in the striatum, and that the abnormal behaviors of this disease complex are mediated by a dysfunctional interaction of this brain region with other, mainly cortical brain regions that, as a direct consequence, must increase their activity to abnormal levels as the individual goes about the business of life. The orbital cortex (and perhaps limbic structures such as the cingulate as well) would be such brain regions called upon in the face of striatal dysfunction. In dealing with possible interactions of other brain regions with the striatum, we recognize that many authorities have expounded upon more extensive circuits, involving other structures (Alexander et al., 1986; Iversen, 1984; Marsden, 1982; Nauta & Domesick, 1984; Parent, 1986; Schneider, 1984). All of these "circuits" were evolved in the context of studying certain conditions wherein support for such circuits could be found—largely in studies of animal motor behavior. Because the striatum in particular is a very complex system within which there are undoubtedly very many circuits, we have chosen to confine our discussion of OCD only to those brain regions that have been implicated directly in OCD brain-imaging studies.

In such a theory, impairment in the gating and screening functions of the striatum would result in a variety of adventitious phenomena—both sensations and thoughts as well as motor behaviors—coming into conscious awareness that normals usually inhibit effectively by evoking striatal system mechanisms in concert with cortical ones during the execution of routine behaviors. Impulses concerning aggression, danger, hygiene and sex—the stuff of obsessions—are related to drives that modern humans must keep under control in order to function in society. In normal adults, this is usually done with little, or at most passing conscious awareness by a functioning striatal-cortical system, but with a dysfunctional striatum, such sensations, thoughts, and impulses would tend to "leak through," again and again, giving the subjective experience of "obsessions." Tic-like motor behaviors and more complex "compulsions" likewise would also be expected, as the latter may be fixed behavioral action patterns executed by this system in response to the sensations and thoughts not being inhibited. Thus, the OCD individual cannot concentrate and pursue goal-directed social behaviors without these distractions—much as the HD patient has to contend with unwanted movements, especially when trying to do some purposeful activity. Also, in OCD as in Huntington's Disease, the functionally appropriate, behaviorally specific cortical region of the brain that would normally work at low levels of neuronal activity in concert with the striatum to deal with such matters would need to increase its own work markedly in an effort to cope with the problem. Conscious efforts to combat these impulses—that is, superstitious thinking, consciously executed rituals, avoidance, and so on—would be seen as such cortical responses. The orbital region of the brain—a major area of "limbic cortex," which when damaged results in an individual prone to violence, socially inappropriate sexual behavior, and a lack of concern with hygiene (Stuss & Benson, 1986)—seems an appropriate candidate for such a cortical region involved in these "control efforts." Other parts of the limbic system proper (e.g., the cingulate) might also be involved—especially in mediating anxiety.

Put more directly, in OCD an impulse or unacceptable thought (sex, dirt, violence) that normal adult individuals easily put aside ("repress") through the action of an intact orbital-striatal system, would leak through into consciousness awareness in OCD because of a dysfunctional striatum, leaving the intact orbital area to try to cope with it through conscious mechanisms, such as ritual. Such an impaired system would also be less likely to be able to "put the concern to rest," resulting in the perseverative nature of OCD symptoms.

An example, for the purpose of illustration, could be the case of a patient with contamination obsessions and washing rituals. Normal individuals may be concerned, momentarily, after contact with a dirty object, but these thoughts are easily put aside in favor of other matters with little conscious thought after washing once. In our theory, this "dropping" of the concern in normals would be accomplished through mechanisms involving an interaction of the striatum and the orbital cortex. In the OCD patient, however, because the striatum is dysfunctional, turning away from the concern with contamination is done only with great conscious effort—if it is successful at all. Instead, there is a tendency for perseveration of the disturbing thoughts because of the defect in striatal inhibition (incomplete "repression"), and actions such as ritualized washing are initiated through conscious orbital mechanisms to deal with the concern.

In this model, the "function" of the caudate might, thus, be viewed similar to "repression," while that of the orbital gyri is viewed as orchestrating more conscious coping mechanisms, or defenses. Obviously humans might vary innately in the "strength" of both parts of this system. In addition, the functional capacity of the two divisions of the postulated system might vary during normal brain development. Strong repression (caudate) or strong magical belief in the power of ritual (orbital) might be equally effective for various persons in avoiding such anxiety. Individuals with a strength in either subsystem, but a weakness in the other, might be able to function well—one person unusually "carefree," the other a member of a highly ritualized society or cult. Others (most) would employ both mechanisms in an adaptive balance.

That these ideas can be fitted into Freud's detailed phenomenological descriptions of OCD pathology has obviously not escaped our attention. This theory of neuroanatomical symptom mediation is, however, entirely neutral as to any theories of causation (see below).

A final important observation from recent research on OCD—and one that must be explained by any modern theory of OCD—is recent evidence that OCD, Gilles de la Tourette's Syndrome (TS), and chronic multiple motor tics (CMT) may run in certain families, and are all apparently inherited as a single autosomal dominant gene with variable expressivity (Pauls & Leckman, 1986. Also see Chapter 4, this volume). Can the cortical-striatal dysfunction theorized here for OCD explain the symptoms of TS and CMT as well? We believe it can indeed.

The striatum has a well-described topographical organization with respect to its afferent cortical connections (Iversen, 1984), and this organization can be used to explain the association of OCD with TS and CMT. In the theory we present, striatal pathology would result in the symptoms of OCD, TS, or CMT, depending on which regions of the striatum are defective above a critical threshold value beyond which the system cannot compensate (see Figure 5.1). (In Parkinson's disease this threshold of damage is approximately 70% of the dopamine system.) Striatal sublocalization is the key to this theory of symptom prediction, thus this theory predicts that the primary lesion would not be further "up or down stream" from the striatum.

Pure obsessional disorder, without compulsions or other motor symptoms, would be expected to show pathology over this critical threshold primarily in the ventral medial region of the head of the caudate nucleus—the region to which limbic structures and orbital cortex project. These pure obsessional patients would not have pathology over this threshold in the putamen, which receives primary and supplementary sensory-motor projections (Young et al., 1986). CMT (simple motor tics, but no abnormal mentation) would show above threshold pathology confined to the putamen. Patients with CMT would also be expected to show activation over that seen in normals in the corresponding primary and supplementary motor areas when the individual so afflicted attempts to perform a purposeful action that requires momentary

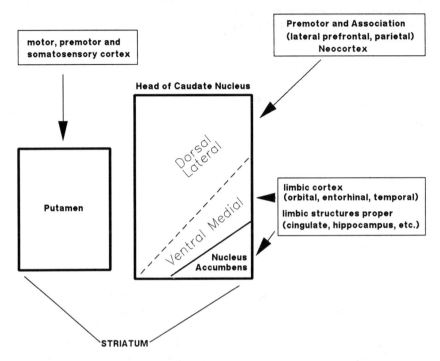

CORTICAL AND LIMBIC PROJECTIONS TO STRIATUM

FIGURE 5.1 Functionally different regions of the cortex and limbic system have predominant projections to different regions of the striatum. Thus, we hypothesize that the symptoms of chronic multiple motor tics, without other emotional or cognitive symptoms, would relate to a dysfunction of the putamen interacting with primary motor cortex. Pure obsessional disorder, without any motor symptoms, on the other hand, would be a disorder of the ventral medial caudate-nucleus accumbens region (not anatomically distinct in humans) interacting with limbic cortex and limbic system structures. Dorsal lateral caudate-cortex dysfunctions would give more complex cognitive and motor behaviors in addition—as seen in typical OCD. Patients with all these behaviors (i.e., Gilles de la Tourette's syndrome with obsessions and compulsions) would have dysfunction throughout the system—the degree of specific symptoms being roughly proportional to the degree of dysfunction above a critical threshold beyond which the system cannot compensate.

(Greatly modified and simplified from Alexander, DeLong, & Strick, 1986.)

suppression of adventitious motor activity. Individuals with mixed motor and cognitive symptoms, such as patients with obsessions, compulsions, complex tics, and simple tics (e.g., TS with OCD), would show suprathreshold pathology throughout the striatum, and over activation in the various appropriate areas of the cortex when attempting to suppress those adventitious behaviors (tics, vocalizations, compulsions,

TABLE 5.1 Proposed Sites of Significant Striatal Substructure Dysfunction Leading to the Different Symptoms of Obsessions, Compulsions and Tics Seen in the OCD-TS-CMT Disease Complex.

	Striatum		
	Caudate		
	Ventral	Dorsal	Putamen
POD	*		
OCD	*	*	
TS OCD	*	*	*
TS without OCD		*	*
CMT			*

obsessions). (It is well known that *all* of these symptoms can be suppressed for at least brief periods of time, although with great conscious effort, if the patient makes a strong enough effort.) The degree of deficit throughout the distribution of striatal pathology would correlate with the severity of symptoms related to those specific areas (see Table 5.1).

With symptomatic improvement after treatment, there would be a corresponding increase in activity in those regions of the striatum associated with the symptoms that improved. Activity would remain increased in the corresponding areas of the cortex and limbic system, however, if there were only partial improvement, that is, the behaviors were not completely, "unconsciously," repressed, and conscious effort still had to be invoked in the total operation.

This theory, while complex and speculative, can be tested. Recently developed high-resolution PET scanners can gather data with equal resolution in three spatial dimensions, giving coronal and saggital projections as well as the traditional horizontal sections (Hoffman, Phelps, & Huang, 1983). This technology could be used to examine the striatum along its known topographical distribution of association with specific regions of the cortex for the predicted correlation of sites of above-threshold pathology with symptoms (see Figure 5.2).

There is even some evidence for a type of process that could attack the striatum in a variable, patchy distribution, as theorized here, to give the varied symptoms of the OCD-TS-CMT complex. A recent report (Swedo et al., 1989a) suggests an association between OCD and Sydenham's

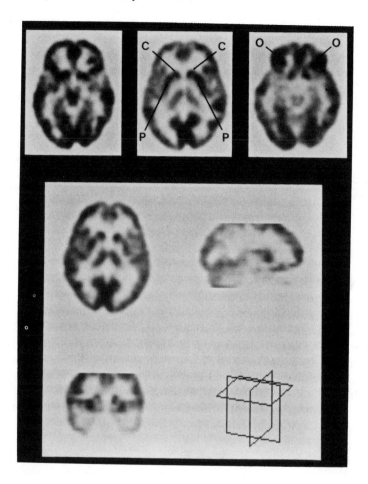

FIGURE 5.2 Selected high resolution FDG-PET scan image reconstructions from a patient with OCD. The top row of images shows three planes from conventional horizontal image reconstructions. *O* = orbital cortex; *C* = head of the caudate nucleus; *P* = putamen. The illustration below that shows horizontal, coronal, and saggital reconstructions through the striatum (caudate and putamen). Studies were done with the Seimens-CTI 831 NeuroECAT.

Chorea, an illness in which antistriatal antibodies have been demonstrated (Husby, Van de Rijn, Zabriskie, Abdin, & Williams, 1976). This or another kind of autoantibody attack on the cells of some striatal subsystem might well result in patchy damage. Streptococci, or a variety of other agents might stimulate the formation of antistriatal antibodies in genetically predisposed individuals. Of course many other sources of such hypothesized damage could be possible, and even developmental and "learned" dysfunctions, might contribute to a suboptimally

functioning cortical-limbic-striatal system. Evidence for damage compatible with an autoantibody attack might be obtained through MRI or
postmortem examinations of the brains of individuals afflicted with
diseases in the OCD-TS-CMT complex.

Despite this last speculation about one possible kind of causative
pathological insult for the whole OCD-TS-CMT disease complex, we
would like to close with a reminder to readers that the available brain-
imaging data do not address the "cause" of OCD in any way whatsoev-
er. All mental activity as well as motor behavior, regardless of "cause,"
is mediated by the biochemical processes of the brain. These brain
imaging data merely provide clues to some of the possible sites of
abnormal cerebral activity that may mediate the complex mentation and
behavioral patterns seen in this most fascinating psychiatric illness,
OCD.

ACKNOWLEDGMENTS

The authors would like to express their gratitude to their UCLA col-
laborators in the experimental investigations reviewed: Michael E.
Phelps, Ph.D., John C. Mazziotta, M.D., Ph.D., Carl E. Selin, M.S., Ron
M. Sumida, Jorg Pahl, M.D., Lynn Fairbanks, Ph.D., and Robert H.
Gerner, M.D. We would also like to thank D. Frank Benson, M.D.,
Joaquin M. Fuster, M.D., and Daniel X. Freedman, M.D. for helpful
critical commmments during the development of the theoretical ideas
presented.

REFERENCES

Alexander, G. E., DeLong, M. R., & Strick, P. L. (1986). Parallel organization of
     functionally segregated circuits linking basal ganglia and cortex. *Annual
     Review of Neuroscience, 9,* 357–381.
Andreasen, N. C. (1988). Brain imaging: Applications in psychiatry. *Science, 239,*
     1381–1388.
Andreasen, N. D. (1989). *Brain imaging: Applications in psychiatry.* Washington,
     DC: American Psychiatric Press.
Baxter, L. R., Phelps, M. E., Mazziotta, J. C., Guze, B. H., Schwartz, J. M., &
     Selin, C. E. (1987a). Local cerebral glucose metabolic rates in obsessive–
     compulsive disorder—A comparison with rates in unipolar depression and
     in normal controls. *Archives of General Psychiatry, 44,* 211–218.
Baxter, L. R., Mazziotta, J. C., Phelps, M. E., Selin, C. E., Guze, B. H., &
     Fairbanks, L. (1987b). Cerebral glucose metabolic rates in normal human
     females vs. normal males. *Psychiatry Research, 21,* 237–245.

Baxter, L. R., Schwartz, J. M., Mazziotta, J. C., Phelps, M. E., Pahl, J. J., Guze, B. H., & Fairbanks, L. (1988). Cerebral glucose metabolic rates in nondepressed obsessive–compulsives. *American Journal of Psychiatry, 145,* 1560–1563.

Baxter, L. R., Schwartz, J. M., Phelps, M. E., Mazziotta, J. C., Guze, B. H., Selin, C. E., Gerner, R. H., & Sumida, R. M. (1989). Reduction of prefrontal cortex glucose metabolism common to three types of depression. *Archives of General Psychiatry, 46,* 243–250.

Behar, D., Rapoport, J. L., Berg, C. J., Denckla, M. B., Mann, L., Cox, C., Fedio, P., Zahn, T., & Wolfman, H. G. (1984). Computerized tomography and neuropsychological test measures in adolescents with obsessive–compulsive disorder. *American Journal of Psychiatry, 141,* 363–369.

Cummings, J. L., & Frankel, M. (1985). Gilles de la Tourette's syndrome and the neurological basis of obsessions and compulsions. *Biological Psychiatry, 20,* 1117–1126.

Emson, P. C. (Ed.). (1983). *Chemical neuroanatomy.* New York: Raven Press.

Engel, J. (1989). *Epilepsy.* Philadelphia: F. A. Davis.

Foa, E. B., & Steketee, G. (1984). Behavioral treatment of obsessive–compulsive ritualizers. In T. R. Insel (Ed.), *New findings in obsessive–compulsive disorder* (pp. 46–69). Washington, DC: American Psychiatric Press.

Hoffman, E. J., Phelps, M. E., & Huang, S. C. (1983). Performance evaluation of a positron tomograph designed for brain imaging. *Journal of Nuclear Medicine, 24,* 245–257.

Husby, G., van de Rijn, I., Zabriskie, J. B., Abdin, Z. H., & Williams, R. C. (1976). Antibodies reacting with cytoplasm of subthalamic and caudate nuclei neurons in chorea and acute rheumatic fever. *Journal of Experimental Medicine, 144,* 1094–1110.

Insel, T. R., Donnelly, E. F., Lalakea, M. L., Alterman, I. S., & Murphy, D. L. (1983). Neurological and neuropsychological studies of patients with obsessive–compulsive disorder. *Biological Psychiatry, 18,* 741–751.

Iversen, S. D. (1984). Behavioral aspects of cortico-subcortical interaction with special reference to frontostriatal relations. In G. Reinoso-Suarez, & C. Ajmone-Marsan (Eds.), *Cortical integration.* New York: Raven Press.

Luxenberg, J. S., Swedo, S. E., Flament, M. F., Friedland, R. P., Rapoport, J., & Rapoport, S. I. (1988). Neuroanatomical abnormalities in obsessive–compulsive disorder determined with quantitative x-ray computed tomography. *American Journal of Psychiatry, 145,* 1089–1093.

MacLean, P. D. (1978). Effects of lesions of globus pallidus on species-typical display behavior of squirrel monkeys. *Brain Research, 149,* 175–196.

MacLean, P. D. (1985). Brain evolution relating to family, play, and the separation call. *Archives of General Psychiatry, 42,* 405–417.

Marks, I. M., Hodgson, R., & Rachman, S. (1975). Treatment of chronic obsessive–compulsives by *in vivo* exposure: A two year follow-up and issue in treatment. *British Journal of Psychiatry, 127,* 349–364.

Marsden, C. D. (1982). The mysterious motor function of the basal ganglia. *Neurology, 32,* 514–539.

Mazziotta, J. C., Phelps, M. E., & Wapenski, J. A. (1985). Human cerebral motor system metabolic responses in health and disease. *Journal of Cerebral Blood Flow and Metabolism, 5*, S213–S214.

Meyer, V. (1966). Modification of expectations in cases with obsessional rituals. *Behaviour Research and Therapy, 4*, 273–280.

Nauta, W. J. H., & Domesick, V. B. (1984). Afferent and efferent relationships of the basal ganglia. *Functions of the basal ganglia* (pp. 3–29). London (CIBA Foundation Symposium #107): Pitman.

Nordahl, T. E., Benkelfat, C., Semple, W. E., Gross, M., King, A. C., & Cohen, R. M. (1989). Cerebral glucose metabolic rates in obsessive–compulsive disorder. *Neuropsychopharmacology, 2*, 23–28.

Parent, A. (1986). *Comparative neurobiology of the basal ganglia.* New York: John Wiley & Sons.

Pauls, D. L., & Leckman, J. F. (1986). The inheritance of Gilles de la Tourette's syndrome and associated behaviors—Evidence for autosomal dominant transmission. *New England Journal of Medicine, 315*, 993–997.

Perse, T. (1988). Obsessive–compulsive disorder a treatment review. *Journal of Clinical Psychiatry, 49*, 48–55.

Phelps, M. E., & Mazziotta, J. C. (1985). Positron emission tomography: Human brain function and biochemistry. *Science, 228*, 799–809.

Phelps, M. E., Mazziotta, J. C., & Shelbert, H. R. (Eds.). (1986). *Positron emission tomography and autoradiography.* New York: Raven Press.

Reiman, E. M., Raichle, M. E., Butler, F. K., Herscovitch, P., & Robins, E. (1984). A focal brain abnormality in panic disorder, a severe form of anxiety. *Nature, 310*, 684–685.

Reiman, E. M., Fusselman, M. J., Fox, P. T., & Raichle, M. E. (1989a). Neuroanatomical correlates of anticipatory anxiety. *Science, 243*, 1071–1074.

Reiman, E. M., Raichle, M. E., Robins, E., Mintun, M. A., Fusselman, M. J., Fox, P. T., Price, J. L., & Hackman, K. A. (1989b). Neuroanatomical correlates of lactate-induced anxiety attack. *Archives of General Psychiatry, 46*, 493–500.

Rolls, E. T., Thorpe, S. J., & Maddison, S. P. (1983). Responses of striatal neurons in the behaving monkey 1. Head of the caudate nucleus. *Behavioral Brain Research, 7*, 179–210.

Schneider, J. S. (1984). Review: Basal ganglia role in behavior: Importance of sensory gating and its relevance to psychiatry. *Biological Psychiatry, 19*, 1693–1710.

Stober, T., Wasso, W., & Schimrigk, K. (1984). Bicaudate diameter—The most specific and simple CT parameter in the diagnosis of Huntington's disease. *Neuroradiology, 26*, 25–28.

Stuss, D. T., & Benson, D. F. (1986). *The frontal lobes.* New York: Raven Press.

Swedo, S. E., Rapoport, J. L., Cheslow, D. L., Leonard, H. L., Ayoub, E. M., Hosier, D. M., & Wald, E. R. (1989a). High prevalence of obsessive–compulsive symptoms in patients with Sydenham's Chorea. *American Journal of Psychiatry, 146*, 246–249.

Swedo, S. E., Schapiro, M. B., Grady, C. L., Cheslow, D. L. Leonard, H. L., Kumar, A., Friedland, R. P., Rapoport, S. I., & Rapoport, J. L. (1989b).

Cerebral glucose metabolism in childhood-onset obsessive–compulsive disorder. *Archives of General Psychiatry, 46*, 518–523.

Young, A. B., Penney, J. B., Starosta-Rubinstein, S., Markel, D. S., Berent, S., Giodani, B., Ehrenkaufer, R., Jewett, D., & Hichwa, R. (1986). PET scan investigations of Huntington's disease: Cerebral metabolic correlates of neurological features and functional decline. *Annals of Neurology, 20*, 296–303.

Zohar, J., & Insel, T. R. (1987). Obsessive–compulsive disorder: Psychobiological approaches to diagnosis, treatment, and pathophysiology. *Biological Psychiatry, 22*, 667–687.

Zohar, J., Insel, T. R., Berman, K. F., Foa, E. B., Hill, J. L., & Weinberger, D. R. (1989). Anxiety and cerebral blood flow during behavioral challenge: Dissociation of central from peripheral and subjective measures. *Archives of General Psychiatry, 46*, 505–510.

6

Neuropsychiatric and Neuropsychological Studies in Obsessive–Compulsive Disorder

Eric Hollander
Michael R. Liebowitz
Wilma G. Rosen

Obsessive Compulsive Disorder (OCD), a disabling and relatively common disorder, has been the object of increasing research in psychopharmacology and neurobiology. Reports documenting altered neurological function in OCD over the past fifty years have generated considerable interest in, and have led to the development of neuropsychiatric and neuropsychological models of OCD. In particular, new studies using imaging techniques (see Chapter 5, this volume) and new theoretical developments based on neuroanatomic lesion studies (see Chapter 11, this volume) have implicated specific neural dysfunction in the pathophysiology of OCD. In this chapter, we will review the clinical evidence for neurological abnormalities using an array of tests for laterality, soft-signs, higher cortical functions, and electrophysiologic responses to exogenous stimuli.

NEUROLOGICAL FINDINGS

Neurological findings include the onset of OCD following head trauma (Hillbom, 1960; McKeon, McGuffin; & Robinson, 1984), epilepsy (Kettl & Marks, 1986), and Von Economo's encephalitis (Claude, Bourke, & Lamache, 1927; Jeliffe & Smith, 1932; Jenike, 1982; Schilder, 1938) (see Table 6.1). There are also reports of a high prevalence of other neurological premorbid illnesses, such as meningitis, encephalitis, seizures, and

TABLE 6.1 Neurological Abnormalities Associated with OCD

head trauma	birth trauma
Sydenham's chorea	Tourette's Syndrome
epilepsy	seizures
diabetes insipidus	chorea
meningitis	Von Economos encephalitis

chorea (Grimshaw, 1964). An association between OCD and birth trauma (Capstick & Seldrup, 1977), and an increased incidence of males with childhood onset OCD (Rapoport et al., 1981) suggests neurologic dysfunction stemming from early developmental trauma in a subgroup of OCD patients.

There are close links between OCD and Tourette's Syndrome (TS). Many Tourette's patients have obsessions and compulsions (Cohen, Detlor, Young, & Shaywitz, 1980; Nee, Caine, Polinsky, Eldridge, & Ebert, 1980; Pitman, Green, Jenike, & Mesulam, 1987), although some have raised the question of whether these are true compulsions or "impulsions" that are not ego-dystonic (Shapiro, Shapiro, Young & Feinberg, 1988). A high rate of OCD in the first-degree relatives of Tourette's patients suggests a genetic linkage (Montgomery, Clayton, & Friedhoff, 1982; Pauls, Towbin, Leckman, Zahner, & Cohen, 1986). Because of this close clinical and familial relationship we will report on neuropsychiatric findings in TS patients as well.

There are reports of nine patients with diabetes insipidus and obsessional neurosis that developed independently (Barton, 1954, 1965). This is suggestive of an association between hypothalamic disturbance and OCD. There are also reports of childhood OCD following Sydenham's chorea (Grimshaw, 1964), suggesting involvement of the basal ganglia in some OCD patients (Rapoport, 1988).

Electrical stimulation of the cingulum during surgery in epileptic patients resulted in increased stereotypic movements (Talairach et al., 1973). Evidence from neurosurgical procedures shows improvement in some OCD patients following surgical lesions of the cingulum (Grey-Walter, 1977; Lewin, 1973; Mitchell-Heggs, Kelly, & Richardson, 1976). However, improvement after a surgical lesion does not prove that an abnormality of the lesioned tract was etiologic in the disorder.

LATERALITY

Assessments of laterality have been made using psycholinguistic techniques, evaluation of handedness, EEG, and dichotic listening tasks.

Rapoport et al. (1981) administered selective subtests of the Neurosensory Center Comprehensive Examination for Aphasia and dichotic listening tasks to investigate left hemispheric function and language function in a small group ($N=9$) of childhood OCD patients and normal controls. Dichotic listening results indicated a lack of laterality in the childhood OCD patients compared to normals, suggesting less dominance of the left hemisphere during competitive processing. However, dichotic listening is not infallible for determining laterality of function in children.

Handedness has also been related to language laterality. Ninety percent of the population is right handed, and of those, 95% are estimated to be left hemisphere dominant for language. Ten percent of the general population is left handed, and of those, only 60% are left hemisphere dominant for language. Studies of adult (Flor-Henry, Yeudall, Koles, & Howarth, 1979) and childhood (Rapoport et al., 1981) OCD find higher prevalence of left handedness, with 27% and 22% respectively.

Lack of left hemispheric predominance on EEG during verbal tasks, a high rate of left handedness, and a lack of laterality during dichotic listening all suggest reduced left hemisphere dominance for language in OCD. However, this may be a nonspecific finding, since absence of laterality has been reported in other psychiatric populations, including depression (Wexler, 1980).

NEUROLOGICAL SOFT-SIGNS

Neurological soft signs are a particular form of nonlocalizing deviant performance on a motor or sensory test in which no other sign of a focal neurological disorder is present (see Table 6.2). Abnormalities may include disorders of coordination, involuntary movements, and sensory signs. Previous studies have documented a link between neurological soft signs and psychiatric illness, such as asocial schizophrenia and emotionally unstable character disorder (Quitkin, Rifkin, & Klein, 1976), as well as childhood hyperactivity and minimal brain dysfunction (Denckla, 1978; Nichols, 1987). In a prospective study, early soft signs at age seven were associated with the development of anxiety disorders in adolescence (Shaffer et al., 1985).

In a small study of seven adolescents with OCD, neurodevelopmental examination yielded a high frequency of age-inappropriate synkinesias and left hemibody signs (Behar et al., 1984).

A larger sample of 54 childhood OCD patients ranging in age from 6 to 20 years was examined by one neurologist with a standard neurological examination (strength, tone, reflexes, sensation, cranial nerves) and

TABLE 6.2 Neurological Findings in OCD

Adolescents	
left hemibody signs age inappropriate synkinesias	(Behar et al., 1984)
choreiform movements nonspecific neurodevelopmental signs left hemisyndrome (associated with impaired spatial tests) miscellaneous	(Denckla, 1986)
Adults	
increased total soft-signs	(Hollander et al., 1987; 1990)
abnormal fine motor coordination abnormal cube drawing cut-off: 5 or more soft-signs	
Soft-Sign Correlates	
lack of exacerbation with 5HT agonist	(Hollander, Rosen, Towey, et al., 1988)
visual memory deficit visual discrimination deficit poor treatment outcome with clomipramine	

with the revised Physical and Neurological Examination for Soft-Signs (PANESS) (Denckla, 1988). The PANESS allows neurodevelopmental status referenced to age-expected performance to be determined (Denckla, 1985). Of the 54 OCD patients, 44 had abnormal neurological findings, and only 10 had no evidence of neurodevelopmental abnormalities (Denckla, 1988). Of these 44 patients with abnormalities, 18 had choreiform movements, 13 had nonspecific neurodevelopmental signs only, 8 had left hemisyndrome, and 5 had miscellaneous findings. There was a nonsignificant increase in personal or family history of tics in the OCD patients with choreiform syndrome. The left hemisyndrome OCD patients were most impaired on spatial tests, such as the Money road map and stylus maze tests compared to controls, with the choreiform patients intermediate between these groups. The 10 neurologically normal OCD patients tended to be older than the others. Denckla suggested that choreiform movements may be a marker for caudate/basal ganglia abnormalities and frontal-caudate disinhibition. There was also a suggestion of "right impaired relative to left" hemisphere imbalance, with greater obsessive severity related to right hemisphere disorder.

We reported on a comprehensive study of neurological soft signs in adult OCD patients (Hollander, Schiffman, & Liebowitz, 1987). Subjects included 19 adult outpatients who met DSM-III-R criteria for OCD, with a mean duration of illness of 16 years. All patients were 2 weeks free from medications, and had no focal neurological disorder or major medical illness. Normal controls (N=10) were free of any DSM-III-R diagnosis or major neurological or medical illnesses. The examination for neurological soft-signs was done blind to the subject's diagnosis.

The soft-sign exam included 20 individual tasks involving four categories: fine motor coordination, involuntary movements, sensory function, and mental status/visuospatial tasks. Previous studies have demonstrated high intra- and inter-rater reliability over time for many of these items. (Quitkin, Rifkin, & Klein, 1976; Shaffer et al., 1985; Stokman et al., 1986).

Coordination was assessed for smoothness and accuracy of the following fine motor movements: finger-to-finger, rapid alternating movements of upper and lower extremitites, mirror movements (of opposite finger and thumb), hopping, toe walking, and heel walking. Two tongue twisters were used to assess speech. Involuntary movements were tested on standing in the Romberg position, with the first 20 seconds assessing station and motor persistence. For the next 20 seconds, assessment of athetosis, chorea, tremor (resting and intention), and abnormal posturing was conducted. Sensory function was assessed for astereognosis (recognition of penny, nickel, dime, quarter), agraphesthesia (recognition of numbers written on the palm), position sense, and direction of cutaneous kinesthesia. Mental status was assessed with the face–hand test, evaluation of right-left confusion on self and examiner, and the drawing of a cube. Laterality was determined for each subject on eye, ear, and upper and lower extremities.

OCD patients had significantly more total soft signs compared to normals. This consisted primarily of a significant increase in abnormalities of fine motor coordination in the OCD patients compared to controls. However, even without abnormalities in coordination, the subtotal soft signs were still significantly increased in the OCD group compared to normals. There was an equal number of right sided and left sided findings in the OCD and control groups, consistent with an absence of unilateral findings. However, there was a significant increase in abnormalities of cube drawing in the OCD patients compared to normals, suggestive of right hemisphere impairment in some patients.

The normal controls all had four or less soft signs. The OCD patients all had at least two abnormal soft signs, and 11 of the 19 patients had 5 or more soft signs. This suggested a bimodal distribution within the OCD group. Perhaps the presence of four or less soft signs represented background noise, whereas the presence of five or more soft signs represented a distinct subgroup of patients with true neuropsychiatric impairment. Setting a cutoff of of greater than four soft signs completely distinguished the OCD group from normal controls.

Our recent report in a larger patient sample (Hollander et al., 1990) confirmed and expanded evidence for neurological abnormalities in a subgroup of OCD patients, and confirmed the usefulness of assessing soft signs in adult anxiety disorder populations.

NEUROPSYCHOLOGY

Neurospychological testing in OCD has revealed inconsistent findings among different investigators. The tests were presumed to reflect functions mediated by particular cortical regions, and deficit performance was presumed to reflect focal cortical dysfunction (see Table 6.3).

Flor-Henry (1979, 1983) studied 11 adult OCD patients with EEG and neuropsychological tests, and proposed that dominant (left) frontal lobe dysfunction was most characteristic of OCD patients. In addition, on the Wechsler Adult Intelligence Scale (WAIS), patients were impaired on digit span and digit symbol subtests. While Flor-Henry concludes that this is consistent with "frontal lobe dysfunction," these findings are also consistent with other types of brain dysfunction. In an expanded sample, Flor-Henry and Lind (1988) compared 28 unmedicated OCD patients to a large group of normal controls. Male and female OCD patients showed deficits on the Purdue Pegboard, Tactual Performance, Halstead Category and Wisconsin Card Sorting tests. The authors suggest that while temporal function is intact, there is discrete bilateral frontal dysfunction in OCD. Insel, Donnelly, Lalakea, Alterman and Murphy (1983) studied 18 adult OCD patients with the Halstead-Reitan Battery (HRB), and found no evidence to support this suggestion. Instead, more than half the subjects in Insel's study were impaired on the tactile performance test, indicating possible difficulty in visuospatial orientation, a finding absent in Flor-Henry's sample. A recent report by Diamond, Albrecht, and Borison (1988) in 18 OCD patients finds abnormalities on the Complex Figure Test (a test of visuoconstructional ability and incidental visual memory). Significant widespread organic deficits were revealed in a small portion of the Insel et al. sample, and a larger segment of the Flor-Henry and Diamond samples.

TABLE 6.3 Neuropsychology of OCD[a]

Adult	
Dominant (left) frontal lobe dysfunction impaired digit span, digit symbol (WAIS)	(Flor-Henry et al., 1979; Flor-Henry, 1983)
Bilateral frontal dysfunction	(Flor-Henry & Lind, 1988)
Deficits on Purdue Pegboard, Tactual performance Halstead Category, and Wisconsin Card Sort	
No frontal dysfunction on Halstead-Reitan Battery impaired tactile performance (visuospatial)	(Insel et al., 1983)
Abnormal Complex Figure Test (visuoconstructional, visual memory)	(Diamond et al., 1988)
Matching Familiar Figures Test (biomodal: fast/inaccurate and slow/accurate) (visual discrimination deficit vs. risk aversive) Benton Visual Retention Test (impaired visual memory) Trail Making, Stroop, WAIS-R administered	(Rosen et al., 1987)
Adolescent	
Stylus Maze, Road Map, Rey-Osterrieth Figure Tests (spatial-perceptual deficits)	(Behar et al., 1984)

[a]*Potential confound:* cortical dysfunction vs. aberrant strategies

In a group of adolescent OCD patients, there was evidence of neurodevelopmental immaturity and bilateral dysfunction (Behar et al., 1984). Seventeen OCD children and adolescents were compared to controls on a battery of neuropsychological tests. There were no significant differences between obsessional subjects and controls on measures of attention, memory, or decision time. However, patients made more errors on the Road Map Test, reflecting an impairment in spatial and directional judgments using their own bodies as a reference. OCD patients also differed from controls on Stylus Maze Learning, indicating a relative inability to discern unstated patterns. Similar patterns of spatial-perceptual deficits have been reported in subjects with confirmed frontal lobe damage (Fedio et al., 1979). On the Rey-Osterrieth Complex Figure copy, patients took longer to copy the figure, and used immature strategies for completion.

In a recent study, 19 adults meeting DSM-IIIR criteria for OCD who were drug-free for 24 to 36 hours were examined for verbal intelligence, visuospatial perception, and frontal lobe function (Harvey, 1986). The OCD patients were impaired on the Nelson's Modified Wisconsin Card Sorting Test. OCD patients had a markedly abnormal tendency to perseverate, which related most significantly to the extent and pervasiveness of the fundamental obsessional characteristics given on the Leyton Obsessional Inventory. Perseveration is a qualitative characteristic of Wisconsin test errors, and is linked to frontal lobe impiarment. In the OCD patient, perseveration may be conceived of as an impairment in set-shifting ability. Category alternation, unlike verbal fluency, related to the obsessional syndrome and was also consistent with an impairment in set-shifting ability.

The findings from these studies indicate that (1) all or nearly all OCD patients have not manifested a common cognitive deficit that could be tapped by a standarized neuropsychological battery (Halstead-Reitan Battery) and psychometric testing (WAIS), (2) there is a small subgroup of patients who exhibit impairments in several areas of cognitive functioning and may represent more globally deficient patients with organicity identifiable as early as adolescence, and (3) there may be subgroups of OCD patients who exhibit visuospatial/visuoperceptual deficits and possibly other circumscribed deficits, such as frontal lobe dysfunction.

To date, only one study (Reed, 1977) has attempted with obsessive–compulsive personality (OCP) patients to investigate selectively the cognitive dysfunctions that may underlie or correlate with aberrant behaviors that characterize the disorder. Other studies (Sher, Frost, & Otto, 1983; Sher, Mann, & Frost, 1984) have employed college students characterized according to the degree of compulsive checking behavior on the Maudsley Obsessional-Compulsive Inventory who did not meet criteria for OCD. These studies focused on faulty memory (did I turn off the light?) and superior memory for details and precision. Patients with obsessional personality disorder compared to other personality disorders showed superior digit span, superior recall of ambiguous anecdotal information, but attenuated and constricted recall of personal events (Reed, 1977). College students identified as "checkers" revealed some memory difficulties, but also underestimated their ability to distinguish between memories of real and imagined events (Sher et al., 1983, 1984). Both poor memory and uncertainty about whether a memory is real or imagined can lead to repeated checking. Checking status was negatively related to memory functioning. The authors suggest that checkers have memory deficits related to everyday activities. It is not clear whether these findings in obsessive personality disorder and obsessive "checkers" lie on a continuum with OCD, or are a discrete entity.

We have conducted a battery of neuropsychological tests in adult OCD patients and normal controls designed to evaluate selective defects of this disorder. To date 34 OCD patients and 14 normal controls have been tested blind to diagnosis. The groups differed in sex distribution but not in mean age.

The tests and the findings were as follows (Rosen, Hollander, Stannick, & Liebowitz, 1988; and unpublished observations):

The Matching Familiar Figures Test (MFFT) is a timed test that requires selecting a matching figure from multiple choice. The target figure is very detailed and the foils differ in a single detail. The OCD group made significantly more errors than the controls, despite the lack of overall difference in latency to first response. The patients showed a significant inverse relationship between latency and total errors, while the controls did not.

OCD patients tended to be fast and inaccurate or slow and accurate on the MFFT. The 18 OCD patients with short latencies had a high error rate, while the 16 patients with long latencies had a low error rate. These patterns contrast with the control group's intermediate latency and low error rate.

These results can be interpreted in the following ways: Patients with a long latency and a low error rate may reflect a low tolerance for risk-taking or decreased certainty in response. Patients with a short latency and high error rate may have visual discrimination difficulties. Alternatively, these two types of patients may have similar deficits but compensate differently.

The Trail Making Tests are sensitive to the presence of compromised brain function and may indicate the ability to conceptually track two sequences. On Trails A, the OCD group was significantly slower than the controls; on the more complex task of Trails B, the same relationship held.

The Stroop Color Word Interference test requires the ability to maintain a response set while ignoring more salient characteristics of the stimuli. The most difficult part of the test requires identifying the color of the ink that a word is printed in (i.e., green) while the word itself is a different color name (i.e., red). The groups did not differ in absolute time to complete the word reading (card 1) and color identification (card 2) tasks. However, on the interference task (card 3), the OCD groups had a significantly greater time to completion compared with the control group. Similarly, on the usual measure of interference (card 3-card 2), the OCD group required significantly greater amounts of time to suppress interference from the more salient stimulus characteristic.

The Benton Visual Retention Test (BVRT) measures the ability to reproduce geometric forms from memory after a 10 second exposure. The OCD group was impaired compared to the control group on both the total number of figures correct and total errors. The latter may be related to the possibility that the estimated mean IQ score of the control goups was somewhat higher (High average range) than that of the OCD group (Average range). Nevertheless, the presence of a possible visual memory impairment is consistent with the idea that the more globally impaired patients experience pathological doubt based on deficient memory mechanisms.

Selected subtests from the Wechsler Adult Intelligence Scale-Revised (WAIS-R) were administered, including Information (fund of general knowledge), Digit Span (immediate memory), Block Design (analysis and synthesis of aspects of space), and Digit Symbol (a number–symbol copying test that reflects response speed, sustained attention, and possible visuoperceptual problems).

Of the four tests administered, the two groups were equivalent on only Digit Span. On the remaining three subtests, the controls' mean scores were in the high average range and significantly greater than the OCD group's mean scores, which were in the average range.

Our preliminary findings indicated that OCD patients exhibit deficits in shifting between conceptual sets and in inhibiting responses to an irrelevant stimulus dimension. Overall, they were less accurate in making decisions requiring fine visual discriminations, although their average response speed was equivalent to the control group's. With greater time, about half of the patients achieved accuracy in the normal range, suggesting that more time is required for assured matching of visual stimuli. Those OCD patients who consistently responded too rapidly on the discrimination task also made an excessive number of errors, suggesting perhaps perseveration in a kind of behavior (i.e., quick response) despite the negative consequences. The OCD patients did not exhibit significant deficits in immediate memory (digit span) or verbal learning, but had a visual memory impairment. The latter may be secondary to deficiencies related to visual discrimination processes. The lack of a robust finding on verbal learning and memory tasks suggests that a memory impairment may not underlie checking behavior in OCD.

In all neuropsychological studies of OCD, one must be concerned with how many of the reported abnormalities really reflect aberrant cortical functions and how many are due to aberrant strategies adopted by these patients. Although these strategies might themselves reflect neuropsychological dysfunction, the interpretation of these results cannot be immediately equated with similar results in patients with known neural lesions.

ELECTROPHYSIOLOGY

Electrophysiologic findings demonstrate abnormalities on EEG (Jenike & Brotman, 1984; Pacella, Polatin, & Nagler, 1944) and power spectral analysis of EEG (Flor-Henry et al., 1979), and similarities with EEG's of temporal lobe epileptics (Epstein & Bailine, 1971). There are abnormalities in sleep EEG's in OCD, with shortened REM latency paralleling findings seen in depression (Insel, et al., 1982). This does not occur only in OCD patients with coexistent depression.

Visual, somatosensory, and auditory stimuli will reliably elicit from the human brain time-locked electrical components recorded at the scalp as event-related potentials (ERPs). Early ERP components (N100, P200) are primarily exogenous, because they are dependent on physical stimulus parameters. Late ERP components (N200, P300, slow wave) are primarily endogneous, as they can be elicited in the absence of stimulation, and vary in amplitude and latency in relation to the role or meaning of the stimulus as defined by the task or perceived by the subject. N200 latency gives a measure of sensory decision time and reflects the stimulus classification stage of information processing. P300 latency reflects the time it takes to make a decision as to the contextual categorization of the eliciting event. P300 amplitude may reflect psychological processes relevant to future events since it is directly related to the probability of item recall or recognition in memory. Slow wave is linked to psychological processes of mental effort, and its amplitude increases with increments in perceptual difficulty. The late ERPs reflect evaluations of decision making and are affected by the novelty and complexity of stimuli. This may be particularly relevant to OCD, because doubting and lack of certainty are core features of this illness, and may be reflected in the late event-related potentials.

Visual evoked potential (EP) studies demonstrate shortened latencies of late event-related potentials in a small group of OCD patients ($N=8$) compared to controls, with group differences becoming greater during more difficult discrimination tasks (Beech, Ciesielski, & Gordon, 1983; Ciesielski, Beech, & Gordon, 1981).

Another study focused on early and middle latency evoked potentials to somatosensory, auditory, and visual stimuli in a group of 14 OCD patients compared to other psychiatric control groups (Shagass, Roemer, Straumanis, & Josiassen, 1984). Although the EP of OCD patients differed from normal controls in several respects, one finding stood out as specific to OCD. Somatosensory evoked potentials revealed increased negative amplitude of N60.

We have studied auditory evoked potentials in adult OCD patients compared to normal controls (Towey et al., 1990; Hollander, DeCaria,

& Liebowitz, 1989). Using the standard oddball paradigm (i.e., detect the rarer and louder of two clicks), the cortical event-related potentials of OCD patients were recorded. The oddball paradigm is known to elicit endogenous late ERP components (N200, P300, SW) that are related to the cognitive and attentional demands of the task. Preliminary ERP data for 10 OCD patients and 10 age and sex matched controls show an abnormal pattern of late ERP components for the OCD patients:

1. Shorter latencies in the regions of N200 and P300 during the difficult discrimination condition, which replicates prior studies (Beech et al., 1983; Ciesielski et al., 1981).
2. Larger negative amplitude in the regions of N200 and slow wave, which is a new ERP finding in OCD research.

This suggests that OCD patients are hypervigilant and react very strongly to novel stimuli. Furthermore, the more difficult the discrimination task, the more hypervigilant the OCD patient becomes and the shorter the P300 latency. In contrast, normals show longer latencies for more difficult discrimination tasks.

The findings of briefer latency of N200 and P300 components in OCD patients is important because patients with other psychiatric disorders (schizophrenia or depression) show either longer latencies or no differences in comparison to normal controls. Further analyses of both pre- and post-treatment ERP data will give information on whether these alterations in OCD patients normalize, or represent more stable state–independent (trait) characteristics, or are predictive of treatment outcome.

RELATIONSHIP OF NEUROPSYCHIATRY, NEUROPSYCHOLOGY, BIOLOGY, AND TREATMENT OUTCOME

Overlapping but not identical subsets of our OCD population were studied with neurological soft signs, neuropsychological testing, and M-chlorophenylpiperazine (M-CPP) challenge (Hollander et al., 1988). M-CPP is a selective 5HT agonist that produces behavioral exacerbation in a subgroup of OCD patients (Hollander, Fay, Cohen, Campeas, Gorman, & Liebowitz, 1988; Zohar, Mueller, Insel, Zohar-Kadouch, & Murphy, 1987). (For a discussion of this challenge, see Chapter 8, this volume). The following preliminary interrelationships were observed:

Patients who experienced an exacerbation of OCD symptoms with M-CPP (M-CPP +) showed a trend toward having less total number of neurological soft signs (SS) than did those without an exacerbation from M-CPP (M-CPP –). This suggests that serotonergic dysfunction and neuropsychiatric impairment might be distinct in terms of patients affected.

Patients who were slow and accurate on the Matching Familiar Figures Test (MFFT) showed exacerbations with M-CPP (M-CPP +). Patients who were fast and inaccurate on MFFT tended not to be behaviorally sensitive to M-CPP (M-CPP –). These data suggest that OCD patients with different patterns of neuropsychological dysfunction may differ in serotonergic (5-HT) sensitivity.

Patients who show exacerbation with M-CPP challenge (M-CPP +) seem to have a better treatment outcome with fluoxetine than do the M-CPP nonresponders. However, this trend occurs in a small group and needs to be replicated.

Patients with an abnormal total number of neurological soft signs (SS +) were more likely to be abnormal on the Benton Visual Retention Test (BVRT +) (a measure of visual memory). In addition, the total number of neurological soft signs correlated positively with the number of BVRT errors and with number of MFFT errors. This suggests that patients with neuropsychiatric impairment also have evidence of neuropsychological impairment, particularly visual memory and visual discrimination deficits.

Patients with an abnormal number of total soft-signs (SS +) were more likely to have a poor treatment outcome with clomipramine than were those with few abnormal soft signs (SS –).

This suggests distinct subgroups of OCD patients. One group appears to have a moderate number of abnormal soft-signs, exhibits exacerbation with oral M-CPP challenge, is slow and accurate on neuropsychological testing (MFFT), and improves with fluoxetine treatment. The other group has a high number of soft signs, is unresponsive to M-CPP challenge, is fast and inaccurate on visual performance tests (MFFT), and has a poor response to treatment with clomipramine and other 5HT reuptake blockers.

NEUROPSYCHIATRIC STUDIES OF TOURETTE'S SYNDROME

Clinical and familial evidence suggests a close relationship between TS and OCD. Thus, it is of interest that there is considerable overlap in neuropsychiatric markers for these two disorders when independently studied.

TS patients have abnormal neurological soft signs. In an examination of 70 TS patients, 57.1% had neurological soft signs (Sweet, Solomon, Wayne, Shapiro, & Shapiro, 1973). In a larger sample of 380 patients, the same investigators found 24% had soft signs and 5% had focal findings (Shapiro et al., 1988). The neurological soft signs were significantly higher in the TS group with coexistent attention deficit disorder with hyperactivity (ADDH).

This is of interest because a subgroup of OCD patients have abnormal choreiform movements suggestive of basal ganglia disease (Denckla, 1988). Choreiform movements have previously been shown to be a marker for attention deficit disorder with hyperactivity (ADDH) and for basal ganglia disturbance (Denckla, 1978). Basal ganglia dysfunction, manifest by involuntary movements, may be a common element in OCD, TS, and ADDH.

There have been few neuropsychological studies in TS, and available studies are limited by lack of appropriate control groups, and inclusion of subjects on medication or with coexistent ADD, learning disabilities, or other CNS impairment. Bornstein, Carroll, and King (1985) administered the Halstead Reitan Neuropsychological Battery (HRNB), Wechsler Intelligence Scale for Children-Revised (WISC-R), and Wide Range Achievement Test (WRAT) to 7 male adolescent TS patients, and reported a pattern of nonverbal and visuospatial deficits suggestive of right cerebral hemisphere dysfunction. Sutherland, Kolb, Schoel, Whishaw, and Davies (1982) used the Montreal Neurological Institute Battery in 32 unmedicated TS patients compared to learning disabled and schizophrenic controls. They reported impaired performance IQ, deficits in memory and copying of visually presented nonverbal material, reduced verbal fluency, and short-term memory for stories.

Findings of right hemisphere visuospatial abnormalities in TS parallel the subgroup of OCD patients with right cerebral visuospatial abnormalities and left hemisyndrome abnormalities.

Surwillo (1981) reported reduced N200 and P300 latencies in TS compared to normals. N200 and P300 amplitudes were reduced, but normalized with haloperidol treatment. Others reported the short latency response in TS did not significantly differ from controls (Krumholz, Singer, Niedermeyer, Burnite, & Harris, 1983). Another study compared the late event related potentials in 6 TS patients on and off pimozide and clonidine to normal controls (Van de Wetering, Martens, Fortgens, Slaets, Van Woerkom, 1985). While there were several differences, the N100 amplitude was smaller in unmedicated TS patients than in normals, and returned towards normal with medication. N100 has been related to selective attention. Some of the TS patients in this study had ADD symptoms. Dopamine blockers have been shown to prolong the latencies of evoked potentials in animals and humans.

Findings of decreased latency of P300 and N200 in both OCD and TS suggest similarities in attention and cognitive processing of novel stimuli, suggestive of hypervigilance.

CONCLUSION

We have reviewed evidence suggesting neuropsychiatric and neuropsychological dysfunction in obsessive–compulsive disorder. Clear differences exist between OCD patients and normal controls, and similarities exist among OCD and TS patients on neurological soft signs, electrophysiology and evoked potentials, and neuropsychology.

OCD patients have abnormal neurological soft signs. These consist of abnormalities of fine motor coordination (nonspecific), involuntary movements such as choreiform movements (suggestive of basal ganglia disorder), and of visuospatial function (suggestive of right hemisphere disorder).

Although limited by methodological shortcomings and lack of specifically designed test batteries, OCD patients exhibit various abnormalities on neuropsychological testing. These include both frontal as well as right hemisphere nonverbal visuospatial abnormalities. There also appear to be subgroups with either visual discrimination deficits or with low tolerance for risk-taking and decreased certainty of correct response.

Evoked potentials demonstrate short latency and increased negative amplitudes of late event-related potentials, suggestive of hypervigilance, which increases on more difficult tasks.

There is also tentative preliminary evidence for subgroups within OCD. Patients who are biochemically responsive to selective serotonergic agonists may have moderate soft-sign abnormalities, be risk aversive on neuropsychological tests, and responsive to 5HT reuptake inhibitors. In rats, M-CPP preferentially binds to 5HT1B receptors located in the basal ganglia. In this first subgroup of OCD patients, M-CPP produces exacerbation of OCD symptoms. This would be consistent with a basal ganglia subtype, which has a moderate number of soft signs (choreiform movements) and is responsive to 5HT drugs.

Another tentative group may have very high soft signs (cube drawing abnormalities), appear to be unresponsive to serotonergic challenges, show visual discrimination and visual memory deficits on neuropsychological tests, and do poorly with drug treatment. Perhaps these are patients with right hemisphere damage, and little serotonergic involvement.

Neuroanatomic models involving dysfunction of the basal ganglia, frontal lobes, right hemisphere, and hippocampus have been proposed based on the available evidence. These models find support from neuropsychiatric studies in children and adults with OCD, localizing studies with other patient populations, imaging studies, and animal models. However, there remains considerable conflicting evidence, which may be partially due to the presence of distinct subgroups of patients within the OCD population. More work needs to be done to identify the presence of distinct subgroups of OCD patients, to compare OCD patients with other anxiety disorder control groups, and to better understand the relationship between biochemical, neuropsychiatric, and genetic factors in this disorder.

REFERENCES

Barton, R. (1954). Diabetes insipidus, obsessional neurosis, and hypothalamic dysfunction. *Proceedings of the Royal Society of Medicine, 47,* 276–277.

Barton, R. (1965). Diabetes insipidus and obsessional neurosis: A syndrome. *Lancet, 1,* 133–135.

Beech, H. R., Ciesielski, K. T., & Gordon, K. T. (1983). Further observations of evoked potentials in obsessional patients. *British Journal of Psychiatry, 142,* 605–609.

Behar, D., Rapoport, J., Berg, C., Denckla, M. B., Mann, L., Cox, C., Fedio, T., Zahn, T., & Wolfman, M. G. (1984). Computerized tomography and neuropsychological test measures in adolescents with obsessive compulsive disorder. *American Journal of Psychiatry, 141,* 363–369.

Bornstein, R. A., Carroll, A., & King, G. (1985). Relationship of age to neuropsychological deficit in Tourette syndrome. *Brain Research Bulletin, 11,* 205–208.

Capstick, N., & Seldrup, U. (1977). Obsessional states. A study in the relationship between abnormalities occurring at birth and subsequent development of obsessional symptoms. *Acta Psychiatrica Scandinavia, 56,* 427–439.

Ciesielski, H. R., Beech, H. R., & Gordon, P. K. (1981). Some electrophysiological observations in obsessional states. *British Journal of Psychiatry, 138,* 479–484.

Claude, H., Bourke, H., & Lamache, A. (1927). Obsessive-impulsions consecutives a l'encephalite epidemique. *Encephale, 22,* 716–722.

Cohen, D. J., Detlor, J., Young, J., & Shaywitz, B. A. (1980). Clonidine ameliorates Gilles de la Tourette syndrome. *Archives of General Psychiatry, 37,* 1350–1357.

Denckla, M. B. (1978). Minimal brain dysfunction. In J. Chall, A. F. Mirsky, & K. J. Relage (Eds.), *Education and the brain.* Chicago: University of Chicago Press.

Denckla, M. B. (1985). Revised PANESS. *Psychopharmacology Bulletin, 21,* 773–800.

Denckla, M. B. (1988). Neurological examination. In J. L. Rapoport (Ed.), *Obsessive compulsive disorder in children and adolescents* (pp. 107–115). Washington, DC: American Psychiatric Press, Inc.

Diamond, B. M., Albrecht, W., & Borison, R. L. (1988). Neuropsychology of obsessive compulsive disorders (abstract 215). *Society of Biological Psychiatry Scientific Program,* Montreal, Canada.

Epstein, A. W., & Bailine, S. H. (1971). Sleep and dream studies in obsessional neurosis with particular reference to epileptic states. *Biological Psychiatry, 3,* 149–158.

Fedio, P., Cox, C., Neophytides, A., Canal, C., Frederick, G., & Chase, T. (1979). Neuropsychological profile of Huntington's disease: Patients and those at risk. In T. N. Chase, N. S. Wexler, & A. Barbeau (Eds.), *Advances in neurology: Huntingtons disease, Vol. 23* (pp. 239–256). New York: Raven Press.

Flor-Henry, P., Yeudall, L. T., Koles, Z. J., & Howarth, B. G. (1979). Neuropsychological and power spectral EEG investigations of the obsessive compulsive syndrome. *Biological Psychiatry, 14,* 119–130.

Flor-Henry, P. (1983). The obsessive-compulsive syndrome. In P. Flor-Henry (Ed.), *Cerebral basis of psychopathology.* Boston: John Coright.

Flor-Henry, P., & Lind, J. (1988). Further neuropsychological studies of obsessive compulsive syndrome (abstract 211). *Society of Biological Psychiatry Scientific Program,* Montreal, Canada.

Grey-Walter, W. G. (1977). Viewpoints of mental illness: Neurophysiologic aspects. *Seminars in Psychiatry, 14,* 211–231.

Grimshaw, L. (1964). Obsessional disorder and neurological illness. *Journal of Neurology, Neurosurgery, and Psychiatry, 27,* 229–231.

Harvey, N. S. (1986). Impaired cognitive set-shifting in obsessive compulsive neurosis. *IRCS Medical Science, 14,* 936–937.

Hillbom, E. (1960). After effects of brain injuries. *Acta Psychiatrica Neurologica Scandanavia, 35,* (suppl. 42).

Hollander, E., DeCaria, C., & Liebowitz, M. R. (1989). Biological aspects of obsessive-compulsive disorder. *Psychiatric Annals, 19,* 80–87.

Hollander, E., Fay, M., Cohen, B., Campeas, R., Gorman, J. M., & Liebowitz, M. R. (1988). Serotonergic and noradrenergic responsiveness in obsessive compulsive disorder: Behavioral findings. *American Journal of Psychiatry, 145,* 1015–1017.

Hollander, E., Schiffman, E., Cohen, B., Rivera-Stein, M., Rosen, W., Gorman, J. M., Fyer, A., Papp, L., & Liebowitz, M. R. (1990). Signs of central nervous system dysfunction in obsessive-compulsive disorder. *Archives of General Psychiatry, 47,* 27–32.

Hollander, E., Schiffman, E., & Liebowitz, M. R. (1987). Neurological soft signs in obsessive compulsive disorders. New Research Abstract 182, *American Psychiatric Association Annual Meeting.* Chicago, Illinois.

Hollander, E., Rosen, W., Towey, J., Bruder, G., Schiffman, E., & Liebowitz, M. R. (1988). Neurologic and biochemical subgroups in obsessive compulsive disorder. New Research Abstract, *American Psychiatric Association Annual Meeting.* Montreal, Canada.

Insel, T., Donnelly, E. F., Lalakea, M. L., Alterman, I. S., & Murphy, D. L. (1983). Neurological and neuropsychological studies of patients with obsessive compulsive disorder. *Biological Psychiatry, 18,* 741–751.

Insel, T. R., Gillin, J. C., Moore, A., Mendelson, W. B., Loewenstein, R. J., & Murphy, D. L. (1982). Sleep in obsessive–compulsive disorder. *Archives of General Psychiatry, 39,* 1372–1377.

Jelliffe, S. E., & Smith, E. (1932). Psychopathology of forced movements in oculogyric crises of lethargic encephalitis. *Nervous and Mental Disorders Monograph Series,* 1–200.

Jenike, M. A. (1982). Behavioral aspects of neurotic syndromes. *Contemporary Psychiatry, 1,* 109–112.

Jenike, M. A., & Brotman, A. W. (1984). The EEG in obsessive compulsive disorder. *Journal of Clinical Psychiatry, 45,* 122–124.

Kettl, P. A., & Marks, M. (1986). Neurological factors in obsessive compulsive disorder: Two case reports and a review of the literature. *British Journal of Psychiatry, 149,* 315–319.

Krumholz, A., Singer, H. S., Niedermeyer, E., Burnite, R., & Harris, K. (1983). Electrophysiological studies in Tourette's syndrome. *Annals of Neurology, 14,* 638–641.

Lewin, W. (1973). Selective leukotomy: A review. In L. V. Laitinen, & K. Livingston (Eds.), *Surgical approaches in psychiatry* (pp. 69–73). Lancaster, England: Medical and Technical Publishing Co.

McKeon, J., McGuffin, P., & Robinson, P. (1984). Obsessive-compulsive neurosis following head injury: A report of four cases. *British Journal of Psychiarty, 144,* 190–192.

Mitchell-Heggs, N., Kelly, D., & Richardson, A. (1976). Stereotactic limbic leukotomy: A follow up at 16 months. *British Journal of Psychiatry, 128,* 226–240.

Montgomery, M. A., Clayton, P. J., & Friedhoff, A. J. (1982). Psychiatric illness in Tourette Syndrome patients and first degree relatives. In A. J. Friedhoff, & T. N. Chase (Eds.), *Gilles de la Tourette Syndrome* (pp. 335–339). New York: Raven Press.

Nee, L. E., Caine, E. D., Polinsky, R. J., Eldridge, R., & Ebert, M. H. (1980). Gilles de la Tourette syndrome: Clinical and family study of 50 cases. *Annals of Neurology, 7,* 41–49.

Nichols, P. L. (1987). Minimal brain dysfunction and soft signs: The collaborative perinatal project. In D. Tupper (Ed.), *Soft neurological signs* (pp. 179–199). Orlando, FL: Grune & Stratton.

Pacella, B. L., Polatin, P., & Nagler, S. H. (1944). Clinical and EEG studies in obsessive–compulsive states. *American Journal of Psychiatry, 100,* 830–838.

Pauls, D. L., Towbin, K. E., Leckman, J. F., Zahner, G. E. P., & Cohen, D. J. (1986). Gilles de la Tourette syndrome and obsessive compulsive disorder. *Archives of General Psychiatry, 43,* 1180–1182.

Pitman, R. K. (1982). Neurological etiology of obsessive compulsive disorders? *American Journal of Psychiatry, 139,* 139–140.

Pitman, R. K., Green, R. C., Jenike, M. A., & Mesulam, M. M. (1987). Clinical comparison of Tourette's disorder and obsessive-compulsive disorder. *American Journal of Psychiatry, 144,* 1166–1171.

Quitkin, F. M., Rifkin, A., & Klein, D. F. (1976). Neurologic soft signs in schizophrenia and character disorders: Organicity in schizophrenia with premorbid asociality and emotionally unstable character disorders. *Archives of General Psychiatry, 33,* 845–853.

Rapoport, J., Elkins, R., Langer, D. H., Sceevy, W., Buchsbaum, M. S., Gillin, J. G., Murphy, D. L., Zahn, T. P., Lake, R., Ludlow, C., & Mendelson, W. (1981). Childhood obsessive–compulsive disorder. *American Journal of Psychiatry, 12,* 1545–1555.

Rapoport, J. L. (1988). *Obsessive compulsive disorder in children and adolescents.* Washington, DC: American Psychiatric Press, Inc.

Reed, G. (1977). Obsessional personality disorder and remembering. *British Journal of Psychiatry, 130,* 177–183.

Rosen, W., Hollander, E., Stannick, V., & Liebowitz, M. R. (1988). Task performance variables in obsessive-compulsive disorder (abstract). *Journal of Clinical and Experimental Neuropsychology, 10,* 73.

Schilder, P. (1938). The organic background of obsessions and compulsions. *American Journal of Psychiatry, 94,* 1397.

Shaffer, D., Schonfeld, I. S., O'Connor, P. A., Stokman, C., Troutman, T., Shafer, S., & Ng, S. (1985). Neurological soft signs and their relationship to psychiatric disorder and intelligence in childhood and adolescence. *Archives of General Psychiatry, 42,* 342–351.

Shagass, C., Roemer, R. A., Straumanis, J. J., & Josiassen, R. C. (1984). Distinctive somatosensory evoked potential features in obsessive compulsive disorder. *Biological Psychiatry, 19,* 1507–1524.

Shapiro, A. K., Shapiro, E. S., Young, J. G., & Feinberg, T. E. (1988). *Gilles de la Tourette Syndrome (2nd Ed).* New York: Raven Press.

Sher, K., Frost, R., & Otto, R. (1983). Cognitive deficits in compulsive checkers: An exploratory study. *Behavior Research and Therapy, 21,* 357–363.

Sher, K., Mann, B., & Frost, R. O. (1984). Cognitive dysfunction in compulsive checkers: Further explorations. *Behavior Research and Therapy, 22,* 493–502.

Stokman, C. J., Shafer, S. O., Shaffer, D., Ng, SK-C., O'Connor, P. A., & Wolff, R. R. (1986). Assessment of neurological soft signs in adolescents: Reliability studies. *Developmental and Medical Child Neurology, 28,* 428–439.

Surwillo, W. W. (1981). Cortical evoked potentials in Gille de la Tourette syndrome: A single case study. *Psychiatry Research, 4,* 31–38.

Sutherland, R. J., Kolb, B., Schoel, W. M., Wishaw, I. Q., & Dovier, D. (1982). Neuropsychological assessment of children and adults with Tourette syndrome: A comparison with learning disabilites and schizophrenia. In A. J. Friedhoff & T. N. Chase (Eds.), *Advances in neurology, Vol. 35, Gilles de la Tourette Syndrome* (pp. 311–322). Raven Press: New York.

Sweet, R. D., Solomon, G. E., Wayne, H. L., Shapiro, E., & Shapiro, A. K. (1973). Neurological features of Gilles de la Tourette's syndrome. *Journal of Neurology, Neurosurgery, and Psychiatry, 36,* 1–9.

Talairach, J., Bancard, J., Geirer, S., Bordas-Ferrer, M., Bonis, A., Szikla, G., & Rusu, M. (1973). The Cingulate gyrus and human behavior. *Electroencephalography and Clinical Neurophysiology, 34,* 45–52.

Towey, J., Bruder, G., Hollander, E., Friedman, D., Erhan, H., Liebowitz, M. R. & Sutton, S. (1990). Endogenous event-related potentials in obsessive-compulsive disorder. *Biological Psychiatry, 28,* 92–98.

Van de Wetering, B. J. M., Martens, C. M. C., Fortgens, C., Slaets, J. P., & Van Woerkom, T. C. (1985). Late components of the auditory evoked potentials in Gille de la Tourette syndrome. *Clinical Neurology and Neurosurgery, 87,* 3.

Wexler, B. E. (1980). Cerebral laterality and psychiatry: A review of the literature. *American Journal of Psychiatry, 137,* 279–291.

Zohar, J., Mueller, E. A., Insel, T. R., Zohar-Kadouch, R. C., & Murphy, D. L. (1987). Serotonergic responsivity in obsessive compulsive disorder. *Archives of General Psychiatry, 44,* 946–951.

7

Biological Markers in Obsessive–Compulsive Disorder

Abraham Weizman
Joseph Zohar
Thomas Insel

Compulsive ideas are not caused by an emotional or affect-like state. Actually, the person afflicted often is in a completely peaceful and indifferent mood condition when the compulsive idea first arises, and is not under the influence of any mood or affect—and I lay special importance on this fact with respect to the concept of this disease and its position vis-á-vis other diseases. Nevertheless, the patients in the course of the disease often complain of a feeling of anxiety . . . Just by closer analysis . . . I have always found that these feelings of anxiety were secondary produced by the pathologic compulsion in thinking.

K. WESTPHAL

Biological markers in psychiatric disorders have generally been of two types: "state" markers and "trait" markers. State markers are evident only in the presence of clinical symptoms and thus, have been explored as possible diagnostic tools. By contrast, trait markers persist following clinical improvement and may therefore prove useful for identifying vulnerability to a particular psychiatric syndrome.

A relatively unexplored application of both "state" and "trait" markers is the use of these markers to investigate the relationship between related but distinct clinical syndromes. If, for instance, two disorders differ in symptomatology but share a variety of biologic features, then similar pathophysiology, response to treatment, or genetic loading may also be present.

Over the past decade psychopharmacological studies provided a new method of treatment (Insel & Murphy, 1981) and also a novel strategy

146

for investigating the etiology of obsessive-compulsive disorder (OCD) (Zohar & Insel, 1987a). However, the relationship of OCD to other forms of psychopathology, mainly to major depressive disorder (MDD), and anxiety disorders remains unclear.

In this chapter we will review a series of studies carried out with OCD patients, that utilized biological markers and were aimed at investigating the relationship between OCD and other clinical syndromes.

BIOLOGICAL MARKERS FOR DEPRESSION TESTED IN OCD

Although OCD is currently classified as an anxiety disorder (APA Task Force, 1986) there has been a long tradition linking OCD and affective illness (Maudsley, 1895). Before the 20th century, OCD was known as melancholy (Hunter & MacAlpine, 1963). In modern times phenomenologic studies have demonstrated not only that depression is the most common complication of OCD (Gittleson, 1966; Goodwin, Guze, & Robins, 1969) but that obsessions are common in primary affective illness as well (Gittleson, 1966; Vaughan, 1976). Moreover the Epidemiologic Catchment Area (ECA) survey (Myers et al., 1984; Robins Helzer, Weissman, Orvaschel, Gruenberg, Burke, & Regier, 1984) like earlier studies (Lewis, 1936; Goodwin, Guze, & Robins, 1969) found significant overlap between OCD and MDD.

One approach to further investigate the link between OCD and affective illness is to examine OCD patients for putative biological markers that have been reported in depression.

Eight types of biological markers for MDD were assessed in patients with OCD: dexamethasone suppression test (DST), rapid eye movement (REM) latency and rapid eye movement density, growth-hormone response to the 2-adrenergic agonist clonidine, platelet ^{3}H-imipramine binding and platelet serotonin uptake, and cerebrospinal fluid (CSF) measure of 5-hydroxy-indoleactetic acid (5HIAA) and of 3-methoxy-4-hydroxyphenyl-glycol (MHPG). All of these markers are summarized in Table 7.1.

ENOCRINE STUDIES

Dexamethasone Suppression Test

In a study carried out in a mixed population of inpatients and outpatients with OCD, about 25% of the patients had abnormally high cortisol levels (> 5 μg/dl), following administration of 1 mg of de-

TABLE 7.1 Biological Markers in Obsessive–Compulsive Disorder (OCD) and Major Depressive Disorder (MDD)

Marker	MDD	OCD	Similarity of OCD to MDD
Endocrine			
DST nonsuppression	+1	+2, 3, 4 −5	+
Blunted growth hormone response to clonidine	+6	+7	+
Blunted TSH response to TRH	+8	+9	+
Electrophysiologic			
Decreased REM latency	+10	+11	+
Increased REM density	+12	−11	−
Platelet			
Reduced ³H-imipramine binding	+13	+14	+
Reduced serotonin uptake	+15	−14, 15	−
CSF amine metabolites			
5-HIAA increased	−16	+15, ±17	−
MHPG decreased	±18	−17	±

1. Carroll et al., 1981; 2. Insel et al., 1983; 3. Cottraux et al., 1984; 4. Asberg et al., 1982; 5. Monterio et al., 1986; 6. Siever et al., 1984; 7. Siever et al., 1983; 8. Loosen & Prange, 1982; 9. Weizman et al., 1988; 10. Kupfer et al., 1978; 11. Insel et al., 1982; 12. Foster et al., 1976; 13. Meltzer et al., 1983; 14. Weizman et al., 1986; 15. Insel et al., 1985; 16. Van Praag, 1982; 17. Thoren et al., 1980; 18. Jimerson & Berrettini, 1985.

xamethasone given at 11p.m. (Insel Kalin, Guttmacher, Ehoen, & Murphy, 1982). Hamilton and Comprehensive Psychiatric Rating Scale (CPRS) scores were nonsignificantly higher in the patients with abnormal DST. This percentage of DST nonsuppressor is somewhat more modest than previous findings with DST in obsessive compulsives including 37.5% DST nonsuppression in one study (Insel & Goodwin, 1983), 41% in another study (Asberg, Thoren, & Bertilsson, 1982), and 30% in a third study (Cottraux, Bouvard, Claustrat, & Juenet, 1984). The difference most likely reflects the greater number of outpatients in the recent study compared to the earlier reports. As outpatients had only one time point sampled for plasma cortisol, the likelihood of finding an abnormality was considerably less than with inpatients for whom three time points were tested. A 25% incidence of nonsuppression approximates the sensitivity of the DST for endogenous depression in some centers and is somewhat higher than the incidence of DST nonsuppression in normals.

While DST abnormalities suggest a link between OCD and affective illness, a similarly high incidence of cortisol levels following administration of dexamethazone exists with a variety of other psychiatric syndromes such as anorexia nervosa, senile dementia, and alcohol withdrawal (Insel & Goodwin, 1983). Moreover, even healthy controls subjected to stress had high incidence of DST nonsuppression (Mullen, Insel, & Parker, 1986). Hence, the physiological link between these conditions and DST nonsuppression remains unclear. DST nonsuppression in Cushing's syndrome, for instance, may result from pituitary, hypothalamic, or even pulmonary lesions. It is therefore premature to assume that all psychiatric patients with DST nonsuppression have the same "lesion." Moroever, the significance of DST nonsuppression in OCD is further diminished as two recent studies report normal DST responses in OCD (Lieberman et al., 1985; Monterio et al., 1986).

Growth Hormone Response to Clonidine Challenge Test

Nine OCD patients and nine healthy volunteers received intravenously 2 μg/kg of the α2-adrenergic autoreceptor agonist clonidine (Siever Insel, Jimerson, Lake, Uhde, & Murphy, 1983). OCD patients showed a significant blunted growth hormone response following this challenge with clonidine; growth hormone increases of greater than 3 ng/ml following clonidine were observed only in two (out of nine) patients with OCD as compare to five (out of nine) normal controls. Baseline growth hormone levels were not significantly different between the two groups.

These results with OCD subjects resembled previously reported results with depressives. However, the blunted growth hormone response was not limited to subjects with secondary depression; of the five OCD subjects with 17-item HDRS scores of less than 12, all but one had blunted growth hormone response to clonidine. Yet, similar to the DST test, the question of the specificity of blunted growth hormone response remains controversial as nondepressed post-menopausal women and schizoaffective patients also show attenuation similar to that seen in depressives (Matussek et al., 1980).

Thyroid-Stimulating Hormone (TSH) Response to Thyrotropin-Releasing Hormone (TRH)

The effect of TRH (0.2 mg, iv in one bolus) on plasma TSH, prolactin (PRL) and growth hormone (GH) levels was studied in 10 drug-free

OCD patients aged 20 to 40 years and 10 age- and- sex-matched heatlhy controls. Nine out of the 10 OCD patients exhibited diminished (Δ max TSH < 6 μU/ml) TSH response to TRH provocation, whereas reduced TSH response was detected in 2 controls only. PRL and GH responses to the neuroendocrine challenge were normal (Weizman, Hermesh, Gilad, Aizenberg, Tyano, & Laron 1988).

A blunted TSH response to TRH has been found to occur significantly more often in depressed patients than controls (Loosen & Prange, 1982). The blunted TSH response to TRH stimulation indicates some dysfunction of the hypothalamic–pituitary axis, and suggests a link between OCD and affective disorders. However, reduced TSH response to TRH have also been found in other neuropsychiatric disorders, including panic disorder, eating disorders, personlaity disorders, mania, alcoholism, and cocaine abuse (Khan, 1988). Thus it seems that the specifity of this test is too low to be a useful laboratory aid in the diagnosis of OCD.

SLEEP EEG STUDIES

The triad of short REM latency, increased REM density and disturbed temporal distribution of REM has been suggested as specific to endogenous depressive illness (Vogel, 1981).

Decreased REM Latency

Patients with OCD had decreased REM latency compared to age-matched normal control and to depressed patients, although in this particular study the OCD as a group was significantly less depressed (p < 0.05) than the primary affective group (mean 24 items Hamilton Depression Rating Scale [HDSR] = 17.9 and 31.4 correspondingly) (Insel, Gillin, Moore, Mendelson, Loewenstein, & Murphy, 1982).

Feinberg, Gillin, Carrol, Greden, and Zis (1982) and Rush, Giles, Roffwarg, and Parker (1982) have studied depressed patients with both DSTs and EEGs. More patients showed short REM latency (defined as < 62 min by Rush et al., 1982) than DST nonsuppression, suggesting that REM latency might be more sensitive than the DST as a diagnostic test of depression. However, the specificity of shortened REM latency for depression remains controversial as a recent report (Hiatt, Floyd, Katz & Feinberg, 1983) described very short REM latencies in a group of well-diagnosed schizophrenic patients.

Increased REM Density

The REM density in the OC patients was reported to be identical to those of the normal and significantly different ($p < .05$ paired t-test) from depressed patients (Insel, Gillin, Moore, Mendelson, Loewenstein, & Murphy, 1982).

The extent to which these sleep variables are state dependent is not entirely clear. Hauri, Chernik, Hawkins, and Mendels (1974) reported normal REM latencies for unipolar patients in remission. Others have found increased REM density and even occasional nights with short REM latency in euthymic bipolar patients (Gillin, 1983). Conceivably, increased REM density may reflect a vulnerability to affective illness whereas REM latency may be more closely related to clinical state, but thus far the data are insufficient to confirm such a proposition.

In summary, patients with OCD resemble patients with MDD only in one variable—decreased REM latency, patients with OCD are identical to normal on the other variable—increased REM density. Moreover, REM latency in the OCD patients was not significantly correlated with any of the clinical ratings (Insel, Gillin, Moore, et al., 1982).

PLATELET STUDIES

High affinity ^{3}H-imipramine binding sites in human platelets closely resemble imipramine binding sites in the human brain (Rehavi, Paul, & Skolnick, 1984). High affinity ^{3}H-imipramine sites and serotonin uptake have been demonstrated to be reduced in patients with depression (Paul, Rehavi, Skolnick, & Goodwin, 1984).

Reduced [3H] Imipramine Binding

[3]H-impraine binding to platelets was reported to be unchanged in one study (Insel, Mueller, Alterman, Linnoila, & Murphy, 1985), although there was a trend for reduced ^{3}H-imipramine binding sites in the OCD patients. However, much of this tendency resulted from two patients with very low values. These patients were the only ones included who had received clomipramine in the past (more than 3 months before the study). Removing them and their two matched controls from the sample

abolishes the difference between the remaining 10 OCD patients and their 10 matched controls (OCD Bmax = 634.4 ± 81.3 fmol/mg protein vs normal Bmax = 634.4 ± 157.8 fmol/mg protein).

The results from this study may be subject to a type-2 error: the variance in ^{3}H-imipramine binding within a normal population is so great that with 12 subjects a significant difference, (i.e., $p < 0.05$) comparable to that reported in depressed patients, would be missed 25% of the time. Indeed a recent study (Weizman, Carmi, Hermesh, Shahar, Apter, Tyano, & Rehavi, 1986) with 18 patients with OCD has demonstrated a significant decrease in the maximal binding of ^{3}H-imipramine (Bmax) of 18 untreated OCD patients (8 adolescents and 10 adults). The decreased Bmax values were detected in both age groups of OCD patients in comparison to their age and sex matched controls. (Bmax values, adolescents: OCD vs controls = 292 ± 186 vs 587 ± 150 fmol/mg protein: adults: OCD vs controls = 334 ± 107 vs 527 ± 129 fmol/mg protein.)

Reduced Serotonin Uptake

Reduced serotonin uptake (Vmax) in the platelets of depressed patients is well established. Studies carried out with OCD (Insel, Mueller, Alterman, Linnoila, & Murphy, 1985; Weizman et al., 1986) reveal no significant difference between OCD patients and age-matched normal controls for serotonin uptake in platelets.

The possibility of a type-2 error for this measure should also be considered. The fact that there was not even a trend toward such a difference in one study (Insel et al, 1985) suggests that even with a much larger sample size, this particular measure of platelet serotonin function would be normal in OCD patients. Indeed, a recent study confirms that there was no reduction in serotonin reuptake in 18 patients with OCD who were examined (Weizman et al., 1986).

Whole blood serotonin content has been reported to be reduced in OCD (Yaryura-Tobias, 1977), although this has not been corroborated in a recent study focusing on platelet 5HT content (Flament, Rapoport, Murphy, Berg, & Lake, 1987). In this latter study, platelet 5HT content appeared highest in patients who responded best to clomipramine treatment, suggesting that this measure—which has previously been correlated to social status in nonhuman primates (see Chapter 10, this volume)—may prove useful in predicting treatment response even if it is not valid as a diagnostic marker.

CSF STUDIES

Two studies have looked at 5-hydroxy-idoleacetic acid (5-HIAA) cere-brospinal fluid (CSF) levels in patients with OCD. Thoren et al. (1980) found a nonsignificant increase (19%) in CSF 5-HIAA levels of 24 pre-treatment hospitalized patients with OCD as compared with 37 paid healthy volunteers (123 ± 53 versus 107 ± 41 nmole/liter 5-HIAA). Insel et al. (1985) found, in a cohort of 8 patients with OCD, that 5-HIAA levels were significantly elevated in comparison to 23 matched controls (OCD vs. controls: 98.9 ± 43.1 vs. 56.9 ± 24.1 pmol/ml). The high variance in the patient sample was largely due to a single outlier, a 55-year-old, postmenopausal woman with a CSF 5-HIAA value of 200 pmol/ml. As there were no postmenopausal females in the control group, the data were reanalyzed excluding this subject. The patient mean decreased to 84.3 ± 13.7 pmol/ml. Correcting both patient and control values for height and weight did not abolish the significant difference between the groups. The patients were shorter than the controls; however, some of the increase that this height difference con-tributed to the 5-HIAA values was offset by the lower weights of the OCD subects. Differences between patients and normals in other monoamine metabolites homovanillic acid (HVA) and 3-methoxy-4-hydroxyphenyl-glycol (MHPG) were not significant (Thoren, Asberg, Bertilsson, Mellstrom, Sjogvist, & Traskman, 1980; Insel et al., 1985).

The possibility of a type-1 error with the CSF study seems likely. Previous reports both in normals and in other psychiatric groups have found a large variance in CSF monoamine metabolites. Some in-vestigators have described a bimodal distribution of CSF 5-HIAA (Post, Ballenger, & Goodwin, 1980), others have suggested that this variable may relate to particular clinical characteristics such as impulsivity or aggression that are not syndrome specific (reviewed by Jimerson & Berrettini, 1985). With so much variance within diagnositc groups, large samples are usually required to demonstrate differences between groups.

Given the complexities of this variable, the CSF data should be in-terpreted very cautiously. Certainly the results with OCD patients do not suggest a lower CSF 5-HIAA as previously reported with violent or psychopathic subjects (Asberg, Ringberger, Sjogvist, Thoren, Trask-man, & Tuck, 1977; Traskman, Asberg, Bertilsson, Sjostrand, 1981; Van Praag, 1982; Brown, Ebert, Goyer, Jimerson, Klein, Bunny, & Goodwin, 1982; Linnoila, Virkkunen, Scheinin, Nuutila, Rimon, & Goodwin, 1983; Roy & Linnoila, 1988). The higher levels of CSF 5-HIAA are of interest, as OCD patients tend to be diametrically opposed to impulsive or violent patients. However, a difference in activity, diet, medication history, or other variables might have contributed to this increase.

DISCUSSION: BIOLOGICAL MARKERS FOR MDD AND OCD

Four out of eight biological markers studied in MDD and OCD are similar in both conditions, three are not and one is doubtful (Table 7.1). The four biological markers that are similar are: DST nonsuppression, blunted growth hormone response to clonidine, decreased REM latency and decreased platelet imipramine binding. However, two out of the four biological markers that are similar in OCD and MDD are coupled to dissimilar findings: In MDD the increased REM density is coupled with decreased REM latency while in OCD the decrease in REM latency is not associated with alteration in REM density. Similarly the decreased imipramine binding in MDD is accompanied by reduced serotonin uptake, whereas in OCD the reduced imipramine binding is not accompanied by diminished serotonin uptake. This lack of correlation between the changes in REM latency and density and between imipramine binding and serotonin uptake in patients with OCD further emphasize the biological differences, rather than the similarity, between MDD and OCD.

The other two similar biological markers are neuroendocrine biological markers (DST, GH response to clonidine and TSH response to TRH). All are present in a variety of psychiatric and nonpsychiatric conditions and thus do not appear to be specific. Another marker, the elevated CSF 5-HIAA level in patients with OCD, is opposite to the reduced or normal CSF 5-HIAA level reported in MDD.

Taken together the findings with biological markers do not support a direct linkage between OCD and MDD. Furthermore, the natural courses of these two illnesses are different; OCD is usually chronic in contrast to primary depression, which tends to be episodic.

The age of onset for OCD patients is younger in comparison to MDD and the male/female ratio is diferent beween these two disorders (lower for depression). Moreover, in contrast to MDD, one particular tricyclic antidepressant—clomipramine—appears to be relatively specific for reducing OCD symptoms (Zohar & Insel, 1987b) while in MDD all the tricyclic antidepressants appear to be equipotent.

It seems, therefore, that although OCD and MDD share some common "markers," the overall biological and clinical perspective indicates that the two disorders are separate psychobiological entities.

ANXIOGENIC CHALLENGES SPECIFIC FOR PANIC DISORDERS ADMINISTERED IN OCD

Although OCD is classified as an anxiety disorder, recent studies with so-called "anxiogenic" challenges appear to differentiate the OCD patients from patients with panic disorder and agoraphobia. (Table 7.2) As detailed description and discussion of these pharmacological challenges are provided in this volume by Goodman et al (Chapter 8, this volume) we will focus our remarks only on what one might learn from these studies regarding the biological interaction between OCD and panic disorder. For instance, lactate infusions were followed by a panic attack in only one of seven patients with OCD as compared to 26 out of 48 patients with panic disorder or agoraphobia with panic attacks (Gorman, Liebowitz, Fyer, Dillon, Davies, Stein, & Klein, 1985). Moreover, three of the patients with OCD actually reported feeling better than usual during the lactate infusion, a phenomenon that was "never seen" during lactate infusions in patients with panic disorder and agoraphobia or with normal volunteers (Gorman et al., 1985). OCD patients also failed to develop increased symptoms following yohimbine (Rasmussen et al, 1987), or caffeine administration (Zohar, Klein, Mueller Insel, Uhde, & Murphy et al., 1987), in contrast to the anxious response of agoraphobic patients following these challenges. Hence, the studies with anxiogenic challenges have questioned the current linkage between OCD and other anxiety disorders, mainy panic disorder.

TABLE 7.2 Pharmacological Challenges in Patients with Panic Disorder, OCD and Normal Controls

| | INDUCTION OF ANXIETY | | |
Challenge	Panic Disorder	O.C.D.	Normal controls
Sodium Lactate	+1	-2	-1
Yohimbine	+3	-4	-3
Caffeine	+5	-6	-5
Carbon dioxide	+7	-7	-7
m CPP	+8	+9	-9

1. Liebowitz et al., 1985; 2. Gorman et al., 1985; 3. Charney et al., 1984; 4. Rasmussen et al., 1987; 5. Boulenger et al., 1984; 6. Zohar et al., 1987c; 7. Gorman et al., 1987; 8. Klein et al., submitted; 9. Zohar et al., 1987d.

BIOLOGICAL MARKERS SPECIFIC TO OCD

Somatosensory Averaged Evoked Response

Shagass and colleagues (1984) have reported an abnormal pattern in the middle latency waves of the somatosensory averaged evoked response (AER) that appears specifically in OCD and not in other psychiatric disorders, including depression (Shagass, Roemer, Straumanis, & Josiassen, 1980).

This study is unique because it describes specific positive biological findings in OCD that do not appear in other clinical entities (including depression) while the previously reported markers were mostly "positive" in other psychiatric disorders and "negative" in OCD.

Cerebral Glucose Metabolic Rate

Specific neuroanatomical findings of OCD are reviewed in Chapter 5, this volume. Briefly, increased regional cerebral metabolic rates for glucose were detected, using positron emission tomography (PET) in both caudate nuclei of patients with OCD as compared to the metabollic rates in the same area of control subjects and MDD patients (Baxter, Phelps, Mazziotta, Guze, Schwartz, & Selin, 1987). The cerebral metabolic abnormalities in OCD were limited to the caudate nuclei and left orbital gyrus.

Quantitative X-Ray Computed Tomography

Ten patients with childhood-onset OCD had significantly smaller caudate nuclei bilaterally than did healthy control subjects. Lenticular nuclei, third ventricle, and lateral ventricle volumes did not differ between OCD patients and the controls, and no abnormal asymmetry of bilateral structures was detected (Luxenberg et al., 1988).

The results obtained from these two recent studies might indicate possible involvement of basal ganglia in OCD, particularly with respect to the basal–frontal lobe relationship. Additional neuroanatomical research is undoubtedly warranted in order to further investigate the involvement of caudate nucleus–frontal lobe circuit in the etiology of OCD.

CONCLUSIONS

The search for biological markers in OCD is a relatively new concept, as, until recently, OCD has been considered to be of psychological origin.

Nevertheless, this approach turned out to be fruitful. Biological markers seem to indicate that OCD is different from MDD as well as from panic disorder. More research directed at psychobiological characteristics unique and specific for OCD is undoubtedly warranted.

REFERENCES

American Psychiatric Association Task Force. (1986). *Diagnostic and statistical manual of mental disorders*, third edition, revised. Washington, DC: American Psychiatric Association.

Asberg, M., Ringberger, V., Sjoqvist, F., Thoren, P., Traskman, L., & Tuck, R. (1977). Monoamine metabolites in the cerebrospinal fluid and serotonin uptake inhibition during treatment with chlorimipramine. *Clinical Pharmacology and Therapeutics, 21*, 201–207.

Asberg, M., Thoren, P., & Bertilsson, L. (1982). Clomipramine treatment of obsessive compulsive disorder—Biochemical and clinical aspect. *Psychopharmacology Bulletin, 18*, 13–21.

Baxter, L. R. Jr., Phelps, M. E., Mazziota, J. C., Guze, B. H., Schwartz, J. M., & Selin, C. E. (1987). Local cerebral glucose metabolic rates in obsessive-compulsive disorder—A comparison with rates in unipolar depression and normal controls. *Archives of General Psychiatry, 44*, 211–218.

Boulenger, J. P., Uhde, T. W., Wolff, E. A., & Post, R. M. (1984). Increased sensitivity to caffiene in patients with panic disorders: Preliminary evidence. *Archives of General Psychiatry, 41*, 1067–1071.

Boyd, J. H., Burke, J. D., Gruenberg, E., Holzer, C. E., Rae, D. S., George, L. K., Karno, M., Stoltzman, R., McEvoy, L., & Nestadt, G. (1984). Exclusion criteria of DSM III. *Archives of General Psychiatry, 41*, 983–989.

Brown, G. L., Ebert, M. H., Goyer, P. F., Jimerson, D. C., Klein, W. J., Bunney, W. E., & Goodwin, F. K. (1982). Aggression, suicide, and serotonin: Relationships to CSF amine metabolites. *American Journal of Psychiatry, 139*, 741–746.

Cameron, O. G., Thyer, B. A., Nesse, R. M., & Curtis, G. C. (1986). Symptom profiles of patients with DSM-III anxiety disorders. *American Journal of Psychiatry, 143*, 1132–1137.

Carroll, B. J., Feinberg, M., Greden, J. F., Tarika, J., Albala, A. A., Haskett, R. F., James, N. McI., Kronfol, Z., Lohr, N., Steiner, M., De Vigne, J. P., & Young, E. (1981). A specific laboratory test for the diagnosis of melancholia. *Archives of General Psychiatry, 38*, 15–22.

Charney, D. S., Heninger, G. K., & Breier, A. (1984). Noradrenergic function in panic anxiety: Effects of yohimbine in healthy subjects and patients with agoraphobia and panic disorder. *Archives of General Psychiatry, 41*, 751–763.

Cottraux, J. A., Bouvard, M., Claustrat, B., & Juenet, C. (1984). Abnormal dexamethasone suppression test in primary obsessive-compulsive patients—A confirmatory report. *Psychiatry Research, 13*, 157–165.

Feinberg, M., Gillin, J. C., Carroll, B. J., Greden, J. F., & Zis, A. P. (1982). EEG studies of sleep in the diagnosis of depression. *Biological Psychiatry, 17,* 305–316.

Flament, M. F., Rapoport, J. L., Murphy, D. L., Berg, C. J., & Lake, C. R. (1987). Biochemical changes during clomipramine treatment of childhood obsessive-compulsive disorder. *Archives of General Psychiatry, 44,* 219–225.

Foster, F. G., Kupfer, D. J., Coble, P., et al. (1976). Rapid eye movement sleep density: An objective indicator in severe medical-depressive syndromes. *Archives of General Psychiatry, 33,* 1119–1123.

Gillin, J. C. (1983). Sleep studies in affective illness: Diagnostic, therapeutic and pathophysiological implications. *Psychiatry Annals., 13,* 367–383.

Gittlesson, N. (1966). The depressive psychosis in the obsessional neurotic. *Archives of General Psychiatry, 112,* 883–887.

Goodwin, D., Guze, S., & Robins, E. (1969). Follow-up studies in obsessional neurosis. *Archives of General Psychiatry, 20,* 182–187.

Gorman, J. M., Fyer, M. R., Liebowitz, M. R., et al. (1987). Pharmacologic provocation of panic attacks. In H. Y. Meltzer (Ed.), *Psychopharmacology, the third generation of progress* (pp. 985–993). New York: Raven Press.

Gorman, J. M., Liebowitz, M. R., Fyer, A. J., Dillon, D., Davies, S. O., Stein, J., & Klein, D. F. (1985). Lactate infusions in obsessive-compulsive disorder. *American Journal of Psychiatry, 142,* 864–866.

Hauri, P., Chernik, D., Hawkins, D., & Mendels, J. (1974). Sleep of depressed patients in remission. *Archives of General Psychiatry, 31,* 386–391.

Hiatt, J. F., Floyd, T. C., Katz, P., & Feinberg, M. (1983). A new look at abnormal NREM sleep in schizophrenia. In *New Research abstracts of 136th APA Meeting*, NR III, New York. Washington, DC: American Psychiatric Association.

Huntrer, R., & Mac Alpine, I. (1963). *Three hundred years of psychiatry*. London: Oxford University Press.

Insel, T. R., Gillin, J. C., Moore, A., Mendelson, W. B., Loewenstein, R. J., & Murphy, D. L. (1982). The sleep of patients with obsessive-compulsive disorder. *Archives of General Psychiatry, 39,* 1372–1377.

Insel, T. R., & Goodwin, F. K. (1983). The promises and problems of laboratory tests in psychiatry: The dexamethasone suppression test as a case example. *Hospital and Community Psychiatry, 34,* 1131–1138.

Insel, T. R., Kalin, N. H., Guttmacher, L. B., Cohen, R. M., & Murphy, D. L. (1982). The dexamethasone suppression test in patients with primary obsessive-compulsive disorder. *Psychiatry Research, 6,* 153–158.

Insel, T. R., Mueller, E. A., Alterman, I., Linnoila, M., & Murphy; D. L. (1985). Obsessive-compulsive disorder and serotonin: Is there a connection? *Biological Psychiatry, 20,* 1174–1188.

Insel, T. R., & Murphy, D. L. (1981). The psychopharmalogical treatment of obsessive-compulsive disorder: A review. *Journal of Clinical Psychopharmacology, 1,* 304–311.

Jimerson, D. C., & Berrettini, W. (1985). Cerebrospinal fluid amine metabolite studies in depression: Research update. In H. Beckmann & P. Riederer (Eds.), *Pathochemical markers in major psychoses* (pp. 129–143). Berlin: Springer-Verlag.

Khan, A. V. (1988). Sensitivity and specificity of TRH stimulation test in depressed and nondepresed adolescents. *Psychiatry Research, 25,* 11–17.

Klein, E., Zohar, J., Geraci, M. F., Murphy, D. L., & Uhde, T. W. (submitted for publication). Anxiogenic effects of mCPP in patients with panic disorder: Comparison to caffiene's anxiogenic effects.

Kupfer, D. J., Foster, F. G., Coble, P., McPartland, R. J., & Ulrich, R. F. (1978). The application of EEG sleep for the differential diagnosis of affective disorders. *American Journal of Psychiatry, 135,* 69–74.

Lewis, A. J. (1936). Problems of obsessional illness. *Proceedings of the Royal Society of Medicine, 29,* 325–336.

Lieberman, J. A., Kane, J. M., Sarantakos, S., Cole, K., Howard, A., Borenstein, M., Novacenko, H., & Puig-Antich, J. (1985). Dexamethasone suppression tests in patients with obsessive-compulsive disorder. *American Journal of Psychiatry, 142,* 747–751.

Liebowitz, M. R., Gorman, J. M., Fyer, A. J., Dillon, D., Appleby, I., Levy, G., Anderson, S., Levitt, S., Palij, M., Davies, S. O., & Klein, D. F. (1984). Lactate provocation of panic attacks. *Archives of General Psychiatry, 41,* 764–770.

Linnoila, M., Virkkunen, M., Scheinin, M., Nuutila, A., Rimon, R., & Goodwin, F. K. (1983). Low cerebrospinal fluid 5-hydroxy-indoleacetic acid concentration differentiates impulsive from nonimpulsive violent behaviour. *Life Sciences, 33,* 2609–2614.

Loosen, P. T., & Prange, A. J. Jr. (1982). The serum thyrotropin (TSH) response to thyrotropin-releasing hormone (TRH) in psychiatric patients: A review. *American Journal of Psychiatry, 139,* 405–416.

Luxenberg, J. S. Swedo, S. E., Flament, M. F., Friedland, R. P., Rapoport, J., & Rapoport, S. I. (1988). Neuroanatomical abnormalities in obsessive-compulsive disorder detected with quantitative x-ray computed tomography. *American Journal of Psychiatry, 145,* 1089–1093.

Maudsley, H. (1895). *The pathology of the mind.* London: MacMillan.

Matussek, N., Ackenheil, M., Hippius, H., Muller, F. Schroder, H. T., Schultes, H., & Wasilewski, B. (1980). Effect of clonidine on growth hormone release in psychiatric patients and controls. *Psychiatry Research, 2,* 25–36.

Meltzer, H. Y., Arora, R. C., & Song, P. (1982). Serotonin uptake in blood platelets as a biological marker for major depressive disorders. In E. Usdin & E. Costa (Eds.), *Biological markers in psychiatry and neurology* (pp. 39–48). New York: Pergamon Press.

Monterio, W., Noshiruani, H., Marks, I. M., & Checkley, S. (1986). Normal dexamethasone suppression test in OCD. *British Journal of Psychiatry, 148,* 326–329.

Mullen, P. E., Linsell, C. R., & Parker, D. (1986). Influence of sleep disruption and calorie restriction on biological markers for depression. *The Lancet, 2,* 1051–1055.

Myers, J. K. Weissman, M. M., Tischler, G. L., Holzer, C. E., Leaf, P. J., Orvaschel, H., Anthony, J. C., Boyd, J. H., Burke, J. D. Jr., Kramer, M., & Stoltzman, R. (1984). Six-month prevalence of psychiatric disorders in three communities. *Archives of General Psychiatry, 41,* 959–971.

Nemiah, J. C., Foreward, I., & Insel, T. R. (Eds.). (1984). *New findings in obsessive-compulsive disorder.* Washington, DC: American Psychiatric Association.

Paul, S. M., Rehavi, M., Skolnick, P., & Goodwin, F. K. (1984). High affinity binding of antidepressants to biogenic amine transport sites in human brain and platelet: Studies in depression. In R. M. Post & J. C. Ballenger (Eds.), *Neurobiology of mood disorder* (pp. 846–853). Baltimore: Williams & Wilkins.

Post, R. M., Ballenger, J. C., & Goodwin, F. K. (1980). Cerebrospinal fluid studies of neurotransmitter function in manic and depressive illness. In J. H. Wood (Ed.), *Neurobiology of cerebrospinal fluid* (pp. 685–695). New York: Plenum Press.

Rachman, S. J., & Hodgson, R. J. (1980). *Obsessions and compulsions.* Englewood Cliffs, NJ: Prentice Hall.

Rasmussen, S. A., Goodman, W. K., Woods, S. W., Heninger, G. R., & Charney, D. S. (1987). Effects of yohimbine in obsessive-compulsive disorder. *Psychopharmacology, 93,* 308–313.

Rehavi, M., Paul, S. M., & Skolnick, P. (1984). High affinity binding sites for tricyclic antidepressants in brain and platelets. In P. J. Marangos, I. C. Campbell, & R. M. Cohen (Eds.), *Brain receptor methodologies, part B* (pp. 279–295). Orlando, FL: Academic Press.

Robins, L. N., Helzer, J. E., Weissman, M. M., Orvaschel, H., Gruenberg, E., Burke, J. D. Jr., & Regier, D. A. (1984). Lifetime prevalence of specific psychiatric disorders in three sites. *Archives of General Psychiatry, 41,* 949–958.

Roy, A., & Linnoila, M. (1988). Suicidal behavior, impulsiveness, and serotonin. *Acta Psychiatrica Scandinavica, 78,* 529–535.

Rush, A. J., Giles, D. E., Roffwarg, H. P., & Parker, C. R. (1982). Sleep–EEG and dexamethasone suppression test findings in unipolar major depressive disorders. *Biological Psychiatry, 17,* 327–341.

Shagass, C., Roemer, R. A., Straumanis, J. J., & Amadeo, M. (1980). Topograhy of sensory evoked potentials in depressive disorders. *Biological Psychiatry, 15,* 183–207.

Shagass, C., Roemer, R. A., Straumanis, J. J., & Josiassen, R. C., (1984). Distinctive somatosensory evoked potential features in obsessive-compulsive disorder. *Biological Psychiatry, 19,* 1507–1524.

Siever, L. J., Insel, T. R., Jimerson, D. C., Lake, C. R., Uhde, T. W., Aloi, J., & Murphy, D. L. (1983). Growth hormone response to clonidine in obsessive-compulsive patients. *British Journal of Psychiatry, 142,* 184–187.

Siever, L. J., & Uhde, T. W. (1984). New studies and perspectives on the noradrenergic receptor system in depression: Effects of the 2-adrenergic agonist clonidine. *Biological Psychiatry, 19,* 131–156.

Thoren, P., Asberg, M., Bertilsson, L., Mellstrom, B., Sjoqvist, F., & Traskman, L. (1980). Clomipramine treatment of obsessive compulsive disorder, II, biochemical aspects. *Archives of General Psychiatry, 37,* 1289–1294.

Traskman, L., Asberg, M., Bertilsson, L., & Sjostrand, L. (1981). Monoamine metabolites in CSF and suicidal behaviour. *Archives of General Psychiatry, 38,* 631–636.

Van Praag, H. M. (1982). Neurotransmitters and CNS disease depression. *Lancet, ii*, 1259–1269.

Vaughan, M. (1976). The relationship between obsessional personality, obsessions in depression and symptoms of depression. *British Journal of Psychiatry, 129*, 36–39.

Vogel, E. W. (1981). The relationship between endogenous depression and REM sleep. *Psychiatry Annals, II*, 423–428.

Weizman, A., Carmi, M., Hermesh, H., Shahar, A., Apter, A., Tyano, S., & Rehavi, M. (1986). High-affinity imipramine binding and serotonin uptake in platelets of eight adolescent and ten adult obsessive-compulsive patients. *American Journal of Psychiatry, 143*, 335–339.

Weizman, A., Hermesh, H., Gilad, I., Aizenberg, D., Tyano, S. & Laron, Z. (1988). Blunted TSH response in obsessive compulsive disorder. Paper presented at the *70th Annual Meeting of the Endocrine Society*, New Orleans, Louisiana (Abstract No. 792).

Westphal, K. (1878). Ueber Zwangsvorstellungen. *Archives of Psychiatry Nervenker, 8*, 734–750.

Yaryura-Tobias, J. A. (1977). Obsessive-compulsive disorders: A serotoninergic hypothesis. *Journal of Orthomolecular Psychiatry, 6*, 317–326.

Zohar, J., & Insel, T. R. (1987a). Obsessive-compulsive disorder: Psychobiological approaches to diagnosis, treatment, and pathophysiology. *Biological Psychiatry, 22*, 667–678.

Zohar, J., & Insel, T. R. (1987b). Drug treatment of obsessive–compulsive disorder. *Journal of Affective Disorder, 13*, 193–202.

Zohar, J., Klein, E. M., Mueller, A., Insel, T. R., Uhde, T. W., & Murphy, D. L. (1987). 5-HT, obsessive–compulsive disorder and anxiety. *Proceedings American Psychiatric Association*, p. 175. Chicago.

Zohar, J., Mueller, E. A., Insel, T. R., Zohar-Kadouch, R. C., & Murphy, D. L. (1987). Serotonergic responsivity in obsessive–compulsive disorder: Comparison of patients and healthy controls. *Archives of General Psychiatry, 44*, 946–951.

8

Pharmacologic Challenges in Obsessive–Compulsive Disorder

Wayne K. Goodman
Lawrence H. Price
Scott W. Woods
Dennis S. Charney

Until recently, hypotheses regarding the possible biological basis of Obsessive–Compulsive Disorder (OCD) have undergone little direct testing. For example, the hypothesis that an alteration in brain serotonin (5-HT) function may be related to the pathophysiology of OCD is largely based on the efficacy of potent 5-HT reuptake inhibitors in the treatment of OCD (Goodman et al., 1989). However, as indicated elsewhere in this book, it has not been established whether the antiobsessional mechanism of action of the potent 5-HT reuptake inhibitors (e.g., clomipramine or fluvoxamine) is due entirely to their effects on serotonergic function (see Chapter 10, this volume). For instance, a therapeutic response usually does not develop until after several weeks of drug administration, by which time (as suggested by preclinical studies) adaptive changes may take place in other neurotransmitter systems [e.g., decreased density of beta-adrenergic receptors after chronic fluvoxamine administration in the rat (Bradford, Tulp, & Schipper, 1987)]. Moreover, the mechanism of action of the treatment may bear little connection to the actual pathogenesis of the disorder. For example, successful treatment of obsessive–compulsive symptoms with potent 5-HT reuptake inhibitors might conceivably enhance the functioning of intact compensatory systems rather than correct a primary 5-HT abnormality. The pharmacologic challenge strategy offers a more direct approach to testing specific biological hypotheses concerning both the pathophysiology and treatment of OCD.

The main objective of the pharmacologic challenge paradigm is to provide better separation of subject groups on the variable of interest than might be obtained by examination of between-group differences in baseline measures alone (Woods & Charney, 1988). True abnormalities in neurochemical function may be masked in the basal state as a result of compensatory actions of other neurochemical systems. When the target neurochemical system is activated by the challenge drug, the other systems may be unable to compensate completely, and the response of the dependent variable(s) may then reveal the dysfunction. Similarly, because the pharmacologic challenge tests the dynamic properties of the target system, it may disclose functional abnormalities in its buffering characteristics not evident during nonstressed conditions.

The typical pharmacologic challenge design consists of measuring the behavioral and/or neurobiological response of an identified group of subjects to a test dose of a drug with relatively well-characterized pharmacological actions and/or behavioral effects (Figure 8.1). In the simplest case, the analysis of the challenge drug effect involves examining the change(s) in the dependent variable(s) (e.g., behavior, physiological measures, neurochemical levels, or regional cerebral blood flow) from baseline (i.e., prior to challenge drug administration). Often, additional within-subject (e.g., active drug vs. placebo on separate test days) and/ or between-subject (e.g., patients vs. healthy subjects) comparisons of response are included in the experimental design.

Current and potential applications of the pharmacologic challenge strategy in OCD research are listed in Table 8.1 (Woods & Charney, 1988). To date, the first two applications (i.e., investigating neurochemical dysfunction and the mechanism of drug action) have been most frequently studied, and will be the focus of the present chapter. The remaining applications (e.g., as a diagnostic test), particularly the last two, reflect potential applications that depend, in large measure, on successfully elucidating the solutions to applications one and two. Before turning to a review of pharmacological challenges in OCD, we will discuss factors that contribute to the selection of independent and dependent variables and which may, in turn, influence the interpretation of the study findings.

METHODOLOGICAL CONSIDERATIONS

Independent Variables

Challenge Drug

For use as a probe in investigating possible neurobiological dysfunction in OCD, the challenge drug should have CNS effects that are (a) relative-

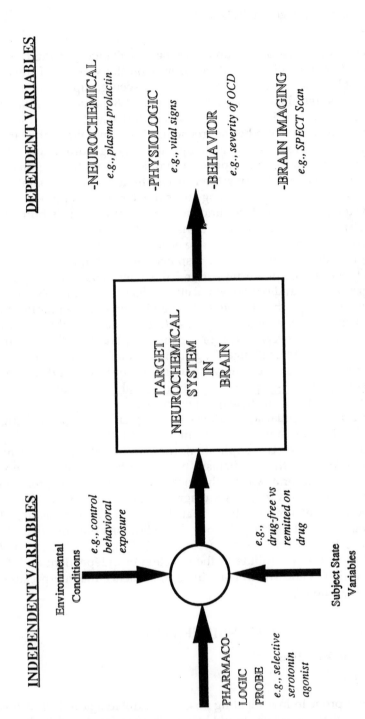

FIGURE 8.1 Simplified schematic diagram of pharmacologic challenge strategy in obsessive–compulsive disorder patients.

TABLE 8.1. Current and Potential Applications of the Pharmacologic
Challenge in Obsessive–Compulsive Disorder Research

1. As a method of testing and generating hypotheses regarding neurotransmitter/receptor dysfunction.
2. As a method of investigating the mechanism(s) of action of treatments of OCD.
3. As a method of identifying neurobiologically distinct subtypes of OCD.
4. As a diagnostic test in atypical cases, or in asymptomatic individuals at risk for the development of the illness.
5. As a method of predicting treatment response, or risk of relapse after discontinuation of successful treatment.

ly well-characterized in preclinical studies, (b) measurable clinically, and (c) reasonably specific to the system of interest. Given the availability of newer and more selective pharmacologic agents (e.g., the 5-HT$_2$ antagonist ritanserin), the pharmacologic challenge paradigm is well suited to investigations of specific subtypes of neurotransmitter receptor systems. Dosage, route, and rate of administration, and bioavailability (including ability to penetrate the blood–brain barrier) may all affect the potency and specificity of the challenge agent. If the challenge drug also has reliable effects on behavior (e.g., severity of obsessive–compulsive symptoms), then it may assist in the identification of the biochemical mediators of that behavior. Induction or modulation of obsessive–compulsive symptoms by the challenge drug strengthens the case that a concomitant abnormal neurobiological response is clinically relevant. In some cases, the challenge drug may be a useful provocative agent, but its neurochemical mechanism of action may be incompletely understood [e.g., sodium lactate in triggering panic attacks in panic disorder patients (Liebowitz et al., 1984)].

Subjects

As discussed elsewhere in this book, there has been considerable interest in the clinical and pathogenetic relationship between OCD and other disorders. Thus, pharmacologic challenges in OCD research may involve comparing the response of OCD patients not only with that of healthy control subjects, but with the response elicited in patients with a different principal psychiatric diagnosis (e.g., panic disorder). The possibility that OCD may represent a heterogenous disorder, both clinically and neurobiologically, may be examined in the pharmacologic challenge paradigm by subtyping OCD patients according to type of obsessive–compulsive symptoms (e.g., agressive vs. nonaggressive obsessions), associated comorbidity (e.g., depressive symptoms), or family history (e.g., Tourette's Syndrome in first-degree relatives). It may be determined whether a finding is state versus trait specific by conducting challenges when patients are either symptomatic versus remitted, respectively. In consideration of the second application listed in Table 8.1 (i.e., examining the mechanism of action of medication treatment), challenges can be performed during the drug-free state and then repeated during chronic medication treatment.

Environmental Conditions

Many OCD patients experience an exacerbation of their symptoms during exposure to certain environmental stimuli (e.g., blood products in a patient with an AIDS obsession). Thus, various aspects of the challenge procedure itself may inadvertently trigger symptoms in susceptible OCD patients. To reduce the risk of "contaminating" the patient, and also the findings, the usual approach is to instruct the research staff to exercise special care when peforming challenges in OCD patients (e.g., extra hand-washing). An alternative is to preselect OCD patients for the challenge study whose symptoms are relatively independent of environmental influences (e.g., patients with very frequent intrusive thoughts that harm will come to loved ones unless mental rituals are performed).

Dependent Variables

The strength of the data generated by a challenge study is only as strong as its weakest link. In general, the sensitivity and specificity of the dependent measures are the major limiting factors. This is because the organ of interest, the brain, is so inaccessable to direct measurement, given our present technology.

Neurochemical

Plasma levels of hormones and neurotransmitters and their metabolites have been utilized most extensively as putative markers of central nervous system response to a pharmacologic challenge. For example, changes in plasma levels of prolactin and the norepinephrine (NE) metabolite 3-methoxy-4-hydroxyphenylglycol (MHPG) have been used as indices of central 5-HT and NE activity, respectively, in a variety of challenge studies (Heninger, Charney, & Steinberg, 1984; Charney, Woods, Goodman, & Heninger, 1987; Charney et al., 1988). The capacity of a plasma measure to reliably reflect changes in pertinent brain activity is influenced by a number of factors, including its specificity as a measure of the system of interest [e.g., plasma prolactin is also influenced by dopamine (Price, Charney, Delgado, Anderson, & Heninger, 1988)], the relative contribution of the periphery and spinal cord to that measure [e.g., approximately 60% of plasma MHPG is derived from sources outside the brain (Charney et al., 1987)], and the sensitivity of the assay itself. In addition, neurochemical levels usually at best reflect "whole-brain" responses, which could mask important "regional brain" variations.

Cerebrospinal fluid (CSF) neurochemical levels are seldom used as dependent measures in pharmacologic challenge studies because of similar sensitivity and specificity limitations, and it is cumbersome to obtain repeated CSF samples before and after drug administration.

Behavior

Evaluation of behavioral response may include clinician and/or self-administered ratings of obsessive–compulsive symptoms, mood states (e.g., depression or anxiety), or somatic symptoms (e.g., nausea or tremors). The assessment of obsessive–compulsive symptoms in the challenge setting is fraught with difficulties. As noted previously, the degree to which obsessive–compulsive symptoms are affected by the challenge setting varies widely among patients. In some patients, obsessive–compulsive symptoms may be confined to times when they are at home (e.g., repeatedly checking household appliances); in others, symptoms may be inadvertently triggered during the challenge procedures (e.g., fear of contamination by germs). The "ideal" patient for evaluation of behavioral response to a phramacologic challenge has moderate symptoms that are relatively autonomous. This allows for unconfounded measurement of either acute improvement or worsening in obsessive–compulsive symptoms (i.e., two-tailed behavioral response).

Another problem with the evaluation of obsessive–compulsive behavior is that, unlike a mood state, OCD severity cannot be assessed during a single, brief slice of time. In fact, one of the major components of measuring symptom severity in OCD is the determination of how much time is occupied by the symptoms. Thus, the shorter the sampling time over which symptoms are rated, the less confident one can be about the reliability of the ratings. In our experience, a 60-minute interval represents the shortest time period over which obsessive–compulsives can be rated without seriously compromising reliability. An example of the OCD challenge rating scales used at our facility appears in the Appendix (Yale-Brown Obsessive Compulsive Challenge Scale [Y-BOCCS]).

Physiological

Measurement of changes in vital signs (e.g., temperature, pulse rate, and blood pressure) in response to a pharmacologic challenge may disclose significant differences between the patient group of interest and control subjects. Preclinical studies have been able to tie changes in some of these variables to specific neurotransmitter systems and/or receptors. In contrast, other peripheral physiological parameters, such as skin conductance, may not yield specific enough data regarding underlying brain mechanisms.

Brain Imaging

Recent advances in Positron Emission Tomography (PET) and Single Photon Emission Tomography (SPECT) technology provide a means to obtaining more direct information about the effects of a pharmacologic challenge on regional brain activity. The marriage of the pharmacologic challenge paradigm with brain imaging has already yielded interesting data about other neuropsychiatric disorders (e.g., panic disorder (Woods et al., 1988), and Schizophrenia (Daniel, Berman, Fawcett, & Weinberger, 1988). SPECT offers the advantage over PET of lower cost and, in general, greater ease in preparation of the radioligand. However, because SPECT images are based on blood flow, the ability of SPECT to provide an accurate measure of brain metabolic activity is determined by the degree of coupling between vascular and tissue activity for the brain region and neurochemical system under study.

REVIEW OF PHARMACOLOGIC CHALLENGES IN OCD

Serotonin (5-HT) Challenges

By far, the 5-HT system has been the subject of the most extensive investigation in pharmacologic challenge studies of patients with OCD (Table 8.2). As discussed elsewhere in this book, there are several lines of evidence that implicate an alteration in brain 5-HT function in at least some aspects of this disorder. The most consistent support for the 5-HT hypothesis is derived from the relative efficacy of potent 5-HT reuptake inhibitors in treating the obsessive–compulsive symptoms of OCD patients (Goodman et al., 1989). Some investigations of putative biological markers of 5-HT function [e.g., platelet tritiated-imipramine binding (Weizmann et al., 1986)] provide additional support for a role of 5-HT in OCD (also see Chapter 7). Studies in laboratory animals suggest that lesions of the brain 5-HT system facilitate the experimental induc-

TABLE 8.2. Summary of Pharmacological Challenges in OCD Patients

Target neuro-chemical system	Reference	Challenge agent	N	Design	Major findings	Implications/comments
A. SEROTO-NINERGIC	Zohar et al., 1987	MCPP (p.o.)	12 20	OCD Pts Healthy Sbs db, pc; MCPP (0.5 mg/kg) single oral dose vs metergoline (given last)	1. OCD sxs exacerbated by MCPP. 2. No signif diff bet Pts and Healthy Ss in PRL, & thermal response to MCPP. 3. Blunted cortisol response in Pts.	1. Suggests behavioral hypersensitivity of one or more subtypes of 5HT receptor systems in OCD.
		Metergoline (MET) (antagonist)	12	OCD Pts db; MET 4 mg p.o.	1. No signif diff bet effects of MET & PLAC on OCD sxs.	1. Nonselective blockade of 5HT function does not significantly affect OCD sxs.
	Hollander et al., 1988	MCPP (p.o.)	8	OCD Pts db, pc; MCPP (0.5 mg/kg) single oral dose vs clonidine (details under noradrenergic). vs fenfluramine (given last)	1. OCD sxs exacerbated by MCPP in 6/8 pts.	1. Replicates finding by Zohar et al. of behavioral supersensitivity to oral dose of 5-HT agonist MCPP. 2. *Discrepant findings with Charney et al. may be related to dose or route of admin.*
		Fenfluramine (FEN) (indirect agonist)	7	OCD Pts db; FEN 60 mg p.o.	1. Effects of FEN & PLAC on OCD sxs not signif different.	1. Unlike oral MCPP, indirect 5HT agonist FEN had no signif effect on OCD sxs.

169

TABLE 8.2. (continued)

Target neuro-chemical system	Reference	Challenge agent	N	Design	Major findings	Implications/comments
	Charney et al., 1988	Tryptophan (TRP) (precursor) Loading	21 21	OCD pts Healthy Sbs 7 gm TRP infused/20 min	1. No signif diff bet Pts & Healthy Sbs in PRL or GH response to TRP 2. No effect of TRP on OCD sxs.	1. Negative TRP findings alone fail to support role of 5HT in OCD. 2. *May need more selective 5HT probes.*
		MCPP (i.v.) (agonist)	21 21	OCD pts (18/21 also had TRP) Healthy Sbs db, pc; MCPP (0.1 mg/kg) infused over 20 minutes	1. PRL response to MCPP blunted in OCD females. 2. Baseline PRL level low in OCD females. 3. No signif effect of MCPP on OCD sxs. 4. No signif diff bet Pts and Healthy Sbs in GH or Cort response to MCPP.	1. Possible subsensitive postsynaptic 5HT function in OCD females. 2. *PRL response may not be adequate measure of 5HT function in males.* 3. Partial support for role of 5HT in OCD.
	DeMeo et al., 1988	Fenfluramine (FEN)	14 12	OCD Pts Healthy Sbs db, pc; FEN 60 mg po	1. PRL response to FEN not signif different in OCD Pts & Healthy Sbs. 2. FEN signif reduced obsessions, but not compulsions.	1. Incomplete effects of FEN on OCD sxs partially supports role of 5HT in OCD. 2. *Interpretation of results confounded by possible age & gender effects.*

170

Study	Probe	N	Design	Findings	Conclusions
Delgado et al., 1988	Tryptophan (TRP) (precursor) Depletion	7	OCD Pts db, pc; 24 hr TRP deficient diet followed by 12-amino acid drink vs PLAC (sham TRP depletion)	1. No signif effect of acute tryptophan depletion on OCD sxs.	1. Contrasts with robust behavioral effects of acute TRP depletion shown in some depressed Pts. 2. Does not support important role of 5HT in tonic control of OCD sxs.
Zohar et al., 1988	MCPP (p.o.) (agonist)	9	Drug-treated OCD Pts db, pc; readministration of oral MCPP (0.5 mg/kg) vs. PLAC in Pts treated with clomipramine (CMI) for four months	1. In contrast to pretreatment, Pts on chronic CMI showed no behavioral hypersensitivity or thermogenic response to oral MCPP. 2. Peak plasma MCPP levels were signif higher after chronic CMI treatment. 3. Baseline plasma PRL levels were signif higher after chronic CMI treatment.	1. Behavioral and thermal hypersensitivity to 5HT stimulation is normalized by CMI treatment. 2. Provides added evidence 5HT is related to pathophysiology and treatment of OCD.
Benkelfat et al., 1989	Metergoline (MET) (antagonist)	10	Improved OCD Pts on CMI. db, pc, crossover; 4 days of MET (4 mg/day) vs PLAC	1. Relatively greater anxiety on Day 4 of MET compared to Day 4 PLAC. 2. OCD sxs tended to be worse with MET. 3. MET lowered plasma PRL levels; consistent with a 5HT blocking action.	1. Modest behavioral effects of MET reflect relative differences from PLAC. 2. Partial support that the clinically relevant mechanism of action of CMI in OCD is related to its serotonergic effects.

TABLE 8.2. (continued)

Target neuro-chemical system	Reference	Challenge agent	N	Design	Major findings	Implications/comments
B. NORAD-RENERGIC	Rasmussen et al., 1987	Yohim-bine (YOH) (alpha-2 antagonist)	12 12	OCD Pts Healthy Sbs db, pc; YOH 20 mg p.o. (YOH always given first)	1. No signif diff bet Pts & Healthy Sbs in their behavioral or MHPG response to YOH. 2. YOH did not increase OCD sxs except in 1 of 2 Pts with a h/o panic disorder 3. OCD Pts had increased Cort response to YOH 4. No signif group diff in baseline MHPG.	1. Suggests OCD may not involve increased noradrenergic sensitivity 2. Suggests pathophysiology of OCD and panic disorder may be distinct.
	Hollander et al., 1988	Cloni-dine (CLON) (alpha-2 agonist)	6	OCD Pts db, pc; CLON (2 ug/kg) slow iv push (*also see under MCPP above*)	1. Decreased OCD sxs after CLON.	1. Suggests OCD sxs exacerbated by increased noradrenergic activity. (*contrasts with findings of YOH in OCD*) 2. *Antiobsessional effects or CLON need to be separated from its nonspecific sedative action.*
	Siever et al., 1983	Cloni-dine (CLON)	9 9	OCD Pts Healthy Sbs CLON (2 ug/kg) iv/5 min	1. Blunted GH response to CLON in OCD Pts compared to Healthy Sbs (but see Hollander et al., 1989; Curtis et al., 1989)	1. Possible subsensitive post-synaptic alpha-2 function.

					Results	Comments
C. MISCEL-LANEOUS panicogenic trigger mechanisms	Gorman et al., 1985	Sodium Lactate	7 48	OCD Pts Panic Disorder Pts sb; 10 mg/kg iv/20 min	1. Sodium lactate induced panic attacks in 1/7 (14%) of OCD Pts compared to 26/48 (56%) of Panic Disorder Pts.	1. OCD as distinct from panic disorder
D. Mixed monominergic agonists	Insel et al., 1983	d-amphetamine	12	OCD Pts db, pc; single dose of d-amphetamine 30 mg p.o. vs. PLAC	1. Signif decrease in ratings of OCD after d-amphetamine but not after PLAC. 2. Improvement in OCD correl signif with improvement in cognitive performance.	1. OCD as a deficit in dopamine function. 2. *Interpretation of findings limited by nonselective effects of amphetamine of monoamine function.*
	Swinson & Joffe, 1988	methylphenidate	13	OCD Pts open; methylphenidate 40 mg p.o. divided doses.	1. No signif effect of methylphenidate on OCD, depression, or anxiety.	1. Lack of behavioral effect of methylphenidate contrasts with findings of amphetamine in OCD (Insel et al., above)
E. Endogenous opiate system (EOS)	Insel & Pickar, 1983	naloxone (nonselective opiate antagonist)	2	OCD Pts (obsessional doubt) db, pc; naloxone 0.3 mg/kg i.v.	1. Worsening of OCD sxs after naloxone, but not after placebo.	1. Suggests involvement of EOS in these sxs of OCD; i.e., already compromised EOS further impaired by naloxone.

Abbreviations: 5HT = serotonin; Pts = patients; Sbs = subjects; MCPP = m-chlorophenylpiperazine; signif = significant; db = double-blind; pc = placebo-controlled; sxs = symptoms; PLAC = placebo; GH = growth hormone; CORT = cortisol; PRL = prolactin; MHPG = 3-methoxy-4-hydroxyphenylglycol.

tion of behaviors (e.g., stereotypies) that resemble compulsive rituals of patients with OCD (Geyer, Puerto, Menkes, Segal, & Mandell, 1976). The application of the pharmacologic challenge strategy has thus far yielded partial, but somewhat inconsistent, evidence for 5-HT dysfunction in OCD. The various challenge agents used in studies of OCD patients have included 5-HT precursors [L-tryptophan loading (Charney et al., 1988) or depletion (Delgado et al., 1988)], 5-HT agonists [m-chlorophenylpiperazine (MCPP)] (Charney et al., 1988; Zohar, Mueller, Insel, Zohar-Kadouch, & Murphy, 1987; Hollander et al., 1988), fenfluramine (Hollander et al., 1988; DeMeo et al., 1988) and MK-212 (Bastani et al., *personal communication*, 1989) and 5-HT antagonists [metergoline (Zohar et al., 1987)]. Plasma prolactin, growth hormone, and cortisol levels have been used to assess the functioning of the brain serotoninergic system in response to these challenge drugs.

The rationales for the use of tryptophan- and MCPP-induced neuroendocrine response as probes of 5-HT function are briefly discussed as follows. Because tryptophan hydroxylase, the enzyme for the rate-limiting step in the synthesis of 5-HT, is normally not fully saturated with its substrate, increased availability of tryptophan leads to an increase in 5-HT synthesis and release (Meltzer, Witta, & Tricou, 1982). The tryptophan-induced increase in prolactin and growth hormone seems to provide a good overall index of serotonergic function, including presynaptic function (Heninger et al., 1984; Price et al., 1988). Meta-chlorophenylpiperazine (MCPP) is a metabolite of the antidepressant trazodone and a relatively selective 5-HT receptor agonist (Charney et al., 1988). There is evidence that the ability of MCPP to increase prolactin, cortisol, and growth hormone levels is mediated by stimulation of postsynaptic 5-HT receptors, and therefore changes following MCPP administration may reflect postsynaptic 5-HT responsivity (Charney et al., 1988; Zohar et al., 1987). However, two caveats about the tryptophan and MCPP challenge paradigms are worth noting. First, because tryptophan competes with the dopamine precursor tryosine for transport into the brain, it is possible that the tryptophan-induced increase in prolactin may also reflect diminished dopamine (vanPraag, Lemus, & Kahn, 1987). [The validity of the plasma prolactin response as a measure of brain 5-HT function is reviewed in Price et al. (1988).] Second, although preclinical studies originally showed MCPP to be a selective 5-HT $_{1B}$ agonist, subsequent work suggests that MCPP may act as agonist at a variety of 5-HT receptor subtypes and possibly at nonserotonergic sites as well (Hamik & Peroutka, 1989). In studies in nonhuman primates, the prolactin response to MCPP appears to be mediated, in roughly equal proportion, by 5-HT1 and 5-HT2 receptors (Heninger, Charney, Price, & Woods, 1988).

5HT-Studies in Drug-free OCD Patients

In double-blind, placebo-controlled studies at two different research centers [NIMH (Zohar et al., 1987) and Columbia (Hollander et al., 1988)] (combined $n = 20$), oral administration of MCPP (0.5 mg/kg) produced an acute exacerbation of obsessive–compulsive symptoms in the majority of OCD patients tested (Table 8.2). The effect was reported to be robust (Zohar et al., 1987). These behavioral findings have been interpreted by Zohar et al. as possible evidence for hypersensitivity of postsynaptic 5-HT receptors in OCD (Zohar et al., 1987). In contrast, a third group [Yale (Charney et al., 1988)] that administered MCPP intravenously over 20 minutes (0.1 mg/kg) ($n = 21$) (also double-blind, placebo-controlled) failed to identify any consistent effect of this challenge agent on obsessive–compulsive behavior. The explanation for these discrepant findings is not clear, but differences in route of administration (e.g., first-pass effects), pharmacokinetics, or dose could conceivably be involved. For example, in the Yale study, MCPP was moderately anxiogenic (excluding ratings of obsessive–compulsive symptoms) in both the patients and healthy control subjects, whereas in the NIMH study, MCPP did not significantly increase ratings of anxiety in the healthy subjects. One interpretation of these findings is that the dose chosen for the intravenous studies was too high and that a ceiling effect obliterated the relative sensitivity of obsessive–compulsive symptoms to MCPP. However, a subsequent pilot study using a lower dose of intravenous MCPP (0.075 mg/mg) ($n = 11$) that produced minimal anxiety and dysphoria in patients and healthy subjects also failed to consistently affect obsessive–compulsive symptoms (Goodman et al., unpublished data, 1988). Hopefully, studies in which both the oral and parenteral forms of MCPP are administered to the same patients, and plasma MCPP levels are measured, might help clarify the contribution of route of administration (and dose) to the pro-obsessive–compulsive effects of this 5-HT probe.

In two of the above studies (the Yale and Columbia groups), the prolactin response to MCPP was significantly blunted in the OCD patients compared to the healthy subjects. In the Yale study, the significant patient–control difference was confined to the female OCD patients (Charney et al., 1988). Charney et al. suggested that the failure to identify a similar patient–control difference in males may reflect the finding that prolactin response is a less sensitive measure of 5-HT function in males in general (Charney et al., 1988). One implication of these prolactin response findings is that some patients with OCD may have reduced postsynaptic 5-HT sensitivity. However, taken together with reports of behavioral exacerbation with orally administered MCPP, these neuroendocrine findings suggest that in some patients with OCD the putative abnormality in brain 5-HT function may involve both hypersensitivity, with respect to behavior, and hyposensitivity, with respect to neuroendocrine response (Hollander, Decaria, Cooper, & Liebowitz, 1989). This dissociation between behavioral and neuroendocrine response to oral MCPP seems difficult to reconcile on the basis of a single abnormality in brain 5-HT function, although it is conceivable that it may reflect regional brain differences in 5-HT function. In the NIMH study, there was no significant difference between patients and healthy subjects in their MCPP-induced prolactin, cortisol, or thermal responses (Zohar et al., 1987). However, the MCPP-induced increase in cortisol was significantly blunted in patients compared to healthy controls (Zohar et al., 1987).

In a companion study to the intravenous MCPP study conducted at Yale, OCD patients ($N = 21$) and healthy subjects ($N = 21$) received a 20-minute infusion of 7 grams of tryptophan (Charney et al., 1988) (Table 8.2). Eighteen of these patients also participated in the MCPP challenge study. Tryptophan had no significant effect on obsessive–compulsive symptoms and its behavioral effects (e.g., drowsiness) were similar in OCD patients and healthy controls. Tryptophan induced significant increases in plasma prolactin in both the healthy subjects and patients at all time points measured. However, there were no significant patient–control differences in prolactin response to tryptophan in either the total or gender-related subject groups. The normal prolactin increase induced by tryptophan in the OCD females, in light of the blunted prolactin response after MCPP (noted earlier), might be explained by a compensatory increase in presynaptic function secondary to reduced postsynaptic function. However, the inability to find a significant negative correlation between the prolactin responses to MCPP and tryptophan among patients who participated in both challenges casts some doubt on this possibility. Alternatively, since the MCPP- and the tryptophan-induced increases in prolactin may be mediated by relatively different sybtypes of 5-HT receptors [mixed 5-HT$_1$ and 5-HT$_2$ vs principally 5-HT$_1$, respectively (Peroutka, Liebovitz, & Snyder, 1981)], it is conceivable that the neuroendocrine abnormality involves only a subgroup of 5-HT receptors (e.g., 5-HT$_2$).

In drug-free OCD patients, neither administration of single challenge doses of the nonselective 5-HT antagonist metergoline nor of the indirect agonist fenfluramine has been very revealing (Table 8.2). In one study, the effect of metergoline on obsessive–compulsive symptoms was not significantly different from that of placebo (Zohar et al., 1987). The prolactin response to fenfluramine was not significantly different in OCD patients and healthy controls (DeMeo et al., 1988) and fenfluramine had minimal (DeMeo et al., 1988) to no (Hollander et al., 1988) effect on obsessive–compulsive symptoms.

Delgado and colleagues at Yale have recently developed a new method for rapidly depleting plasma tryptophan (> 90% depletion) in humans utilizing a 24-hr, 160 mg/day, low tryptophan diet followed the next morning by a tryptophan-free, 16-amino acid drink (Delgado et al., 1988). There were two challenge sessions approximately one week apart; during one of these tests the diet and drink were supplemented with tryptophan (sham diet) in a randomized, double-blind fashion. Studies on protein metabolism had previously shown that ingestion of large amounts of amino acids with a deficiency in one essential amino acid will produce a rapid reduction in plasma levels of the deficient amino acid. [The theory and methodology of this paradigm are discussed in greater detail elsewhere (Peroutka & Snyder, 1980).] In a pilot study of 7 drug-free OCD patients, acute tryptophan deprivation had no significant effects on obsessive–compulsive symptoms (Delgado et al., 1988). Together, the tryptophan-loading and tryptophan-depletion challenge data from studies in OCD suggest that the severity of obsessive–compulsive symptoms does not seem to be critically dependent on availability of 5-HT precursor, or presumably, levels of 5-HT itself. However, it should be noted that the possible behavioral effects of *chronic* tryptophan loading or depletion were not addressed by these challenge studies.

5-HT Studies in Drug-treated OCD Patients

On the basis of the observed worsening of obsessive–compulsive symptoms in response to orally administered MCPP, it was proposed by Zohar that OCD may involve behavioral hypersensitivity of one or more subtypes of 5-HT receptor systems (Zohar et al., 1987). Furthermore, it was suggested that the therapeutic action of clomipramine in OCD may be related to its ability to downregulate 5-HT function (Zohar, Insel, Zohar–Kadouch, Hill, & Murphy, 1988). Studies showing decreased 5-HT$_2$ binding with chronic administration of potent 5-HT reuptake inhibitors provide some preclinical support for this possibility (Peroutka & Snyder, 1980). On the other hand, chronic treatment with potent 5-HT reuptake inhibitors is associated with a net increase in 5-HT function on the basis of electrophysiological data (Chaput, deMontigny, & Blier, 1986) and clinical challenge studies in humans [e.g., enhancement of the prolactin response to tryptopham with chronic fluvoxamine treatment (Price et al., 1988)]. To further examine the antiobsessional mechanism of action of potent 5-HT reuptake inhibitors, and to indirectly learn more about the pathophysiology of OCD, serotonin challenges have been conducted in OCD patients during chronic drug treatment.

In another study by Zohar, the behavioral hypersensitivity and thermogenic response to oral MCPP noted during pretreatment conditions was absent when oral MCPP was readministered to OCD patients treated with clomipramine for an average of four months (Zohar et al., 1988). This finding is consistent with a normalization of 5-HT function during chronic clomipramine treatment. In another recent study from NIMH, OCD patients improved on clomipramine were treated for four days with either active metergoline or placebo metergoline in a randomized, double-blind, crossover design (Benkelfat et al., 1989). Obsessive–compulsive symptoms tended to be worse after four days of metergoline treatment, but the effect was modest. The first study [readministration of MCPP during drug treatment] supports the hypothesis that clomipramine downregulates 5-HT function; however the second study [metergoline administration on drug treatment] suggests clomipramine enhances 5-HT function. These apparently disparate findings may eventually be reconciled by consideration of effects of treatment on various subtypes of 5-HT receptors. Thus, these two challenge studies provide partial support for the hypothesis that the anti-obsessional efficacy of clomipramine is related to its effects on 5-HT function, but the exact nature of those effects requires further elucidation. Based on these data, the most conservative conclusion to draw is that the apparent effect of clomipramine treatment in OCD is to stabilize a dysregulation in brain 5-HT function.

Noradrenergic Challenges

To our knowledge the first published challenge study in OCD involved an investigation of the adrenergic system. In 1935 Erich Lindemann reported on the behavioral and physiological response to administration of epinephrine in a 36-year-old minister with symptoms of OCD (Lindemann, 1935). There were two test sessions on consecutive days. The first challenge dose had no apparent effect on obsessive–compulsive symptoms. Prior to the next challenge dose, the psychiatrist suggested to the patient "that the objects of his obsessional thoughts might . . . be . . . symbols of homosexual interest." A marked increase in obsessional thinking was noted following the second dose of epinephrine, however, the patient's baseline anxiety level was already elevated (compared to day 1) in apparent response to the psychiatrist's interpretation of his symptoms. Because of the obvious methodological limitations of this case report (including use of a probe with poor entry into the brain), this study is best appreciated from a historical perspective.

Presently, the principal rationale for considering abnormalities of brain noradrenergic systems in the pathophysiology of OCD is that altered NE activity has been implicated in panic disorder, which, like OCD, is classified in DSM-III-R as an anxiety disorder. Furthermore, recent epidemiological studies suggest a clinically significant degree of comorbidity between panic disorder and OCD (Breier, Charney, & Heninger, 1986; Mellman & Uhde, 1987). Administration of the alpha-2 adrenergic antagonist yohimbine acts at presynaptic sites to block the normal negative feedback effect of released NE. Thus, yohimbine enhances release of NE, as reflected in increased plasma levels of the NE metabolite MHPG. In panic disorder, yohimbine induces panic attacks in the majority of patients but not in healthy subjects, and leads to a greater rise in plasma MHPG in patients who experience panic attacks (Charney et al., 1987).

In one study, 12 drug-free OCD patients and 12 healthy subjects received placebo capsules on the first day and active yohimbine (20 mg) on the second test day in the morning after an overnight fast (Rasmussen et al., 1987) (Table 8.2). Yohimbine had no consistent effect on severity of obsessive–compulsive symptoms in the patients. Yohimbine was anxiogenic in OCD patients and healthy subjects to a similar degree. A panic attack was induced in one of two OCD patients who had histories of panic attacks. The yohimbine-induced increase in plasma MHPG was not significantly different in patients and healthy subjects. The similarity of OCD patients and healthy subjects in their behavioral and MHPG responses to yohimbine seems to indicate that abnormal noradrenergic sensitivity may not be important to the pathophysiology of OCD.

In contrast to yohimbine, the alpha-2-adrenergic autoreceptor agonist clonidine acts to decrease noradrenergic activity. In one small study in OCD patients, a single dose of clonidine but not placebo produced a reduction in obsessive–compulsive symptoms (Hollander et al., 1988) (Table 8.2). Unlike the yohimbine findings, this study suggests altered alpha-2-adrenergic function may be relevant to OCD. In another study, the growth hormone response to clonidine, which may be a measure of postsynaptic alpha-2-adrenergic receptor function, was blunted in OCD patients but not in healthy controls (Siever et al., 1983; however, see Hollander et al., 1989; Curtis et al., 1989).

Miscellaneous Panicogenic Trigger Mechanisms

Although the mechanism of action remains undetermined, infusion of sodium lactate induces panic attacks in more than 50% of panic disorder patients but infrequently in healthy subjects (Liebowitz et al., 1984). In a small study, sodium lactate produced a panic attack in only one of seven OCD patients (Gorman et al., 1985) (Table 8.2). Similarly, administration of the adenosine receptor antagonist caffeine, which often provokes panic attacks in panic disorder patients (Charney et al., 1984), had little affect on OCD patients (Zohar et al., *personal communication*). Together, the results with yohimbine, sodium lactate, and caffeine in OCD patients suggest that the anxiogenic mechanisms underlying the obsessive–compulsive symptoms of OCD patients may be different from those that mediate panic attacks in panic disorder patients.

Mixed Monominergic (and Dopaminergic) Agonists

In a study in 12 OCD patients, the severity of obsessive–compulsive symptoms was diminished after single doses of d-amphetamine (30 mg po) but not after placebo (Insel & Pickar, 1983) (Table 8.2). Given amphetamine-induced stererotypy as a model for compulsive behavior, these findings are somewhat surprising. However, since amphetamines may bolster self-confidence, an improvement in obsessional doubt (a cardinal feature of some OCD patients) after amphetamine is not totally inexplicable. In another study, open administration of methylphenidate had no significant behavioral effects in 13 OCD patients (Swinson & Joffe, 1988). Methylphenidate and d-amphetamine may act on different neuronal dopamine pools (Clemens & Fuller, 1979). Because dopamine, NE, and 5-HT are all released by d-amphetamine (and methylphenidate), it is difficult to draw conclusions about monominergic mechanisms pertinent to OCD on the basis of these challenge studies.

There is a published report from the Soviet Union of pharmacological challenges with the dopamine precursor L-dopa in OCD patients, however, because of unclear diagnostic and assessment criteria it is difficult to interpret the findings (Vasilev, Chugunov, Derbeneva, & Eremeev, 1988). Other studies of L-dopa administration in OCD are currently in progress (Goodman et al., unpublished data).

Endogenous Opiate System

The endogenous opiate systems (EOS) has been insufficiently studied in OCD. In two published cases, low doses of the nonselective opiate antagonist naloxone, but not placebo, produced a worsening of obsessive–compulsive symptoms (Insel & Pickar, 1983) (Table 8.2). The intuitively appealing rationale for this study was that OCD may involve an inability to experience the sense of relief—possibly mediated by the reward circuits of the EOS—normally associated with the satisfactory completion of a task (Insel & Pickar, 1983). Thus, worsening of OCD symptoms after naloxone reflects an already compromised EOS further impaired by antagonist administration. However, preliminary findings from a study in which higher doses of naloxone (0.1 mg/kg) were administered to 15 OCD patients revealed more variable behavioral effects (Goodman et al., unpublished data).

SUMMARY OF CHALLENGE FINDINGS

Pharmacologic challenge studies of the 5-HT system (particularly with the putative 5-HT agonist MCPP) lend partial support to the hypothesis that 5-HT may play a role in the pathogenesis and/or drug treatment of OCD. However, the precise nature of the 5-HT dysfunction in OCD remains unclear. For example, studies with MCPP in OCD provide evidence for both hypersensitivity and hyposensitivity of 5-HT function. Oral administration of MCPP produces a temporary exacerbation of obsessive–compulsive symptoms in many drug-free OCD patients, but not in clomipramine-treated patients, suggesting that 5-HT hypersensitivity may be related to the symptoms of OCD. On the other hand, a blunted prolactin response to MCPP, which may be indicative of post-synaptic 5-HT subsensitivity, was found in two of three studies. It is also unclear whether possible alterations in 5-HT function represent a primary, or a secondary adaptational, event.

The evidence for a disturbance in noradrenergic function in OCD is based chiefly on preliminary data that clonidine may ameliorate obsessive–compulsive symptoms. If this proves to be a specific anti-obsessional effect of clonidine, as opposed to a nonspecific sedative effect, then these findings will have to be reconciled with the unimpressive actions of yohimbine in OCD. Studies with several different anxiogenic challenge agents (yohimbine, sodium lactate, and caffeine) suggest that the pathophysiology of OCD is distinct from that of panic disorder.

Challenge studies of the dopamine and endogenous opiate systems are too limited to draw firm conclusions about the relevance of these systems to the pathophysiology OCD. Improvement in obsessional symptoms after administration of the mixed monoamine agonist amphetamine is intriguing, but it is unclear which neurotransmitter(s) is(are) related to the behavioral response.

FUTURE DIRECTIONS

A likely next step in OCD challenge research is to combine selective pharmacological probes with brain imaging. This approach would take advantage of the neurotransmitter receptor specificity of newer agents and the enormous potential of a dependent measure that is closely tied to the organ of interest. In challenges that utilize brain imaging techniques, it will be especially important to specify the behavioral state of the patient at the time of the scan. For example, in recent PET scan studies of OCD, neuropsychiatric activation procedures (i.e., the continuous performance test) were used to control for attention and activity of the subject. It is unclear, however, what behavioral conditions would best highlight the functional-neuroanatomical disturbance germane to OCD. If and when evidence begins to emerge that OCD is heterogenous, it will be important to attend to putative clinical and pathogenetic subtypes of the disorder (e.g., OCD with family or personal history of tics) when analyzing the challenge findings. There is also a need to investigate other neurochemical systems and the interactions between systems (e.g., interactions between dopamine and 5-HT systems).

ACKNOWLEDGMENTS

Supported in part by NIMH grants MH-25642, MH-36229, MH-38006, MH-40140, and MH-30920 and the State of Connecticut. We thank the clinical, research, and secretarial (Betsy Kyle) staff of the Clinical Neuroscience Research Unit for their expert assistance.

Appendix: Yale-Brown Obsessive Compulsive Challenge Scale (Y-BOCCS) (Patient-Rated, Analog)

Name _____ Date_____ Time_____ Elapsed Time____

RATE OVER THE LAST 60 MINUTES, INCLUDING NOW. Please discuss the definitions of "obsessions" and "compulsions" with your clinician. Place a vertical mark on line corresponding to severity of your symptoms. For example:

	None 0	Mild 1	Moderate 2	Severe 3	Extreme 4
1. Time Spent on Obsessive Thoughts					

	None 0	Mild 1	Moderate 2	Severe 3	Extreme 4
1. Time Spent on Obsessive Thoughts					
2. Anxiety Due to Obsessive Thoughts					
3. Time Spent Performing Compulsive Behaviors					
4. Intensity of Compulsion to Perform the Behavior					
5. Degree of Indecisiveness (Difficulty in Choosing Between Simple Alternatives)					
6. Guilt (concerned that did, or will do, something terrible or wrong)					

	Complete Control 0	Much 1	Moderate 2	Little 3	No Control 4
7. Degree of Control Over Obsessive Thoughts and/or Compulsive Behavior.					

	Certain Won't Happen 0	Unlikely 1	Not Sure 2	Likely 3	Certain Will Happen 4
8. Conviction that Something Awful Will Happen Unless Behavior Performed					

	None 0	Mild 1	Moderate 2	Severe 3	Extreme 4
9. Overall Severity of Obsessions					
10. Overall Severity of Compulsions					

REFERENCES

Benkelfat, C., Murphy, D. L., Zohar, J., Hill, J. L., Grover, G., & Insel, T. R. (1989). Clomipramine in obsessive-compulsive disorder. *Archives of General Psychiatry, 46,* 23–28.

Bradford, L. D., Tulp, M. Th. M., & Schipper, J. (1987). Biochemical effects in rats after long term treatment with fluvoxamine and clovoxamine: Postsynaptic changes. Society for Neuroscience Abstract #233. 12, p. 774, November 16–21, New Orleans.

Breier, A., Charney, D. S., & Heninger, G. R. (1986). Agoraphobia and panic disorder: Development, diagnostic stability and course of illness. *Archives of General Psychiatry, 43,* 1029–1036.

Chaput, Y., deMontigny, C., & Blier, P. (1986). Effects of a selective 5-HT reuptake blocker, citalopram, on the sensitivity of 5-HT autoreceptors: Electrophysiological study in the rat brain. *Naunyn-Schmiedeberg's Archives of Pharmacology, 333,* 342–348.

Charney, D. S., Galloway, M. P., & Heninger, G. R. (1984). The effects of caffeine on plasma MHPG subjective anxiety, autonomic symptoms and blood pressure in healthy humans. *Life Sciences, 35,* 135–144.

Charney, D. S., Goodman, W. K., Price, L. H., Woods, S. W., Rasmussen, S. A., & Heninger, G. R. (1988). Serotonin function in obsessive–compulsive disorder. *Archives of General Psychiatry, 45,* 177–185.

Charney, D. S., Woods, S. W., Goodman, W. K., & Heninger, G. R. (1987). Neurobiological mechanism of panic anxiety: Biochemical and behavioral correlates of yohimbine-induced panic attacks. *American Journal of Psychiatry, 144,* 1030–1036.

Clemens, J. A., & Fuller, R. W. (1979). Differences in the effects of amphetamine and methylphenidate on brain dopamine turnover and serum prolactin concentration in reserpine-treated rats. *Life Sciences, 24,* 2077–2082.

Curtis, G., Lee, M. A., Glitz, D. A., Cameron, O. G., Abelson, J., & Bronzo, M. (1989). Growth hormone response to clonidine in anxiety disorders. Proceedings of the Annual Meeting of Biological Psychiatry, #32, May 4–8, San Francisco.

Daniel, D. G., Berman, K. F., Fawcett, R., & Weinberger, D. R. (1988). Apomorphine and rCBF in schizophrenia. Proceedings of the American Psychiatric Association Annual Meeting, New Research Abstract NR3, p. 23, May 7–12, Montreal, Canada.

Delgado, P. L., Charney, D. S., Price, L. H., Goodman, W. K., Aghajanian, G. K., Landis, H., & Heninger, G. R. (1988). Behavioral effects of acute tryptophan depletion in depressed and obsessive compulsive disorder (OCD) patients. Society of Neuroscience Abstract, November 13–18, Toronto, Canada.

DeMeo, M. D., McBride, P. A., Shear, M. K., Halper, J. P., Chen, J-S, & Mann, J. J. (1988). Behavioral and prolactin responses to fenfluramine in OCD. American Psychiatric Association Annual Meeting Abstract #NR266, May 7–12, Montreal, Canada.

Geyer, M. A., Puerto, D. B., Menkes, D. B., Segal, D. S., & Mandell, A. J. (1976). Behavioral studies following lesions of mesolimbic and mesostriatal serotonergic pathways. *Brain Research, 106,* 257–270.

Goodman, W. K., Price, L. H., Rasmussen, S. A., Delgado, P. L., Heninger, G. R., & Charney, D. S. (1989). Efficacy of fluvoxamine in obsessive–compulsive disorder. A double-blind comparison with placebo. *Archives of General Psychiatry, 46,* 36–44.

Gorman, J. M., Liebowitz, M. R., Fyer, A. J., Dillon, D., Davies, S. O., Stein, J., & Klein, D. F. (1985). Lactate infusions in obsessive–compulsive disorder. *American Journal of Psychiatry, 142,* 864–866.

Hamik, A., & Peroutka, S. J. (1989). l-(m-Chlorophenyl)piperazine (mCPP) interactions with neurotransmitter receptors in the human brain. *Biological Psychiatry, 25,* 569–575.

Heninger, G. R., Charney, D. S., & Smith, A. (1987). Effects of serotonin receptor agonists and antagonists on neuroendocrine function in rhesus monkeys. Society for Neuroscience Abstract #224.9, November 17–21, New Orleans.

Heninger, G. R., Charney, D. S., & Sternberg, D. E. (1984). Serotonergic function in depression. *Archives of General Psychiatry, 41,* 398–402.

Hollander, E., Decaria, C., Cooper, T., & Liebowitz, M. R. (1989). Neuroendocrine sensitivity in obsessive–compulsive disorder. Proceedings of the Annual Meeting of Biological Psychiatry, #11, May 4–8, San Francisco.

Hollander, E., Fay, M., Cohen, B., Campeas, R., Gorman, J. M., & Liebowitz, M. R. (1988). Serotonergic and noradrenergic sensitivity in obsessive–compulsive disorder: Behavioral findings. *American Journal of Psychiatry, 145,* 1015–1017.

Insel, T. R., Hamilton, J. A., Guttmacher, L. B., & Murphy, D. L. (1983). D-Amphetamine in obsessive–compulsive disorder. *Psychopharmacology, 80,* 231–235.

Insel, T. R., & Pickar, D. (1983). Naloxone administration in obsessive–compulsive disorder: Report of two cases. *American Journal of Psychiatry, 140,* 1219–1220.

Liebowitz, M. R., Fyer, A. J., Gorman, J. M., Dillon, D., Appleby, I. Levy, G., Anderson, S., Levitt, M., Palij, M., Davies, S. O., & Klein, D. F. (1984). Lactate provocation of panic attacks, I: Clinical and behavioral findings. *Archives of General Psychiatry, 41,* 764–770.

Lindemann, E. (1935). Psychopathological effect of adrenalin. *American Journal of Psychiatry, 14,* 983–1008.

Mellman, T. A., & Uhde, T. W. (1987). Obsessive–compulsive symptoms in panic disorder. *American Journal of Psychiatry, 144,* 1573–1576.

Meltzer, H. Y., Wiita, B., & Tricou, B. J. (1982). Effect of serotonin precursors and serotonin agonists on plasma hormone levels. In B. T. Ho, J. C. Schoolar, & E. Usdin (Eds.), *Serotonin in biological psychiatry* (pp. 117–138). New York: Raven Press.

Peroutka, S. J., Lebovitz, R. M., & Snyder, S. H. (1981). Two distinct central serotonin receptors with different physiological functions. *Science, 212,* 827–829.

Peroutka, S. J., & Snyder, S. H. (1980). Chronic antidepressant treatment decreases sprioperidol-labeled serotonin receptor binding. *Science, 210,* 88–90.

Price, L. H., Charney, D. S., Delgado, P. L., Anderson, G. M., & Heninger, G. R. (1989). Effects of desipramine and fluvoxamine treatment on the prolactin response to tryptophan: Serotonergic function and the mechanism of antidepressant action. *Archives of General Psychiatry, 46,* 625–631.

Rasmussen, S. A., Goodman, W. K., Woods, S. W., Heninger, G. R., & Charney, D. S. (1987). Effects of yohimbine in obsessive compulsive disorder. *Psychopharmacology, 93,* 308–313.

Siever, L. J., Insel, T. R., Jimerson, D. C., Lake, C. R., Uhde, T. W., Aloi, J., & Murphy, D. L. (1983). Growth hormone response to clonidine in obsessive–compulsive patients. *British Journal of Psychiatry*, 142, 184–187.

Swinson, R. P., & Joffe, R. T. (1988). Biological challenges in obsessive compulsive disorder. *Progress in Neuro-Psychopharmacology and Biological Psychiatry*, 12, 269–275.

vanPraag, H. M., Lemus, C., & Kahn, R. (1987). Hormonal probes of central serotonergic activity: Do they really exist? *Biological Psychiatry*, 22, 86–98.

Vasilev, V. N., Chugunov, V. S., Derbeneva, L. M., & Eremeev, M. S. (1988). The L-DOPA test in patients with obsessive fear neurosis. *Voprosy Meditsinskoi Khimii*, 34, 115–120.

Weizmann, A., Carmi, M., Hermesh, H., Shahar, A., Apter, A., Tyano, S., & Rehavi, M. (1986). High affinity imipramine binding and serotonin uptake in platelets of eight adolescent and ten adult obsessive–compulsive patients. *American Journal of Psychiatry*, 143, 335–339.

Woods, S. W., & Charney, D. S. (1988). Applications of the pharmacologic challenge strategy in panic disorders research. *Journal of Anxiety Disorders, 2*, 31–49.

Woods, S. W., Koster, K., Krystal, J. K., Smith, E. O., Zubal, I. G., Hoffer, P. B., & Charney, D. S. (1988). Yohimbine alters regional cerebral blood flow in panic disorder. *The Lancet*, 678.

Zohar, J., Insel, T. R., Zohar–Kadouch, R. C., Hill, J. L. & Murphy, D. L. (1988). Serotonergic responsivity in obsessive–compulsive disorder: Effects of chronic clomipramine treatment. *Archives of General Psychiatry*, 45, 167–172.

Zohar, J., Mueller, E. A., Insel, T. R., Zohar–Kadouch, R. C., & Murphy, D. L. (1987). Serotonergic responsivity in obsessive–compulsive disorder: Comparison of patients and healthy controls. *Archives of General Psychiatry*, 44, 946–951.

9

Pharmacologic Treatment of Obsessive–Compulsive Disorder

Joseph DeVeaugh-Geiss

For years, Obsessive Compulsive Disorder (OCD) has been viewed as a treatment-resistant illness. Psychotherapy has generally been of little benefit, and behavioral therapy, while helpful to some patients, is not useful for many patients with OCD. A variety of drug treatments had been tried with limited success. Antidepressants were the earliest form of drug treatment employed, most likely because of the common association of depression with OCD (American Psychiatric Association [APA], 1987). Although most antidepressants did not specifically affect the symptoms of OCD in patients with OCD alone, they were found to relieve the depressive symptoms in patients with both OCD and depression (Foa, Steketee, Kozak, & Dugger, 1987).

There have been very few well-controlled, clinical studies conducted to evaluate the effectiveness of drug therapy in OCD. The widely held belief that OCD was of psychological origin and that OCD had a low prevalence rate contributed to the paucity of studies (Jenike, 1986). However, recent studies suggest a biological etiology, while community studies indicate that mild forms of the disorder may be relatively common (Berg, Whitaker, Davies, Flament, & Rapoport, 1988; Flament et al., 1988; Karno, Golding, Sorenson, & Burnam, 1988). These recent findings have stimulated a growing interest in pharmacologic treatments for this disorder. Consequently, several specialized referral centers in the United States have recently been developed, providing researchers with a larger number of OCD patients and making studies of this disorder more feasible (Jenike, 1986).

TREATMENT WITH SEROTONINERGIC DRUGS

In recent years, drug treatment for OCD has focused primarily on serotoninergic drugs. These drugs have proven to be the most effective to date. Of the compounds that have received the most attention—clomipramine, fluvoxamine, and fluoxetine—clomipramine has been the most extensively studied, with numerous studies demonstrating its effectiveness in OCD.

Clomipramine

Clomipramine hydrochloride (Anafranil®, Geigy) is a tricyclic compound that is similar in chemical structure to imipramine. It differs from imipramine only in the substitution of chlorine for hydrogen at the 3 position of the tricyclic ring (Figure 9.1). Early studies implicating clomipramine's effectiveness in depressed patients with associated obsessive–compulsive symptoms set the stage for more carefully designed studies to investigate clomipramine's effectiveness in patients with primary Obsessive Compulsive Disorder.

Early Studies

In 1967 Fernandez-Cordoba and Lopez-Ibor Alino (1967) first reported that Anafranil was effective in the treatment of obsessive neurosis. Subsequently, this group reported that 13 of 16 patients with OCD responded to intravenous clomipramine (Lopez-Ibor Alino, 1969). At

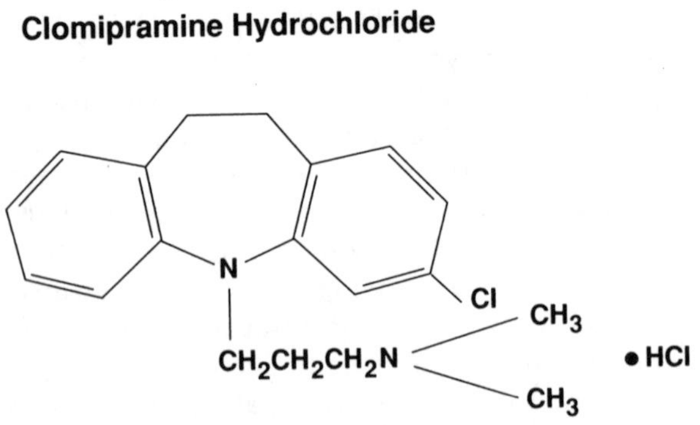

Clomipramine Hydrochloride

FIGURE 9.1 Clomipramine hydrochloride.

the same time, Jimenez-Garcia (1967) reported improvement in obsessive symptoms with clomipramine, while Laboucarie, Rascol, Jorda, Guraud, and Leinadier (1967) found clomipramine to be ineffective in depressed patients with obsessive symptoms. Subsequent studies tended to confirm initial positive findings. Karabanow (1977) found clomipramine superior to placebo in a double-blind study of 20 depressed patients with obsessive-compulsive and phobic traits. Amin, Ban, Pecknold, & Klingner (1977) found clomipramine plus behavioral therapy superior to either of these treatments alone in a placebo controlled trial with six obsessive compulsive and six phobic patients.

A number of other studies also reported improvement with clomipramine in obsessional states (Capstick, 1977; Marshall & Micev, 1973; Rack, 1977; Waxman, 1977; Wyndowe, Solyom, & Ananth; 1975 Yaryura-Tobias, Neziroglu, & Bergman 1976).

The interpretation of these studies is complicated by the differences in doses employed, diagnostic heterogeneity and small numbers of patients studied, and other methodologic issues such as study design and selection of rating instruments.

These early reports of the effectiveness of clomipramine in OCD all pointed, however, to a specific antiobsessional effect independent of antidepressant effects, a finding that would be followed up in later controlled trials.

Double-Blind, Placebo-Controlled Studies

It was not until the 1980s that reports of well-designed, placebo-controlled studies appeared in the literature. These studies (Jaskari, 1980; Kasvikis & Marks, 1988; Marks, Stern, Mawson, Cobb, & McDonald, 1980; Marks et al., 1988; Mavissakalian, Turner, Michelson, & Jacob, 1985; Montgomery, 1980; Thoren, Asberg, Cronholm, Jornestedt, & Traskman 1980) showed clomipramine to be significantly more effective than placebo in relieving obsessive–compulsive symptoms in adult patients. The studies are summarized in Table 9.1. In a 4-week, double-blind, placebo-controlled study of clomipramine and mianserin in 40 patients, Jaskari (1980) reported that both clomipramine and mianserin "have a favorable effect on obsessive-compulsive symptoms." Marks et al. (1980) studied 40 chronic obsessive–compulsive ritualizers treated with clomipramine or placebo for 8 months. Significant improvement was noted in rituals, mood, and social adjustment in patients with depressed mood following treatment with clomipramine. Fourteen patients with obsessional neurosis were studied in a double-blind, placebo-controlled, crossover study (Montgomery, 1980). Significant im-

TABLE 9.1 Double-Blind Studies of Clomipramine in OCD

Adult Studies	Comparative Agent	Dose (mg/day)	I/O[a]	N[b]	Design	Duration on CMI	Outcome[c]	Comments
Marks et al. (1980)	Placebo	CMI – 225	I + O	40 (20CMI, 20P)	randomized, parallel groups	10 weeks	CMI>P	Behavioral therapy also evaluated. Double-blind followup assessments continued up to 36 weeks of treatment.
Montgomery (1980)	placebo	CMI – 75	—	14 (14CMI, 14P)	crossover	4 weeks	CMI>P	Concomitant behavioral therapy.
Mavissakalian et al. (1985)	placebo	CMI to 300	O	12 (7CMI, 5P)	randomized, parallel groups	12 weeks	CMI>P	
Marks et al. (1988)	placebo	CMI to 200	I + O	49 (37CMI, 12P)	randomized, parallel groups	27 weeks	CMI>P	Behavioral therapy also evaluated.
Thoren et al. (1980)	nortriptyline placebo	CMI – 150 N – 150	I	24 (8CMI, 8N, 8P)	Randomized, parallel groups	5 weeks	CMI>P N>P	
Jaskari (1980)	mianserin placebo	M – 60 CMI – 150	O	27 (9CMI, 10M, 8P)	randomized parallel groups	4 weeks	CMI>P M>P	
Ananth et al. (1981)	amitriptyline	CMI to 300 AMI to 300	I + O	20 (10CMI, 10AMI)	randomized parallel groups	4 weeks	CMI> AMI	

Study	Drug	Dose	I/O[a]	N[b]	Design	Duration	Results[c]	Comments
Insel et al. (1983) Volavka et al. (1985)	clorgyline placebo imipramine	C – 30 CMI to 300 CMI to 300 I to 300	I + O O	13 (12CMI, 11C, 12P) 16 (8CMI, 8I)	randomized crossover randomized, parallel groups	6 weeks 12 weeks	CMI>P CMI>C CMI>I	Partial improvement with I and CMI; CMI superior.
Zohar & Insel (1987)	desmethyl-imipramine	CMI to 300 D to 300	—	10 (10CMI, 10P)	randomized, crossover	6 weeks	CMI>D	
Child and Adolescent Studies								
Rapoport et al. (1980)	placebo desmethyl-imipramine	CMI – 150 D – 150	I + O	8 (8CMI, 8D)	randomized, crossover	5 weeks	No sifnigicant differences	This was a preliminary report of ongoing study. Final report (Flament et al, 1985) found CMI>P.
Flament et al. (1985)	placebo	CMI to 200	I + O	19 (19CMI, 19P)	randomized, crossover	5 weeks	CMI>P	Includes all but two of the patients included in preliminary report (Rapoport et al, 1980)
Leonard et al. (1989)	desmethyl-imipramine	CMI to 250 D to 250	O	48 (48CMI, 48D)	randomized, crossover		CMI>D	

[a]I/O=inpatient/outpatient status;
[b]Patients completing the study;
[c]>significantly better improvement; = no difference between treatment.
CMI=clomipramine; AMI=amitriptyline; N=nortriptyline; I=imipramine; P=placebo; C=clorgyline; M=mianserin; D=desmethylimipramine.

provement was seen with clomipramine compared to placebo. Thoren et al. (1980) investigated the use of clomipramine, nortriptyline, and placebo in 24 patients with severe obsessive–compulsive disorder. Superior results were obtained only with clomipramine, while nortriptyline was no better than placebo after a 5-week, randomized, double-blind trial. In the study by Mavissakalian et al. (1985), specific antiobsessional effects were noted with clomipramine in a 12-week, placebo-controlled trial with 12 OCD patients who completed the trial. In this study, the effects of clomipramine on OCD appeared to be at least partially independent of antidepressant effects. In a recent study of rather complex design, various behavioral treatments combined with clomipramine or placebo were compared in 49 obsessive-compulsive ritualizers (Marks et al., 1988). After eight weeks of treatment, clomipramine effects were superior to placebo in patients who also had therapist-aided exposure (Kasvikis & Marks, 1988).

Adolescent patients with OCD were studied by Rapoport, Elkins, and Mikkelsen (1980), who showed clomipramine to be ineffective in their treatment. However, a subsequent study by the same investigators (Flament et al., 1985) showed significant improvement in young patients with OCD who were treated with clomipramine. This was a 5-week, placebo-controlled, double-blind study of 19 children and adolescents with OCD. Seventy-four percent showed marked to moderate improvement with clomipramine.

Clomipramine versus Other Antidepressants

In comparative studies, clomipramine has been shown to be more effective in OCD than other antidepressants. These studies are also summarized in Table 9.1. Clomipramine and amitriptyline were compared in a 4-week randomized, double-blind trial of 20 OCD patients (Ananth, Pecknold, Van Den Steen, & Engelsmann 1981). Statistically significant improvement was noted with clomipramine but not with amitriptyline. In another study, patients with OCD were enrolled in a double-blind, placebo-controlled, randomized, crossover comparison study of clomipramine and clorgyline (Insel et al., 1983). Significant improvement in obsessions, anxiety, and depression was noted for 12 patients who received clomipramine. No significant improvement was noted for the group of 11 patients receiving clorgyline; however, some individual patients did respond to the drug. A 12-week double-blind clinical trial of clomipramine and imipramine was conducted in 23 OCD patients (Volavka, Neziroglu, & Yaryura-Tobias, 1985). Of the 16 patients who completed the study, partial improvement was noted with clomipramine or imipramine, although clomipramine was somewhat more effective than imipramine.

More recent studies have compared clomipramine with desmethylimipramine (Zohar & Insel, 1987; Leonard et al., 1989). Zohar and Insel conducted a double-blind, randomized, crossover study in 10 OCD patients. Clomipramine was found to have significantly more anti-obsessional effects in these patients than desmethylimipramine. Leonard et al. conducted a double-blind crossover study of clomipramine and desmethylimipramine in 48 children and adolescents with OCD which showed that clomipramine was significantly superior to desmethylimipramine.

Large-Scale Trials with Clomipramine

Clomipramine has recently been studied in large-scale multicenter clinical trials. These double-blind, placebo-controlled trials were conducted by CIBA-GEIGY in 1986 and 1987, and included two studies in adult patients with OCD, employing a total of 21 study centers, and one study in child and adolescent patients with OCD, employing 5 study centers. Preliminary analyses were conducted after the trials were completed at all centers but utilizing only data from 384 patients at 16 of the adult centers completing the trials early (DeVeaugh-Geiss, Landau, & Katz, 1989).

One of the adult studies was a fully randomized trial and was conducted at nine U.S. centers. The other adult study employed a stratification based on baseline Hamilton Depression Rating Scale (HDRS) scores prior to randomization and was conducted at 12 U.S. centers. Each study utilized a 2-week, single-blind, placebo run-in at which time baseline evaluations were undertaken. The child and adolescent study was conducted at four U.S. and one Canadian center and was of similar design.

In the adult studies, patients were randomly assigned to either the clomipramine or placebo treatment groups. A 10-week, double-blind treatment period followed randomization. Patients received an initial dose of 25 mg/day of clomipramine, which was increased to 100 mg/day by the end of the second week of treatment. Dosage was flexible for the remainder of the trial. Final daily dosages of clomipramine ranged from 100 mg to 300 mg, with the majority of patients receiving 200 to 250 mg daily.

Safety and efficacy evaluations were conducted weekly throughout the studies. Efficacy evaluations included the Yale–Brown Obsessive Compulsive Scale (Y-BOCS) (Goodman et al., 1989; see also Chapter 8,

TABLE 9.2 Patient Self-Rating Scale

Compared with How I Felt Before Beginning this Study, I Now Am:

1. Very much improved
2. Much improved
3. Minimally improved
4. Unchanged
5. Minimally worse
6. Much worse
7. Very much worse

this volume), the NIMH Global Obsessive Compulsive Scale, a Physician's Global Rating Scale, and a Patient Global Self-Rating Scale (Table 9.2). The 17-item HDRS was used for screening only.

Mean Y-BOCS scores from five centers that completed the first study are represented in Figure 9.2. Although a 5% reduction in mean Y-BOCS scores occurred in the placebo group, this group remained essentially unchanged throughout the 10-week study. The group of patients receiving clomipramine achieved a 40% reduction at the end of 10 weeks, with a monotonic decrease occurring throughout the study. Between-treatment group differences were statistically significant ($p < .05$) beginning at week 2 and for each subsequent week. A similar response was noted with the Patient Self-Rating Scale. No change was reported by patients in the placebo group throughout the 10 weeks of treatment, whereas the clomipramine group showed a decrease over the duration of the trial, achieving scores of approximately 2.5 (minimally improved to much improved) by weeks 6 through 10 of treatment. A statistically significant difference ($p < .05$) between the placebo group and the clomipramine group was noted at each week of treatment.

In the second study, Y-BOCS scores from 11 completed centers were analyzed (Figure 9.3). A 4% reduction in the mean Y-BOCS scores was noted in the placebo group over the 10 weeks of treatment. The group of patients receiving clomipramine achieved a 45% reduction at the end of 10 weeks, with a monotonic decrease also noted throughout the study. Between-treatment group differences were statistically significant ($p < .05$) beginning at week 2 and for each subsequent week. Again, a similar response was noted with the Patient Self-Rating Scale. Mean scores for placebo patients actually increased slightly, representing worsening of their clinical condition, by week 10, while the mean score for clomipramine-treated patients improved to a score of approximately 2.5 at weeks 6 through 10 of treatment. A statistically significant difference ($p < .05$) between treatments was noted at week 2 and for each subsequent week.

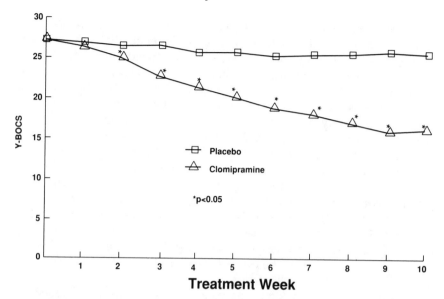

FIGURE 9.2 Study 1—Mean total Y-B.O.C.S. scores.

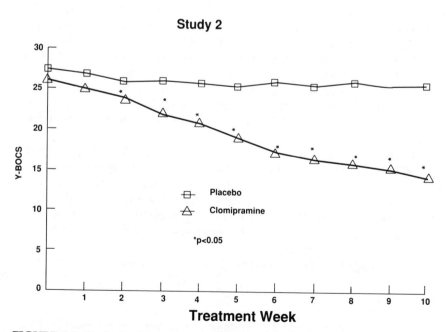

FIGURE 9.3 Study 2—Mean Total Y-B.O.C.S. scores.

A recent analysis of data from all 21 centers, including a total of 520 patients completing the trials (DeVeaugh-Geiss et al., 1991), has shown results consistent with those reported here. In addition, the NIMH Global Obsessive Compulsive Rating Scale results paralleled those found with the Y-BOCS, and the Physician's Gobal Rating Scale results paralleled those of the Patient Global Self-Rating Scale.

Subgroups analyses of patients with Hamilton Depression Rating Scale scores of < 17 or 17 to 21, and of patients with or without a secondary diagnosis of depression found no differences among these subgroups in terms of outcome; that is, clomipramine was efficacious in treating symptoms of OCD in nondepressed patients as well as in patients with mild to moderate affective disturbances and in patients with a secondary diagnosis of depression. As mentioned previously, the majority of patients received clomipramine in doses of 200 to 250 mg daily, suggesting that a therapeutic dose for the treatment of OCD may be somewhat higher than the dose range typically used in the treatment of depression with tricyclic drugs.

A study of similar design was conducted in child and adolescent patients at four U.S. centers and 1 Canadian center. Sixty patients enrolled in the study, of which 54 completed participation. The study included a 2-week, single-blind, placebo run-in and 8 weeks of randomized double-blind treatment with clomipramine (up to 200 mg daily) or placebo. The mean Y-BOCS scores showed an 8% improvement for the placebo group and a 37% improvement for the clomipramine group after 8 weeks of treatment (difference statistically significant, $p < .05$).

The side effects noted in these studies were those typically seen with tricyclic antidepressants and included sedation, dry mouth, blurred vision, tremor, and sexual dysfunction. Four of the 575 patients (0.7%) enrolled in the two adult studies experienced seizures, the incidence of which may be dose related. No seizures occurred among the 60 children and adolescents studied.

These preliminary data indicate a statistically significant improvement of OCD symptoms with clomipramine (40%–45% mean improvement) over placebo (4%–5% mean improvement) in adult patients and similar results with child and adolescent patients. These data also suggest that a further improvement in OCD symptoms may occur if clomipramine treatment is continued beyond 10 weeks. Analyses of data from 1-year double-blind extensions of the two adult studies indicate that improvement is maintained with continued treatment beyond 10 weeks, up to one year.

Fluoxetine

Another serotonin reuptake inhibitor, fluoxetine hydrochloride (Prozac®, Dista), recently approved in the United States for the treatment of depression, has also shown promise in the treatment of patients with OCD. Eight patients with OCD completed a 10-week, single-blind trial of fluoxetine that followed 2 weeks of placebo washout (Turner, Jacob, Beidel, & Himmelhoch, 1985). Fluoxetine had a beneficial effect on symptoms of depression and anxiety as well as the self-reported measures of obsessions and ritualistic behavior. In a follow-up study, comparing the antiobsessional effects of fluoxetine and behavioral treatment (Turner, Beidel, Stanley, & Jacob, 1988), 5 of the patients who had participated in the first study (Turner et al., 1985) were given 10 sessions of exposure and response prevention following fluoxetine treatment. The results of this 12-week study showed that fluoxetine had a clinically significant effect on mood and obsessional behavior for 3 patients experiencing more severe pretreatment symptoms of anxiety, depression, and obsessions and compulsions. The 10-day program of intensive flooding and response prevention had a clinically significant effect in reducing obsessive–compulsive symptoms for all patients in the study. In an uncontrolled, open-label study, 7 patients with OCD were treated with fluoxetine (Fontaine & Chouinard, 1986). The trial consisted of 1 week of placebo washout and 8 weeks of fluoxetine treatment. Significant improvement was noted in 5 of the 7 patients, with the greatest therapeutic effect being noted in obsessive–compulsive symptoms.

In a recently published case report (Riddle, Leckman, Hardin, Anderson, & Cohen, 1988), 3 patients with Tourette's syndrome reported marked reductions in the severity of associated obsessive and compulsive symptoms after three months of fluoxetine treatment.

While it appears that fluoxetine may have promise in the treatment of OCD, no well-controlled trials have been conducted and additional studies are needed.

Fluvoxamine

Fluvoxamine (Faverin®, Duphar) has been reported to be a more potent serotonin reuptake inhibitor than clomipramine (Claasen, 1983). Fluvoxamine is a 2-aminoethyloxime aralkylketone and is structurally unrelated to tricyclic or tetracyclic antidepressants (Perse, Greist, Jefferson, Rosenfeld, &Dar, 1987). Fluvoxamine has only recently been studied in OCD patients and is still an investigational drug in the United States.

A double-blind crossover trial with fluvoxamine and placebo was conducted in 16 patients with OCD (Perse et al., 1987). At the end of the 20-week study, 13 patients (81%) improved with fluvoxamine and 3 (19%) improved with placebo. Fluvoxamine significantly improved measures of OCD symptoms, anxiety, and depression. Price, Goodman, Charney, Rasmussen & Heninger (1987) conducted a single-blind study with fluvoxamine in 10 patients with OCD. A minimum of 4 weeks of fluvoxamine treatment followed at least 2 weeks of placebo treatment. Significant improvement was noted based on several clinical scales and self-rating measures. In this study, 6 of 10 patients responded favorably to fluvoxamine treatment. More recently, this group reported results from a double-blind, placebo-controlled trial in 42 patients (Goodman et al., 1989). About half of the patients were considered nondepressed based on Hamilton Depression Rating Scale scores. In this study, patients were randomly assigned to receive fluvoxamine or placebo for 6 to 8 weeks. Nine of 21 patients receiving fluvoxamine responded, independently of baseline level of depression. A case report of fluvoxamine in the treatment of one woman with panic disorder and with obsessive–compulsive symptoms has also recently been published (Servant, Bailly, & Parquet, 1988). Substantial improvement was noted in the patient's obsessive–compulsive symptoms, and no panic attacks were noted after 6 weeks of fluvoxamine treatment.

These studies provide preliminary evidence of the safety and efficacy of fluvoxamine in the treatment of patients with OCD. However, more studies are needed to confirm these findings.

Zimelidine

Zimelidine hydrochloride (Astra) has had limited success in the treatment of OCD. Three studies were conducted with zimelidine in patients with OCD before it was withdrawn from the market. Two studies demonstrated modest improvement while one study was negative. Zimelidine and desipramine were compared using several measures of serotoninergic function in a double-blind controlled study (Insel, Mueller, Alterman, Linnoila, & Murphy 1985). Zimelidine was clinically ineffective in this group, while desipramine yielded weak but significant clinical improvement. In another study, 6 patients with OCD received zimelidine or imipramine (Prasad, 1984). Patients treated with zimelidine showed significant improvement over the imipramine-treated group after 4 weeks of treatment. Kahn, Westenberg, & Jolles (1984) treated 6 patients with OCD for 8 weeks with zimelidine in an uncontrolled trial. Each patient had cognitive deficits before treatment. Five patients showed an improvement in OCD symptoms and 4 of these showed an improvement in their cognitive deficits.

Buspirone

Fourteen patients with OCD were treated with buspirone (Buspar®, Mead Johnson) (Jenike & Baer, 1988), an anxiolytic drug that acts as an agonist at serotonin 1A receptors. No patient showed improvement with buspirone after an 8-week open trial. However, in a double-blind study in 20 patients, Pato et al. (1989) found both buspirone and clomipramine to be effective after 6 weeks. Augmentation with buspirone will be discussed in the section on adjunctive treatments.

Trazodone

Trazodone hydrochloride (Desyrel®, Mead Johnson) is an antidepressant drug that is chemically unrelated to tricyclic, tetracyclic, or other known antidepressants, and is also a serotonin reuptake inhibitor (Barnhart, 1988). Two patients with severe symptoms of OCD and depression who were treated with trazodone (Baxter, 1985) experienced rapid and impressive improvement in both depression and OCD. Prasad (1986) treated 8 OCD patients with trazodone for 4 weeks. Six patients showed a significant reduction in obsessional symptoms. Two case reports further suggest efficacy of trazodone, in an 18-year-old man (Lydiard, 1986) and in a 49-year-old woman with OCD (Kim, 1987).

OTHER SEROTONINERGIC TREATMENTS

Tryptophan

Tryptophan is an amino acid that is converted by the enzyme tryptophan hydroxylase to 5-hydroxytryptophan (5-HTP) and then to serotonin (5-hydroxytryptamine) by the enzyme aromatic amino acid decarboxylase (Jenike, 1986). Because tryptophan is a serotonin presursor, it has been used in research on OCD. An open study with tryptophan in 7 OCD patients (Yaryura-Tobias & Bhagavan, 1977) showed considerable improvement in these patients after one month of treatment; however, this study has not been replicated. The use of tryptophan in conjunction with other drugs in OCD patients will be discussed in more detail in the section on adjunctive treatment.

LSD

Another serotoninergic drug that has been used in OCD treatment is lysergic acid diethylamide (LSD). A compulsive–neurotic patient was reported to have had a complete remission of symptoms with LSD treatment over a course of $1\frac{1}{2}$ years (Brandrup & Vanggaard, 1977).

Obsessive-compulsive symptoms have been reported to be relieved by the use of LSD and psilocin in an OCD patient who had abused these drugs (Leonard & Rapoport, 1987).

ADJUNCTIVE TREATMENT

Numerous studies of adjunctive treatment have been conducted, employing numerous combinations of serotoninergic drugs, including trazodone, tryptophan, buspirone, and lithium. In one study, 11 patients were treated with trazodone and lithium (Mattes, 1986) with little effect. Lithium has also been used in combination with antidepressants with success. Lithium proved effective when added to a treatment regimen of doxepin, which alone was ineffective in one patient with OCD reported by Golden, Morris, & Sack (1988). In the same report, lithium and clomipramine were found to be effective in a patient who had not responded to clomipramine monotherapy. In another study, clomipramine was combined with tryptophan in one patient and with lithium in another patient (Rasmussen, 1984). Improvement was noted with both drug combinations. Another case report (Eisenberg & Asnis, 1985) recorded improvement with desmethylimipramine when combined with lithium in an OCD patient who had not responded satisfactorily to desmethylimipramine alone.

Markovitz, Stagno, & Calabrese (1989) have reported an open-label trial of buspirone and fluoxetine in 12 patients, in which partial response to fluoxetine was enhanced in all patients by the addition of buspirone.

TRICYCLIC ANTIDEPRESSANTS

Other than clomipramine, the tricyclic antidepressants are not particularly effective in reducing obsessive–compulsive symptoms. In a preliminary report (Insel, Mueller, Gillin, Siever, & Murphy, 1985), desmethylimipramine (desipramine) was administered to 6 OCD patients in a double-blind, placebo-controlled trial. The preliminary results indicated that desipramine did not produce antiobsessional effects in this group of patients. The lack of efficacy of desmethylimipramine was further confirmed by Zohar and Insel (1987) in 10 adult patients, and by Leonard et al. (1989) in 48 children and adolescents. In another study (Foa et al., 1987), 37 OCD patients were treated with imipramine or placebo for 6 weeks. While imipramine reduced depression in highly depressed OCD patients, it was not more effective than placebo in reducing the obsessive–compulsive symptoms in highly depressed or moderately depressed patients.

OTHER ANTIDEPRESSANTS

MAO Inhibitors

Like other drugs that have been used in OCD patients, MAO inhibitors have produced conflicting results. In the previously mentioned comparison of clorgyline and clomipramine (Insel et al., 1983), clorgyline was ineffective. In another study, 12 patients with OCD were treated with clomipramine, clorgyline, or placebo (Zahn, Insel, & Murphy, 1984). After 6 weeks of treatment, significant improvement was noted with clomipramine but not clorgyline.

However, a series of nonblind case reports indicates that MAO inhibitors may have beneficial effects for some patients. Mahgoub (1987) described a patient with OCD who had a good response to phenelzine after 13 weeks of treatment. In one study, 8 patients with OCD were treated with phenelzine or tranylcypromine (Jenike, Surman, Cassem, Zusky, & Anderson, 1983). Three patients responded to phenelzine and 1 patient responded to tranylcypromine. Four patients did not respond to MAO inhibitors. Other case reports have documented the efficacy of MAO inhibitors in some patients with obsessive–compulsive symptoms (Annesley, 1969; Jain, Swinson, & Thomas, 1970; Isberg, 1981; Jenike, 1981; Swinson, 1984).

ANXIOLYTICS

Because OCD is classified as an anxiety disorder, and anxiety often accompanies the obsessive and compulsive symptoms, it is not surprising that anxiolytics have been used in the treatment of OCD. OCD patients experience anxiety if they attempt to resist the obsessions or compulsions (APA, 1987).

The results of anxiolytic treatment in patients with OCD have been inconsistent (Insel & Murphy, 1981). As was mentioned previously, buspirone is an anxiolytic drug with serotoninergic properties that may be useful in treating OCD. Alprazolam (Xanax®, Upjohn) was reported to produce moderate to marked improvement in four patients with OCD (Tollefson, 1985). While other anxiolytics have been tried in OCD, the results have not been very positive.

CONCLUSIONS

Many drugs have been employed in attempts to treat OCD. It is not an easy disease to treat, nor is it likely that a single medication will work in all cases. Furthermore, it is unlikely that drug treatment alone is the optimal treatment for some patients who may benefit from behavioral therapy or a combined pharmacologic and behavioral approach. However, it is abundantly clear that there are effective drug therapies for OCD, where there were none 10 years ago. At this time, the serotonin reuptake inhibitors, particularly clomipramine, fluoxetine, and fluvoxamine, are the most promising. Of these, clomipramine alone has been demonstrated to be efficacious in numerous small studies as well as in large-scale, multicenter studies. Additional well-controlled studies of fluoxetine and fluvoxamine, employing larger numbers of patients, are needed to properly evaluate their role in the future treatment of OCD.

The recent interest in the biology of OCD and its pharmacologic treatment offer significant hope for future progress. One very interesting fact that has emerged early in the course of these investigations is that, so far, OCD is the only psychiatric disorder for which serotoninergic drugs, and only serotoninergic drugs, appear to be therapeutically effective.

ACKNOWLEDGMENTS

The author thanks the following people for their contributions: Richard Katz, Phyllis Landau, Georges Moroz, Alyse Cooper, Joanne Cedrone, and Sylvia Sullivan who assisted in the implementation of the Anafranil clinical trials; Steven Freitag and Ching-Ming Yeh, who performed the statistical analyses; and Suzanne Swanson who provided editorial assistance.

Principal Investigators in the Anafranil clinical trials were: Study 1: James Ballenger, Wayne Goodman, John Greist, Jonathan Himmelhoch, Michael Jenike, Suck Won Kim, Michael Liebowitz, Matig Mavissakalian, and Steven Rasmussen.

Study 2: Hagop Akiskal, Jambur Ananth, Wilmer Betts, Bruce Diamond, Alan Feiger, Edna Foa, David Fogelson, Rudolf Hoehn-Saric, Philip Ninan, Russell Noyes, Alan Ringold, and Katherine Shear.

Study 3: Joseph Biederman, Dennis Cantwell, Rejean Fontaine, John Greist, and Robert Reichler.

REFERENCES

American Psychiatric Association (1987). *Diagnostic and statistical manual of mental disorders*, (3rd ed. Revised). pp. 235, 245–247, Washington, DC: Author.

Amin, M. M., Ban, T. A., Pecknold, J. C., & Klingner, A. (1977). Clomipramine (Anafranil) and behavior therapy in obsessive-compulsive and phobic disorders. *Journal of International Medical Research, 5* (suppl. 5), 33–37.

Ananth, J., Pecknold, J. C., Van Den Steen, N., & Engelsmann, F. (1981). Double-blind comparative study of clomipramine and amitriptyline in obsessive neurosis. *Progress Neuro-Psychopharmacology, 5,* 257–262.

Annesley, P. T. (1969). Nardil response in a chronic obsessive compulsive. *British Journal of Psychiatry, 115,* 748.

Barnhart, E. (1988). *Physician's Desk Reference* (42nd ed., p. 1270). Oradell, NJ: Medical Economics Company.

Baxter, L. R. (1985). Two cases of obsessive–compulsive disorder with depression responsive to trazodone. *Journal of Nervous and Mental Disease, 173,* 432–433.

Berg, C. Z., Whitaker, A., Davies, M., Flament, M. F., & Rapoport, J. L. (1988). The survey form of the Leyton obsessional inventory child version: Norms from epidemiological study. *The Journal of the American Academy of Child and Adolescent Psychiatry, 27,* 759–763.

Brandrup, E., & Vanggaard, T. (1977). LSD treatment in a severe case of compulsive neurosis. *Acta Psychiatrica Scandinavica, 55,* 127–141.

Capstick, N. (1977). Clinical experience in the treatment of obsessional states (1). *Journal of International Medical Research, 5*(Suppl. 5), 71–80.

Claassen, V. (1983). Review of the animal pharmacology and pharmacokinetics of fluvoxamine. *British Journal of Clinical Pharmacology, 15*(Suppl. 3), 349S–355S.

DeVeaugh-Geiss, J. et al. (1991). Clomipramine in the treatment of patients with obsessive compulsive disorder. *Archives of General Psychiatry, 48.*

DeVeaugh-Geiss, J., Landau, P., & Katz, R. (1989). Treatment of Obsessive Compulsive Disorder with clomipramine. *Psychiatric Annals, 19,* 97–101.

Eisenberg, J., & Asnis, G. (1985). Lithium as an adjunct treatment in obsessive-compulsive disorder. *American Journal of Psychiatry, 142,* 663.

Fernandez-Cordoba, E., & Lopez-Ibor Alino, J. (1967). La monoclorimiprimina en enfermos psiquiatricos resistentes a otros tratamientos. *Actas Luso-Espanolas de Neurologia Y Psiquiatria, 26,* 119–147.

Flament, M. F., Rapoport, J. L., Berg, C. J., Sceery, W., Kilts, C., Mellstrom, B., & Linnoila, M. (1985). Clomipramine treatment of childhood obsessive-compulsive disorder. A double-blind controlled study. *Archives of General Psychiatry, 42,* 977–983.

Flament, M. F., Whitaker, A., Rapoport, J. L., Davies, M., Berg, C. Z., Kalikow, K., Sceery, W., & Shaffer, D. (1988). Obsessive compulsive disorder in adolescence: An epidemiological study. *The Journal of the American Academy of Child and Adolescent Psychiatry, 27,* 764–771.

Foa, E. B., Steketee, G., Kozak, M. J., & Dugger, D. (1987). Effects of imipramine on depression and obsessive-compulsive symptoms. *Psychiatry Research, 21,* 123–136.

Fontaine, R., & Chouinard, G. (1986). An open clinical trial of fluoxetine in the treatment of obsessive-compulsive disorder. *Journal of Clinical Psychopharmacology, 6,* 98–101.

Golden, R. N., Morris, J. E., & Sack, D. A. (1988). Combined lithium-tricyclic treatment of obsessive-compulsive disorder. *Biological Psychiatry, 23,* 181–185.

Goodman, W. K., Price, L. H., Rasmussen, S. A., Mazure, C., Fleischmann, R., Hill, C., Heninger, G., & Charney, D. (1989). The Yale-Brown Obsessive-Compulsive Scale (Y-BOCS): Part I. Development, Use, and Reliability. *Archives of General Psychiatry, 46,* 1006–1011.

Goodman, W. K., Price, L. H., Rasmussen, S. A., Delgado, P. L., Heninger, G. R., & Charney, D. S. (1989). Efficacy of fluvoxamine in obsessive-compulsive disorder. A double-blind comparison with placebo. *Archives of General Psychiatry, 46,* 36–44.

Insel, T. R., & Murphy, D. L. (1981). The psychopharmacological treatment of obsessive-compulsive disorder: A review. *Journal of Clinical Psychopharmacology, 1,* 304–311.

Insel, T. R., Murphy, D. L., Cohen, R. M., Alterman, I., Kilts, C., & Linnoila, M. (1983). Obsessive-compulsive disorder. A double-blind trial of clomipramine and clorgyline. *Archives of General Psychiatry, 40,* 605–612.

Insel, T. R., Mueller, E. A., Gillin, J. C., Siever, L. J., & Murphy, D. L. (1985). Tricyclic response in obsessive-compulsive disorder. *Progress in Neuropsychopharmacology and Biological Psychiatry, 9,* 25–31.

Insel, T., Mueller, E., Alterman, I., Linnoila, M., & Murphy, D. L. (1985). Obsessive-compulsive disorder and serotonin: Is there a connection? *Biological Psychiatry, 20,* 1174–1188.

Isberg, R. S. (1981). A comparison of phenelzine and imipramine in an obsessive-compulsive patient. *American Journal of Psychiatry, 138,* 1250–1251.

Jain, V. K., Swinson, R. P., & Thomas, J. G. (1970). Phenelzine in obsessional neurosis. *British Journal of Psychiatry, 117,* 237–238.

Jaskari, M. O. (1980). Observations on mianserin in the treatment of obsessive neurosis. *Current Medical Research Opinion, 6,* 128–131.

Jenike, M. A. (1981). Rapid response of severe obsessive-compulsive disorder to tranylcypromine. *American Journal of Psychiatry, 138,* 1249–1250.

Jenike, M. A. (1986). Somatic Treatments. In M. A. Jenike, L. Baer, W. E. Minichiello (Eds.), *Obsessive compulsive disorders* (pp. 77–111). Littleton, Mass: PSG Publishing Company, Inc.

Jenike, M. A., & Baer, L. (1988). An open trial of buspirone in obsessive-compulsive disorder. *American Journal of Psychiatry, 145,* 1285–1286.

Jenike, M. A., Surman, O. S., Cassem, N. D., Zusky, P., & Anderson, W. H. (1983). Monoamine oxidase inhibitors in obsessive-compulsive disorder. *Journal of Clinical Psychiatry, 44,* 131–132.

Jimenez-Garcia, P. (1967). Experimencia clinica con clomipramina en enfermos psychiatricos. *Libro de Becas Cursos, 58,* 179–201.

Kahn, R. S., Westenberg, H. G. M., & Jolles, J. (1984). Zimelidine treatment of obsessive-compulsive disorder. *Acta Psychiatrica Scandinavica, 69,* 259–261

Karabanow, O. (1977). Double-blind controlled study in phobias and obsessions. *Journal of International Medical Research, 5,*(Suppl.), 42–48.

Karno, M., Golding, J. M., Sorenson, S. B., & Burnam, M. A. (1988). The epidemiology of obsessive-compulsive disorder in five U.S. communities. *Archives of General Psychiatry, 45,* 1094–1099.

Kasvikis, Y., & Marks, I. M. (1988). Clomipramine in obsessive-compulsive ritualizers treated with exposure therapy: Relations between dose, plasma levels, outcome and side effects. *Psychopharmacology, 95,* 113–118.

Kim, S. W. (1987). Trazodone in the treatment of obsessive-compulsive disorder: A case report. *Journal of Clinical Psychopharmacology, 7,* 278–279.

Laboucarie, J., Rascol, A., Jorda, P., Guraud, R., & Leinadier, H. (1967). New prospects in the treatment of melancholic states. Therapeutic study of a major antidepressant, chlorimipramine. *Revue Medicale de Toulouse,* (3), 863–872.

Leonard, H. L., & Rapoport, J. L. (1987). Relief of obsessive-compulsive symptoms by LSD and psilocin. *American Journal of Psychiatry, 144,* 1239–1240.

Leonard, H., Swedo, S., Koby, E., Rapoport, J. L., Lenane, M., Cheslow, D., & Hamburger, S. (1989). Treatment of obsessive compulsive disorder with clomipramine and desmethylimipramine in children and adolescents: A double-blind crossover comparison. *Archives of General Psychiatry, 46,* 1088–1092.

Lopez-Ibor Alino, J. (1969). Intravenous perfusion of monochlorimipramine. Techniques and results. *Proceedings of the International College of CINP, Teragone, April, 1968 (International Congress Series, 180, 519).* Netherlands. Excerpta Medica.

Lydiard, R. B. (1986). Obsessive-compulsive disorder successfully treated with trazodone. *Psychosomatics, 27,* 858–859.

Mahgoub, O. M. (1987). A remarkable response of chronic severe obsessive-compulsive neurosis to phenelzine. *Acta Psychiatrica Scandinavica, 75,* 222–223.

Markovitz, P. J., Stagno, S. J., & Calabrese, J. R. (1989). Buspirone augmentation of fluoxetine in Obsessive-Compulsive Disorder. *Biological Psychiatry, 25,* 186A.

Marks, I. M., Stern, R. S., Mawson, D., Cobb, J., & McDonald, R. (1980). Clomipramine and exposure for obsessive-compulsive rituals:I. *British Journal of Psychiatry, 136,* 1–25.

Marks, I. M., Lelliott, P., Basoglu, M., Noshirvani, H., Monteiro, W., Cohen, D., & Kasvikis, Y. (1988), Clomipramine, self-exposure and therapist-aided exposure for obsessive-compulsive rituals. *British Journal of Psychiatry, 152,* 522–534.

Marshall, W. K., & Micev, V. (1973). Clomipramine (Anafranil) in the treatment of obsessional illnesses and phobic anxiety states. *Journal of International Medical Research, 1,* 403–412.

Mattes, J. A. (1986). A pilot study of combined trazodone and tryptophan in obsessive-compulsive disorder. *International Clinical Psychopharmacology, 1,* 170–173.

Mavissakalian, M., Turner, S. M., Michelson, L., & Jacob, R. (1985). Tricyclic antidepressants in obsessive-compulsive disorder: Antiobsessional or antidepressant agents? II. *American Journal of Psychiatry, 142,* 572–576.

Montgomery, S. A. (1980). Clomipramine in obsessional neurosis: A placebo-controlled trial. *Pharmaceutical Medicine, 1,* 189–192.

Pato, M. T., Pigott, T. A., Hill, J. A., Grover, G., Bernstein, S. E., & Murphy, D. L. (1989). Clomipramine versus buspirone in OCD: A controlled trial. *New Research Abstracts. American Psychiatric Association 142nd Annual Meeting,* Abstract #NR14, p. 34.

Perse, T. L., Greist, J. H., Jefferson, J. W., Rosenfeld, R., & Dar, R. (1987). Fluvoxamine treatment of obsessive-compulsive disorder. *American Journal of Psychiatry, 144,* 1543–1548.

Prasad, A. (1984). A double-blind study of imipramine versus zimelidine in treatment of obsessive compulsive neurosis. *Pharmacopsychiatry, 17,* 61–62.

Prasad, A. (1986). Efficacy of trazodone as an anti-obsessional agent. *Neuropsychobiology, 15*(Suppl. 1), 19–21.

Price, L. H., Goodman, W. K., Charney, D. S., Rasmussen, S. A., & Heninger, G. R. (1987). Treatment of severe obsessive-compulsive disorder with fluvoxamine. *American Journal of Psychiatry, 144,* 1059–1061.

Rack, P. H. (1977). Clinical experience in the treatment of obsessed states (2). *Journal of International Medical Research, 5*(Suppl. 5), 81–90.

Rapoport, J., Elkins, R., & Mikkelsen, E. (1980). Clinical controlled trial of chlorimipramine in adolescents with obsessive-compulsive disorder. *Psychopharmacology Bulletin, 16,* 61–63.

Rasmussen, S. A. (1984). Lithium and tryptophan augmentation in clomipramine-resistant obsessive-compulsive disorder. *American Journal of Psychiatry, 141,* 1283–1285.

Riddle, M. A., Leckman, J. F., Hardin, M. T., Anderson, G. M., & Cohen, D. J. (1988). Fluoxetine treatment of obsessions and compulsions in patients with Tourette's Syndrome. *American Journal of Psychiatry, 145,* 1173–1174.

Servant, D., Bailly, D., & Parquet, P. (1988). Fluvoxamine in the treatment of panic disorder with obsessive-compulsive symptoms. *American Journal of Psychiatry, 145,* 1174–1175.

Swinson, R. P. (1984). Response to tranylcypromine and thought stopping in obsessional disorder. *British Journal of Psychiatry, 144,* 425–427.

Thoren, P., Asberg, M., Cronholm, B., Jornestedt, L., & Traskman, L. (1980). Clomipramine treatment of obsessive-compulsive disorder I. A controlled clinical trial. *Archives of General Psychiatry, 37,* 1281–1285.

Tollefson, G. (1985). Alprazolam in the treatment of obsessive symptoms. *Journal of Clinical Psychopharmacology, 5,* 39–42.

Turner, S. M., Beidel, D. C., Stanley, M. A., & Jacob, R. G. (1988). A comparison of fluoxetine, flooding and response prevention in the treatment of obsessive-compulsive disorder. *Journal of Anxiety Disorders, 2,* 219–225.

Turner, S. M., Jacob, R. G., Beidel, D. C., & Himmelhoch, J. (1985). Fluoxetine treatment of obsessive-compulsive disorder. *Journal of Clinical Psychopharmacology, 5,* 207–212.

Volavka, J., Neziroglu, F., & Yaryura-Tobias, J. A. (1985). Clomipramine and imipramine in obsessive-compulsive disorder. *Psychiatry Research, 14,* 85–93.

Waxman, D. (1977). A clinical trial of clomipramine and diazepam in the treatment of phobic and obsessional illness. *Journal of International Medical Research, 5*(Suppl. 5), 99–110.

Wyndowe, J., Solyom, L., & Ananth, J. (1975). Anafranil in obsessive compulsive neurosis. *Current Therapeutic Research, 18,* 611–618.

Yaryura-Tobias, J. A., & Bhagavan, H. N. (1977). L-tryptophan in obsessive-compulsive disorders. *American Journal of Psychiatry, 134,* 1298–1299.

Yaryura-Tobias, J. A., Neziroglu, F., & Bergman, L. (1976). Chlorimipramine for obsessive-compulsive neurosis: An organic approach. *Current Therapeutic Research, 20,* 541–548.

Zahn, T. P., Insel, T. R., & Murphy, D. L. (1984). Psychophysiological changes during pharmacological treatment of patients with obsessive compulsive disorder. *British Journal of Psychiatry, 145,* 39–44.

Zohar, J., & Insel, T. (1987). Obsessive–compulsive disorder: Psychobiological approaches to diagnosis, treatment, and pathophysiology. *Biological Psychiatry, 22,* 667–687.

10

Neuroethological Models of Obsessive–Compulsive Disorder

James T. Winslow
Thomas R. Insel

Any attempt to develop animal models for obsessive–compulsive disorder (OCD) soon runs into a fundamental dichotomy in the current approaches to this illness. One approach focuses on the cognitive processes of obsessions, worry, and guilt as the primary symptoms, with rituals (i.e., washing and checking) viewed as secondary manifestations. Generally, these cognitive symptoms are assumed to reflect some underlying conflict (intra- or interpersonal), which is either etiologic or at least temporally associated with the emergence of symptoms. Although this approach does not require any behavioral manifestations, one might be able to experimentally pursue OCD from this perspective in animals by focusing on behaviors associated with conflict. For instance, displacement behaviors, even those that superficially appear quite different from the classic compulsive symptoms of washing and checking, could be investigated for their face, construct, and predictive validity as models of OC behavior.

A second approach to OCD focuses on the compulsions: washing, checking, even repetitive intrusive thoughts as primary manifestations of a neural lesion, analogous to the repetitive acts associated with temporal lobe seizures. In this scheme, obsessions of contamination or uncertainty are secondary cognitive explanations that the patient uses to explain uncontrollable behavior. From this perspective, research localizing the neural sites for grooming and checking might point to the presumed "lesion" in OCD. At the outset, we wish to emphasize that those animal behaviors, such as grooming, which phenotypically resemble the motor acts of OCD may not be useful models of the clinical symptoms. What makes a patient's behavior pathologic is not the motor act *per se*, but its excessiveness, its ritualized character, and its inappropriateness for the social context. When grooming becomes stereotyped or perseverative, then the analogy with OCD becomes more useful. Although this might emerge as displacement behavior, stereotyped or perseverative behavior has also been described following a number of pharmacologic and neuroanatomic experimental interventions. In particular, lesions of the hippocampal formation and its primary afferent, the entorhinal cortex, produce perseverative behavior in the rat (Devenport, 1978; Devenport, Devenport, & Holloway, 1981). Lesions of this circuit and the associated afferent system from the septal nuclei (see Gray, 1981) may provide a model of checking behavior due to deficits in spatial memory or mismatches between expected and perceived inputs to the hippocampus. These models, which presume a neurological lesion in OCD, have been discussed elsewhere (Gray, 1982; Pitman, 1989; see also Chapter 11, this volume).

In this chapter, we will adopt a neuroethologic perspective to examine displacement behavior. Following the lead of Ingle and Crews (1985), we view behavior as a link between social influences and neural events—so that both the social context and the neural substrates associated with the behavior may be as relevant as the behavior itself for extending our understanding of compulsive rituals in man. In addition to these specific models of OC behavior, we will describe some recent data regarding a model predictive of anti-obsessional drug efficacy. Finally, given the evidence implicating serotonin in the pathophysiology of OCD (see Chapter 9, this volume), we will review data regarding serotonin and the modulation of aggression in a variety of mammals.

DISPLACEMENT BEHAVIOR

Displacement behaviors, described in elegant detail by classical ethologists (see, for instance, Tinbergen, 1953; Lorenz 1966), are stereotyped motor acts that appear excessive or inappropriate and thus, resemble compulsive rituals (Holland 1974). The particular behaviors, such as pecking, grooming, digging, or head turning, are typical within a species but vary greatly between species. They are nearly ubiquitous across vertebrate phyla and share three features. First, displacement behaviors appear to be invariably triggered or "released" by a conflict—presumably a conflict between two opposing tendencies (e.g., drives). For instance, the ritualized pecking behavior of male birds at the boundary of their territories may reflect both a tendency to attack and a tendency to escape. Indeed, as Tinbergen (1953) has noted, elements of both attack and escape behaviors are evident in many of the stereotyped rituals or displays associated with territorial conflicts. The second feature of this class of behaviors is that once started they continue in an apparently autonomous fashion. The term "fixed action pattern" has been used to describe this "all or nothing" quality of displacement behavior. The term "fixed action pattern" may suggest that the behavior is complete in and of itself. Actually, the signal value of displacement behavior resides not only in the display but in its repetition—the frequency of pecking may be as important as the pecking itself. Finally, although less is known about the factors that terminate the fixed-action pattern once it begins, in most cases either the removal of the conflict or its replacement with a more urgent conflict is sufficient to end the behavior.

Adjunctive behavior refers to behavior spontaneously emitted by animals, sometimes at excessive rates, during intervals between regularly scheduled presentations of rewards. Falk (1971b) proposed that adjunctive behaviors may represent an experimentally induced form of displacement behavior. In the prototypic paradigm, hungry rats exposed to the periodic presentation of small pellets of food, with regular temporal delay, develop excessive drinking (Falk, 1961). This excessive drinking is not due to a physiologic need nor is it due to "superstitious" pairing of drinking with food delivery (Falk, 1971a). The form of adjunctive behavior is not limited to drinking and appears to be significantly influenced by what "releasing" stimuli are available. For example, wheel running, foraging behavior, and aggressive attack behavior have also been identified as potential adjunctive behaviors if appropriate stimuli are pressent (Staddon, 1977). Although the conditons eliciting excessive rates of behavior are not clear, an explanation proposed by Goodrich (1959) for displacement may be applicable: frustration generated by disruption of ongoing behavior may produce a general increase in drive (arousal?) and result in the increased probability and expression of apparently irrelevant behavior.

An interesting variant of displacement is the well-described syndrome of stereotypy or "zoo behavior" in animals that are confined, isolated, or chronically frustrated (Hediger, 1955; Berkson, 1967). In the case of zoo animals, stereotypies can range from scratching, hair pulling, or masturbation behavior to complex motor acts involving prolonged pacing rituals (Hediger, 1955). Foraging mammals, such as bears, appear particularly susceptible to such behaviors when confined. Rapoport has recently described several cases of "acral lick," an apparently dysfunctional grooming behavior in cats and dogs. More interesting still, this syndrome is responsive to anti-obsessional, but not anti-depressant drugs (Rapoport, *personal communication*).

Displacement behavior clearly satisfies criteria for face validity as a model of compulsive rituals in that it is often repetitive and contextually inappropriate, and expressed as motor acts that actually resemble the grooming, hoarding, and checking of OCD patients. The association of both obsessional symptoms and displacement behavior with threat may provide construct validity for this comparison, however unlike displacement behavior, in OCD the threat may not be explicit (or external). In fact, in many OCD patients the expressed fear is not of being attacked, but of attacking or hurting others. A further difference is that displacement behaviors are potent social signals, which may serve to attract a female or thwart attack by an intruding male. Thus far there is little evidence that compulsive rituals such as handwashing or checking have communicative value. Indeed, OCD patients are notoriously secretive about these behaviors, rarely performing them in a social setting.

An important criterion for the evaluation of an animal model of human psychopathology is predictive validity: the accuracy of a model in predicting the efficacy of treatments, particularly pharmacological treatments. For example, symptoms of OCD have been successfully reduced by chronic administration of serotonergic reuptake inhibitors (e.g., clomipramine, zimeldine), but not by administration of selective noradrenergic reuptake inhibitors (e.g., desipramine, nortriptyline). In addition, OC symptoms have been aggravated by acute oral administration of m-CPP, a compound that is an agonist at 5-HT1 receptors (Zohar & Insel, 1987). What is known about the pharmacologic interruption of displacement behaviors?

PHARMACOLOGIC STUDIES OF DISPLACEMENT

Relatively few pharmacological studies of adjunctive behavior are available (Sanger, 1987). Adjunctive drinking was reduced by scopalamine, chlorpromazine, and haloperidol, increased by diazepam and chlordiazepoxide (Sanger & Blackman, 1978) and was unaffected by naloxone (Brown & Holtzman, 1981; Cooper & Holtzman, 1983). Amphetamine has also been shown to reduce the rate of adjunctive drinking and wheel running (Sanger & Corfield-Sumner, 1979; Williams & White, 1984). Robbins and Koob (1980) demonstrated that 6-OHDA lesions of the nucleus accumbens prevented the development of adjunctive drinking without affecting drinking associated with water deprivation. This evidence suggests mesolimbic dopamine terminals may be particularly important in the development of a ritualized or excessive stereotyped behavior associated with frustration.

Although not specifically designed as studies of displacement, pharmacological studies of "excessive" grooming elicited by novel environments and mildly stressful testing stimuli often refer to this behavior as displacement activity (Fentress, 1988). However, grooming behavior is also associated with a variety of functionally unrelated stimulus conditions including cleaning, thermoregulation, distribution of pheromones, and sexual and aggressive encounters (Theissen, 1988). Clearly, each of these may be mediated by different brain mechanisms and interpretation of data must include reference to the behavioral context.

A growing research literature details the sensitivity of grooming behavior to the central administration of several neuropeptides (Colbern & Gispen, 1988). The earliest and most pervasive relationship to be studied was "excessive" grooming elicited by intraventricular administration of adrenocorticotropin hormone (ACTH) (Bertolini, Poggioli, & Vergoni, 1988; Dunn, 1988; Ferrari, Gessa, & Vargiu, 1963), however, similar increases have also been reported following central administration of CRF (Morley & Levine, 1982), vasopressin (Aloyo, Spruijt, Zweirs, & Gispen, 1983), oxytocin (Pedersen et al., 1988), bombesin (Katz, 1980), substance P and other neurokinins (Wilcox, 1988), and low doses of opiate peptides (Dunn, 1988). Although the functional significance of chemically stimulated grooming is unclear, the morphology and sequence of the elicited behavior conforms to that observed in a novel environment (Spruijt, Welberger, Brakkee, & Gispen, 1988). In addition, grooming expressed in a novel environment may be blocked by hypophysectomy or pretreatment with ACTH antiserum (Dunn, Green, & Isaacson, 1979). ACTH-induced grooming and grooming in a novel cage are comparably sensitive to pharmacological treatment: "excessive" grooming is selectively reduced by the opioid, dopaminergic, muscarinic, and alpha-2-adrenergic receptor inhibitors (Dunn, 1988), but not by the beta-adrenergic blocker propranolol. A similar selective reduction of novelty and ACTH-induced grooming has been reported following administration of 5HT1A but not 5HT1B or nonspecific 5HT receptor agonists (Traber, Spencer, Glaser, & Gispen, 1988). Rodriguez Eschandia et al. (1983, 1988) also report that prenatal exposure to clomipramine is associated with increased emotionality, specifically excessive grooming in a novel cage in offspring tested at 30 and 60 days postnatal. These findings indicate a modulatory role for 5HT in the expression of "excessive" grooming by rats similar to that proposed for the control of obsessive–compulsive behavior (Zohar & Insel, 1987), although there clearly is a need for further analysis of the contribution of different serotonergic receptor subtypes.

Efforts to localize the neural substrate of ACTH-induced grooming in rats include studies of application of ACTH to discrete brain areas and lesion studies. Injection of ACTH directly into the substantia nigra (Gispen & Isaacson, 1981) or periaqueductal gray (Spruijt, Cools, & Gispen, 1986) has been reported to elicit grooming. Central effects of ACTH on grooming can also be effectively eliminated by lesions in the substantia nigra or hippocampus (Colbern, Isaacson, Bohus, & Gispen, 1977), and the periaqueductal gray (Spruijt et al., 1986). This network appears to depend on dopaminergic innervation (Cools, Wiegant, & Gispen, 1978). Hippocampal dysfunction has been assigned a central role in the mediation of anxiety-related disorders, primarily in the mediation of cognitive strategies for coping with novelty (Gray, 1982). Although these findings appear to reinforce the value of "excessive" grooming behavior as an example of anxious behavior, it is noteworthy that dopaminergic antagonists are not useful treatments for anxiety-related pathologies (Ananth, 1985; Insel et al., 1983).

Although the morphology of rodent grooming appears to satisfy some of the criteria of face and construct validity for a model of OCD, test animals are typically individually housed and tested in isolation. A paradigm that may be useful in clarifying the role of social context in the development of displacement behavior in rodents is the resident-intruder test. For example, Raab et al. (1986) measured the development of behavioral and physiological measures of dominance in a resident–intruder rat dyad over a 10-day cohabitation. Based on measures of the direction and frequency of attacks and threats, subordinate rats showed significant increases in plasma glucocorticoids and decreased measures of immune function. In addition, subordinate rats showed a four-fold increase in the time spent grooming and significantly less time exploring a novel, open field compared to dominant rats. These findings suggest that social experience may be an important determinant of the likelihood that individual animals will express "displacement" behaviors in stressful situations. A similar relationship between autogrooming and social contingencies has been described for old world primates, Macaca fascicularis (Trioso & Schino, 1986) and Macaca arctoides (Goosen, 1974): autogrooming appears to be elicited in threatening social situations and may be used more often by subordinate than dominant monkeys.

To our knowledge, very few systematic pharmacologic studies of zoo behaviors have been undertaken. Ridley and Baker (1982) reported reduced stereotypy following administration of amphetamine to monkeys exhibiting cage stereotypies. This is of considerable interest as acute administration of amphetamine appeared to decrease the symptoms of OCD (Insel, Mueller, Gillin, Siever, & Murphy, 1983). Separation of infant macaque monkeys from their mothers also produces in-

creased incidence of stereotyped behavior, which is reversed by imipramine (Suomi, Seaman, Lewis, DeLizio, & McKinney, 1971), but the
selectivity of this drug response has not been investigated.

A TEST OF DISPLACEMENT BEHAVIOR AS A MODEL OF OCD

We studied the effects of the acute administration of clomipramine and
desipramine on anticipatory behavior and social interactions during
resident and intruder confrontations between male mice. In a preliminary experiment, we focused on the behavior of intruder mice
placed in the home cage of a male mouse partitioned to prevent direct
social interaction until 5 min after the beginning of the test. Similar
exposure to the soiled bedding of the resident mouse has been associated with the development of a nonopioid analgesia (Rodgers & Randall, 1986), and more recently a role for 5HT1A receptors have also been
associated with nonopioid mediated defeat-induced analgesia (Rodgers
& Shepherd, 1989). Initial findings indicate that desipramine and clomipramine have significantly different effects on the grooming behavior
of intruders, depending on the test contingencies (Figure 10.1). Intruder
mice exhibited many more bouts of grooming during the 5-min
preconfrontation interval as compared to the confrontation interval.
Desipramine increased the frequency of grooming during the preconfrontation phase of the test. During the resident–intruder confrontation, the frequency of grooming by intruder mice was reduced by clomipramine but unaffected by desipramine. These data suggest that the
resident–intruder paradigm may successfully predict differences in the
effects of clomipramine and desipramine on displacement behavior.
Drug-induced changes may depend on immediate social contingencies,
and are very likely to be influenced by previous experience as a victor or
subordinate in aggressive interactions.

PREDICTING ANTIOBSESSIONAL DRUG EFFICACY

Ignoring face and construct validity for the moment, and "putting the
cart before the horse," one might ask the predictive question: What
other behaviors are insensitive to NE uptake inhibitors but sensitive to
5HT uptake inhibitors. This approach has some logical pitfalls as these
drugs have multiple effects that preclude a simple etiological link between two symptoms that respond to the same compound. For instance,
discovering that fever and headache both respond to aspirin does not

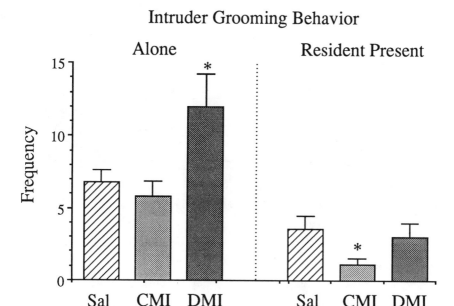

FIGURE 10.1 The effects of desipramine (5 mg/kg, I.P.) and clomipramine (5 mg/kg, I.P.) on the frequency of autogrooming bouts exhibited by a male intruder mouse during a 5 min interval in the partitioned home cage of an aggressive resident mouse (alone), and during a subsequent 5 min resident–intruder confrontation. Asterisks represent Dunnet's t comparisons between saline vehicle and each drug (p < 0.05).

demonstrate a common etiology for fever and headache. Nevertheless, this pharmacologic approach has been extensively used in the screening of drugs for their efficacy in treating other affective disorders (Katz, 1981) and may provide some curious insights for OCD.

We have recently discovered one such instance for which clomipramine and desipramine have quite distinct effects. Rat pups from birth until about day 14 emit ultrasonic isolation or distress calls when they are separated from their parents and littermates. We have previously shown that these species-typical calls are decreased by anxiolytics such as diazepam, and increased by anxiogenic compounds such as pentylenetetrazol (Insel, Hill, & Mayor, 1986). Pups genetically selected for fearfulness also emit more calls than same-aged pups of nonfearful congeners (Insel & Hill, 1987). Clomipramine in acute doses as low as 1 mg/kg(sc), decreases these calls, whereas desipramine (1–20 mg/kg, sc) increases them. These differential effects appear to be related to the 5HT vs NE uptake properites of these drugs since related drugs selected for

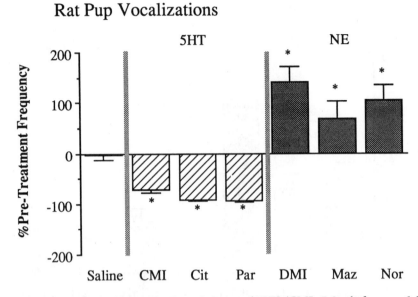

FIGURE 10.2 The effects of selected doses of 5HT (CMI, 5.0; citalopram 1.0; paroxetine, 1.0 mg/kg, sc) and NE (DMI, 5.0; mazindol, 0.5; nortriptyline, 1.0 mg/kg, sc) specific reuptake inhibitors on the frequency of vocal behavior emitted by rat pups during 2 min mother–infant separations. Data are expressed as percentages of pretreatment frequency. Asterisks represent Dunnett's t comparisons of drug effects with saline control (p < 0.05).

5HT uptake inhibition also reduce the calls, while other NE uptake blockers increase the number of calls (Figure 10.2). Rat pup isolation calls are clearly not a valid model of OCD, but this simple, reproducible behavior may prove helpful in screening drugs for their antiobsessional efficacy.

SEROTONIN AND AGGRESSION

The role of social status in the expression of displacement behaviors in primates has been noted previously. Behavioral differences imposed by primate social contingencies are also associated with well-documented differences in hormonal, physiological, and immunological characteristics attributable to social status. Particularly relevant to this discussion are differences in testosterone and 5HT metabolite measures: significantly lower levels of serum testosterone, and higher levels of serum cortisol and CSF 5HIAA have been reported in subordinate male monkeys of both new and old world species (for review see Coe, Smith, &

Levine, 1985; McGuire & Raleigh, 1987; Winslow, DeBold, & Miczek, 1988). These differences may parallel sex-related and physiological characteristics of obsessive–compulsive disorder (Insel et al., 1984; Insel, 1984).

Serotonin has a prominent role among the possible brain mechanisms modulating aggressive behavior (Brown et al., 1982; Valzelli, 1984). Although early efforts to demonstrate a monolithic relationship have been largely discounted (Miczek & Winslow, 1987), there remains substantial evidence for a significant, albeit complex relationship between reduced availability of 5HT and some forms of aggression. The formalization of species differences and social and environmental contingencies in the experimental study of aggressive behavior has provided an important foundation for the interpretation of biochemical and pharmacological data. Table 10.1 summarizes the findings of representative experiments designed to investigate the relationship between 5HT and aggression. At least three clearly defined groups of behavior: offensive, defensive, and predatory aggression have been the focus of an

TABLE 10.1 Serotonin and Aggressive Behavior

Animal species experimental paradigms	Manipulation	Consequence	Reference
OFFENSIVE AGGRESSION			
Typical paradigms include introducing an intruder into the home enviornment of a conspecific animal. Resident may be male or a lactating female. Aggression is measured as frequency of attack and threat by the resident animal. In monkeys, studies often focus on the attack and threat behavior exhibited in the establishment and maintenance of dominance hierarchies.	reduced dietary tryptophan	increased	Lasley and Thurmond, 1985
	5,7DHT or PCPA induced 5HT depletion	increased	Vergnes et al., 1988 Vergnes et al., 1986
	acute administration of 5HT antagonists on habituation of aggression	no change	Winslow and Miczek, 1983
	Blood, brain or CSF levels of 5HT and/ or 5HT turnover of aggressive animals	lower	Sahakian et al., 1986 Kempf et al., 1984 Lee et al., 1987 Raleigh et al., 1984, 1986 Steklis et al., 1984

TABLE 10.1 *(continued)*

Animal species experimental paradigms	Manipulation	Consequence	Reference
	DEFENSIVE AGGRESSION		
Typical paradigms include application of non-specific stressor such as electric foot shock to pairs of conspecifics. Aggression is measured as frequency of attacks directed at partner.	neonatal treatment with endosulfan 5,6 DHT, PCPA, 5,7 DHT induced 5HT depletion	increased	Zaidi et al., 1985 Romaniuk et al., 1987 Puciöwski et al., 1985
	brain levels of 5HT, 5HIAA in shocked compared to nonshocked controls	decreased	Kantak et al., 1984
	PREDATORY AGGRESSION		
Typical paradigm includes introduction of a prey stimulus (mouse to rat; cricket to mouse) into the home environment of the focal animal. Aggression is measures as the latency to kill.	5,7DHT induced 5HT depletion Reduced dietary tryptophan	increased	Vergnes et al., 1988 Kantak et al., 1980
	measured monamines in selected brain	lower	Tani et al., 1987 Broderick et al., 1985
	HUMAN VIOLENCE		
Studies of suicide	CSF 5HIAA ^{3}H imipramine binding in platelets	lower	Goodwin and Post, 1983 Paul et al., 1984 Brown et al., 1982 Åsberg et al., 1976
Criminal population studies	CSF 5HIAA	lower	Linnoila et al., 1983 Lidberg et al., 1984, 1985

intensive research effort. Depletion of serotonin by a variety of different methods has been consistently associated with increased offensive attack behavior, defensive aggression elicited by electric-shock, and predatory attack by mice and rats. Furthermore, aggressive rats, mice, and monkeys appear to have lower brain and CSF levels of 5HIAA compared to nonaggressive conspecifics. This finding may parallel reports of reduced CSF 5HIAA among suicide victims and violent criminals.

The recent identification of several subtypes of 5HT receptors along with the development of selective ligands (Peroutka, 1986) has provided new tools for studying the relationship between aggression and serotonin. Olivier et al. (1987, 1989) describe the effects of subtype-selective 5HT agonists and reuptake inhibitors on several types of aggressive behavior. Based on drug effects measured on offensive, defensive, and predatory behaviors these authors propose a specific modulatory role for the 5HT1B receptor in the control of aggressive behavior. Electrical stimulation of discrete areas of the hypothalamus of a rat also elicits specific, highly stereotyped aggressive attack behaviors (Kruk et al., 1984). The behaviors elicited are comparable to attack behaviors exhibited in resident–intruder confrontations, although typical threat postures are not evident. These behaviors were selectively attenuated by the 5HT1B agonist TFMPP, but were unaffected by the 5HT1A agonist 8-OH-DPAT (Kruk et al., 1987). While attack and threat behavior as such do not appear to have high face validity, the aggressive mental imagery often associated with OCD suggests studies of animal aggression may provide important insights into the neural basis of this disorder. It is particularly interesting that 5HT1B receptor agonists have been associated with decreased aggression in rodents and increased OC symptoms in patients with OCD. Before concluding that OCD is exacerbated by a treatment that decreases aggression, or at least alters the perception of aggression, we need additional data regarding the receptor distribution and function in man.

CONCLUSION

Behaviors analogous to compulsive rituals are evident in several social contexts. Are these contexts (conflicts over territory or dominance, frustration of appetitive drives), which induce repetitive, ritualistic behavior in other mammals, relevant to the etiopathology of OCD? Aggressive impulses and guilt are certainly associated with most compulsive rituals, but it is not clear that these are etiologic rather than symptoms of the disorder. Family conflicts over power or control are also common in the social contexts of OCD patients (Hoover & Insel, 1984), but these conflicts are not temporally associated with compulsive rituals and although most adolescents suffer through major conflicts over personal boundaries, relatively few develop obsessive–compulsive symptoms.

It may be most parsimonious to think of OCD as a disorder involving several etiologies that share a common route of expression built on phylogenetically old patterns of behavior. These patterns include grooming, checking, and hoarding behaviors—all of which can emerge in the context of displacement, but any one of which might also be elicited by spontaneous, intrinsic neural activity unrelated to environmental contingencies. The neural loci for these behaviors are not yet known, but a frontal cortex-basal–ganglia-thalamic circuit has been suggested (Rapoport & Wise, 1989). In addition, as noted above, the mesolimbic dopamine system has been implicated in the control of adjunctive behavior (Robbins & Koob, 1980). Hippocampal circuits should also be considered in the ontogeny of perseverative behavior.

Whatever the ultimate circuitry for these behaviors, one should recognize that animal studies are likely to model only selective features of this complex disorder. In this chapter we have examined the hypothesis that behaviors associated with conflict in several mammalian species resemble some of the symptoms of OCD and thus may also model pathological substrates. While there are ethological, pharmacological, and even neuroanatomical studies to test this hypothesis, the role of human conflict in the etiopathology of OCD has been woefully ignored. An ethological approach to the clinical syndrome now seems warranted to systematically examine the environmental factors that turn on, maintain, and turn off OC symptoms.

REFERENCES

Aloyo, V. J., Spruijt, B., Zwiers, H., & Gispen, W. H. (1983). Peptide-induced excessive grooming in the rat: The role of opiate receptors. *Peptides, 4,* 833–836.

Ananth J. (1985). Pharmacotherapy of obsessive–compulsive disorder. In M. Mavissakalian, S. M. Turner, & L. Michelson (Eds.), *Obsessive–compulsive disorder: Psychological and pharmacological treatment* (pp. 167–211). New York: Plenum.

Åsberg, M., Traskman, L., & Thoren, P. (1976). 5-HIAA in the cerebrospinal fluid: A biochemical suicide marker? *Archives of General Psychiatry, 33,* 1193–1197.

Berkson, G. (1967). Abnormal sterotyped motor acts. In J. Zubin & H. F. Hunt (Eds.), *Comparative psychopathology* (pp. 74–96). New York: Grune and Stratton.

Bertolini, A., Poggioli, R., & Vergoni, V. (1988). Cross-species comparison of the ACTH-induced behavioral syndrome. In D. L. Colbern and W. H. Gispen (Eds.), *Neural mechanisms and biological significance of grooming behavior*. New York: New York Academy of Science.

Broderick, P. A., Barr, G. A., Sharpless, N. S., & Bridger, W. H. (1985). Biogenic amine alterations in the limbic regions of muricidal rats. *Research Communications in Chemical and Pathological Pharmacology, 48,* 3–15.

Brown, D. R., & Holtzman, S. G. (1981). Suppression of drinking by naloxone in the rat: A further characterization. *European Journal of Pharmacology, 69,* 331–340.

Brown, G. L., Ebert, M. H., Goyer, P. F., Jimerson, D. C., Klein, W. J., Bunney, W. E., & Goodwin, F. K. (1982). Aggression, suicide, and serotonin: Relationships to CSF amine metabolites. *American Journal of Psychiatry, 139,* 741–746.

Coe, C. L., Smith, E. R., & Levine, S. (1985). The endocrine system of the squirrel monkey. In: L. A. Rosenblum and C. L. Coe (Eds.), *Handbook of squirrel monkey research*. New York: Plenum.

Colbern, D. L., & Gispen, W. H. (1988). *Neural mechanisms and biological significance of grooming behavior*. New York: New York Academy of Science.

Colbern, D. L., Isaacson, B., Bohus, B., & Gispen, W. H. (1977). Limbic-midbrain lesions and ACTH-induced excessive grooming. *Life Sciences, 21,* 393–401.

Cools, A. R., Wiegant, V. M., & Gispen, W. H. (1978). Distinct dopaminergic systems in ACTH-induced grooming. *European Journal of Pharmacology, 50,* 265–268.

Cooper, S. J., & Holtzman, S. G. (1983). Patterns of drinking in the rat following administration of opiate antagonists. *Pharmacology Biochemistry and Behavior, 19,* 505–511.

Devenport, L. D. (1978). Schedule-induced polydipsia in rats: Adrenocortical and hippocampal modulation. *Journal of Comparative and Physiological Psychology, 92,* 651–660.

Devenport, L. D., Devenport, J. A., & Holloway, F. A. (1981). Reward-induced stereotypy: Modulation by the hippocampus. *Science, 212,* 1280–1281.

Dunn, A. J. (1988). Studies on the neurochemical mechanisms and significance of ACTH-induced grooming. In D. L. Colbern & W. H. Gispen (Eds.), *Neural mechanisms and biological significance of grooming behavior*. New York: New York Academy of Science.

Dunn, A. J., Green, E. J., & Isaacson, R. L. (1979). Intracerebral adrenocorticotropic hormone mediates novelty-induced grooming in the rat. *Science, 203,* 281–283.

Falk, J. L. (1961). Production of polydipsia in normal rats by an intermittent food schedule. *Science, 133,* 195–196.

Falk, J. L. (1971a). The nature and determinants of adjunctive behavior. *Physiology and Behavior, 6,* 577–588.

Falk, J. L. (1971b). The origins and functions of adjunctive behavior. *Animal Learning and Behavior, 5,* 325–355.

Fentress, J. C. (1988). Expressive contexts, fine structure, and central mediation of rodent grooming. In D. L. Colbern & W. H. Gispen (Eds.), *Neural mechanisms and biological significance of grooming behavior.* New York: New York Academy of Science.

Ferrari, W., Gessa, G. L., & Vargiu, L. (1963). Behavioral effects induced by intracisternally injected ACTH and MSH. *Annals of the New York Academy of Sciences, 105,* 330–345.

Gispen, W. H., & Isaacson, R. L. (1981). ACTH-induced excessive grooming in the rat. *Pharmacological Therapeutics, 12,* 209–216.

Goodrich, K. P. (1959). Performance in different segments of an instrumental response chain as a function of reinforcement schedule. *Journal of Experimental Psychology, 57,* 57–62.

Goodwin, F. K., & Post, R. M. (1983). 5-hydroxytryptamine and depression: a model for the interaction of normal variance with pathology. *British Journal of Clinical Pharmacology, 15(Suppl 3),* 393–405.

Goosen, C. (1974). Some causal factors in autogrooming behavior of adult stump-tailed macaques (Macaca arctoides). *Behavior, 49,* 111–129.

Gray, J. A. (1982). *The neuropsychology of anxiety.* New York: Oxford University Press.

Hediger, H. (1955). *Studies of the psychology and behavior of captive animals in zoos and circuses.* New York: Criterion Press.

Holland, H. C. (1974). Displacement activity as a form of abnormal behavior in animals. In: H. R. Beech (Ed.), *Obsessional States.* London: Methuen Press.

Hoover, C. F., & Insel, T. R. (1984). Families of origin in obsessive-compulsive disorder. *Journal of Nervous and Mental Disorders, 172,* 207–215.

Ingle, D., & Crews, D. (1985). Vertebrate neuroethology: Definitions and paradigms. *Annual Review of Neuroscience, 8,* 457–494.

Insel, T. R. (1984). Obsessive-compulsive disorder: The clinical picture. In: T. R. Insel (Ed.), *New Findings in Obsessive-Compulsive Disorder.* American Psychiatric Press: Washington, DC.

Insel, T. R., Hamilton, J. A., Guttmacher, L. B., & Murphy, D. L. (1983). d-Amphetamine in obsessive–compulsive disorder. *Psychopharmacology, 80,* 231–235.

Insel, T. R., & Hill, J. L. (1987). Infant separation distress in genetically fearful rats. *Biological Psychiatry, 22,* 783–786.

Insel, T. R., Hill, J. L., & Mayor, R. B. (1986). Rat pup ultrasonic isolation call: Possible mediation by the benzodiazepine receptor complex. *Pharmacology Biochemistry and Behavior, 24,* 1263–1267.

Insel, T. R., Mueller, E. A., Gillin, J. C., Siever, L. J., & Murphy, D. L. (1984). Bilogical markers in obsessive-compulsive and affective disorders. *Journal of Psychiatric Research, 18,* 407–425.

Kantak, K. M., Hegstrand, L. R., & Eichelman, B. (1980). Dietary tryptophan modulation and aggressive behavior in mice. *Pharmacology, Biochemistry and Behavior, 12,* 675–679.

Kantak, K. M., Hegstrand, L. R., & Eichelman, B. (1984). Regional changes in monoamines and metabolites following defensive aggression in rats. *Brain Research Bulletin, 12*, 227–232.

Katz, R. (1980). Grooming induced by intracerebroventricular bombesin and elediosin in the mouse. *Neuropharmacology, 19*, 143–146.

Katz, R. J. (1981). Animal models and human depressive disorders. *Neuroscience and Biobehavioral Reviews, 5*, 231–246.

Kempf, E., Puglisi-Allegra, S., Cabib, S., Schleef, C., & Mandel, P. (1984). Serotonin levels and turnover in different brain areas of isolated aggressive and non-aggressive strains of mice. *Progress in Neuro-Psychopharmacology & Biological Psychiatry, 8*, 365–371.

Kruk, M. R., Van der Laan, C. E., Mos, J., Van der Poel, A. M., Meelis, W., & Olivier, B. (1984). Brain-stimulation induced agonistic behavior: A novel paradigm in ethopharmacological research. In K. A. Miczek, M. R. Kruk, B. Olivier (Eds.), *Ethopharmacological Aggression Research*. New York: Alan R. Liss.

Kruk, M. R., Van der Poel, A. M., Lammers, J. H. C. M., Hagg, Th., De Hey, A. M. D. M., & Oostwegel, S. (1987). Ethopharmacology of hypothalamic aggression in the rat. In: B. Olivier, J. Mos, P. F. Brain (Eds.), *Ethopharmacology of agonistic behavior in animals and humans*. Dordrecht, The Netherlands: Martinus Nijhoff.

Lasley, S. M., & Thurmond, J. B. (1985). Interaction of dietary tryptophan and social isolation on territorial aggression, motor activity, and neurochemistry in mice. *Psychopharmacology, 87*(3), 313–321.

Lee, E. H., Lin, H. H., & Yin, H. M. (1987). Differential effects of different stressors upon midbrain raphe neurons in rats. *Neuroscience Letters, 80*, 115–119.

Lidberg, L., Asberg, M., & Sundqvist-Stensman, U. B. (1984). 5-Hydroxyindoleacetic acid levels in attempted suicides who have killed their children. *Lancet, 2*, 928.

Lidberg, L., Tuck, J. R., Asberg, M., Scalia-Tomba, G. P., & Bertilsson, L. (1985). Homocide, suicide and CSF 5-HIAA. *Acta Psychiatria Scandinavica, 71*, 230–236.

Liebowitz, M. R., & Hollander, E. (1991). Obsessive–compulsive disorder: Psychobiological integration. In J. Zohar, T. Insel, & S. Rasmussen (Eds.), *The psychobiology of obsessive–compulsive disorder* (pp. 227–255). New York: Springer Publishing Company.

Linnoila, M., Virkkunen, M., Scheinin, M., Nuutila, A., Rimon, R., & Goodwin, F. K. (1983). Low cerebrospinal fluid 5-hydroxyindoleacetic acid concentration in differentiates between impulsive and non-impulsive violent behavior. *Life Science, 33*, 2609–2614.

Lorenz, K. (1966). *On aggression*. New York: Bantam Books.

McGuire, M. T., & Raleigh, M. J. (1987). Serotonin, social behavior, and aggression in vervet monkeys. In B. Olivier, J. Mos, & P. F. Brain (Eds.), *Ethopharmacology of agonistic behavior in animals and humans* (pp. 207–222). Dordrecht, The Netherlands: Martinus Nijhoff.

Miczek, K. A., & Winslow, J. T. (1987). Psychopharmacology research on aggressive behavior. In A. J. Greenshaw & C. T. Dourish (Eds.), *Experimental psychopharmacology*. Clifton, NJ: Humana Press.

Morley, J. E., & Levine, A. S. (1982). Corticotropin-releasing factor, grooming and injestive behavior. *Life Sciences, 31*, 1459–1464.

Olivier, B., Mos, J., Heyden, J. v. d., & Hartog, J. (1989). Serotonergic modulation of social interactions in isolated male mice. *Psychopharmacology, 97*, 154–157.

Olivier, B., Mos, J., Heyden, J. v. d., Schipper, J., Tulp, M., & Berkelmans, B. (1987). Serotonergic modulation of agonistic behavior. In B. Olivier, J. Mos, & P. F. Brain (Eds.), *Ethopharmacology of agonist behavior in animals and humans* (pp. 162–186). Dordrecht, The Netherlands: Martinus Nijhoff.

Paul, S. M., Rehavi, M., Skolnick, P., & Goodwin, F. K. (1984). In R. M. Post & J. C. Ballenger (Eds.), *Neurobiology of mood disorders, Vol. 1*. Baltimore: Williams and Wilkins.

Pedersen, C. A., Caldwell, J. D., Drago, F., Noonan, L. R., Petersen, G., Hood, L. E., & Prange, A. J. (1988). Grooming behavioral effects of oxytocin. In D. L. Colbern & W. H. Gispen (Eds.), *Neural mechanisms and bilogical significance of grooming behavior* (pp. 247–256). New York: New York Academy of Science.

Peroutka, S. J. (1986). Pharmacological differentiation and characterization of $5HT_{1A}$, $5HT_{1B}$, and $5HT_{1C}$ binding sites in rat frontal cortex. *Journal of Neurochemistry, 47*, 529–540.

Pitman, R. K. (1989). Animal models of compulsive behavior. *Biological Psychiatry, 26*(2), 189–198.

Puciöwski, O., Päznik, A., & Kostowski, W. (1985). Aggressive behavior inhibition by serotonin and quipazine injected into the amygdala in the rat. *Behavioral and Neural Biology, 43*, 58–68.

Raab, A., Dantzer, R., Michaud, B., Mormede, P., Taghzouti, K., Simon, H., & Le Moal, M. (1986). Behavioral, physiological and immunological consequences of social status and aggression in chronically coexisting resident-intruder dyads of male rats. *Physiology and Behavior, 36*, 223–228.

Raleigh, M. J., McGuire, M. T., Brammer, G. L., & Yuwiler, A. (1984). Social and environmental influences on blood serotonin concentrations in monkeys. *Archives of General Psychiatry, 41*, 405–410.

Raleigh, M. J., Brammer, G. L., Ritvo, E. R., Geller, E., McGuire, M. T., & Yuwiler, A. (1986). Effects of chronic fenfluramine on blood serotonin, cerebrospinal fluid metabolites, and behavior in monkeys. *Psychopharmacology, 90*, 503–508.

Rapoport, J. L., & Wise, S. P. (1989). Obsessive-compulsive disorder: A basal ganglia disease? In J. L. Rapaport *Childhood obsessive-compulsive disorder*. Washington, DC: American Psychiatric Press.

Ridley, R. M. & Baker, H. F. (1982). Stereotypy in monkeys and humans. *Psychological Medicine, 12*, 61–72.

Robbins, T. W., & Koob, G. F. (1980). Selective disruption of displacement behaviour by lesions of the mesolimbic dopamine system. *Nature, 285*, 409–412.

Rodgers, R. J., & Randall, J. I. (1986). Resident's scent: A critical factor in acute analgesic reaction to defeat experience in male mice. *Physiology and Behavior*, *37*, 317–322.

Rodgers, R. J., & Shepherd, J. K. (1989). 5HT1A agonist, 8-hydroxy-2-(DI-n-propylamino)tetralin (8-OH-DPAT), inhibits non-opioid analgesia in defeated mice: Influence of route of administration. *Psychopharmacology*, *97*, 163–166.

Rodriguez Eschandia, E. L., Broitman, S. T., & Foscolo, M. R. (1983). Effects of serotonergic and catecholaminergic antagonists on mild stress-induced excessive grooming in the rat. *Behavioral Neuroscience*, *97*, 1022–1024.

Rodriguez Eschandia, E. L., Foscolo, M. R., & Gonzalez, A. (1988). Effect of perinatal exposure to therapeutic doses of chlorimipramine on grooming behavior in the adult rat. In D. L. Colbern & W. H. Gispen (Eds.), *Neural mechanisms and biological significance of grooming behavior* (pp. 80–85). New York: New York Academy of Science.

Romaniuk, A., Filipczak, M., & Fryczak, J. (1987). The influence of injection of 5,6 dihydroxytryptamine to dorsal raphe nucleus on carbachol-induced defensive behavior and regional brain amine content in the cat. *Polish Journal of Pharmacology and Pharmacy*, *39*, 17–25.

Sahakian, B. J., Sarna, G. S., Kantamanemi, D. B., Jackson, A., Hutson, P. H., & Curzon, G. (1986). CSF tryptophan and transmitter amine turnover may predict social behavior in the normal rat. *Brain Research*, *399*, 162–166.

Sanger, D. J. (1987). Effects of drugs on schedule-controlled behavior. In A. J. Greenshaw & C. T. Dourish (Eds.), *Experimental Psychopharmacology* (pp. 213–262). Clifton NJ: Humana Press.

Sanger, D. J., & Blackman, D. E. (1978). The effect of drugs on adjunctive behavior. In D. E. Blackman & D. J. Sanger (Eds.) *Contemporary Research in Behavioral Pharmacology* (pp. 73–83). New York: Plenum Press.

Sanger, D. J., & Corfield-Sumner, P. K. (1979). Schedule-induced drinking and thirst: A pharmachological analysis. *Pharmacology Biochemistry and Behavior*, *10*, 471–474.

Spruijt, B. M., Welbergen, P., Brakkee, J., & Gispen, W. H. (1988). An ethological analysis of excessive grooming in young and aged rats. In D. L. Colbern & W. H. Gispen (Eds.), *Neural mechanisms and biological significance of grooming behavior* (pp. 89–100). New York: New York Academy of Science.

Spruijt, B. M., Cools, A. R., & Gispen, W. H. (1986). The periaqueductal gray: A prerequisite for ACTH-induced excessive grooming. *Behavioral Brain Research*, *20*, 19–25.

Staddon, J. E. R. (1977). Schedule-induced behavior. In W. K. Honig & J. E. R. Staddon (Eds.), *Handbook of operant behavior* (pp. 125–152). Englewood Cliffs, NJ: Prentice-Hall.

Steklis, H. D., Brammer, G. L., Raleigh, M. J., & McGuire, M. T. (1984). Serum testosterone, male dominance, and aggression in captive groups of vervet monkeys *(Cercopithecus aetiops sabaeus)*. *Hormones and Behavior*, *19*, 154–153.

Suomi, S. J., Seaman, S. F., Lewis, J. K., DeLizio, R. D., & McKinney, W. T. (1971). Effects of imipramine treatment of separation-induced social disorders in rhesus monkeys. *Archives of General Psychiatry*, *35*, 321–325.

Tani, Y., Kataoka, Y., Sakurai, Y., Yamashita, K., Ushio, M., & Ueki, S. (1987). Changes of brain monoamine contents in three models of experimentally induced muricide in rats. *Pharmacology Biochemistry and Behavior, 26,* 725–729.

Theissen, D. D. (1988). Body temperature and grooming in the mongolian gerbil. In D. L. Colbern & W. H. Gispen (Eds.), *Neural mechanisms and biological significance of grooming behavior* (pp. 27–39). New York: New York Academy of Science.

Tinbergen, N. (1953). *Social Behaviour in Animals.* London: Chapman and Hall.

Traber, J., Spencer, D. G., Glaser, T., & Gispen, W. H. (1988). Actions of psychoactive drugs on ACTH- and Novelty-induced behavior in the rat. In D. L. Colbern and W. H. Gispen (Eds.), *Neural mechanisms and biological significance of grooming behavior* (pp. 270–280). New York: New York Academy of Science.

Trioso, A., & Schino, G. (1986). Environmental and social influences on auto-grooming behaviour in a captive group of Java monkeys. *Behaviour, 100,* 292–302.

Valzelli, L. (1984). Psychobiology of aggression. *Biological Psychiatry, 8,* 311–325.

Vergnes, M., DePaulis, A., & Boehrer, A. (1986). Parachlorophenylalanine-induced serotonin depletion increases offensive but not defensive aggression in male rats. *Physiology and Behavior, 36,* 653–658.

Vergnes, M., DePaulis, A., Boehrer, A., & Kempf, E. (1988). Selective increases of offensive behavior in the rat following intrahypothalamic 5,7-DHT-induced serotonin depletion. *Brain Behavior Research, 29,* 85–91.

Williams, J. L., & White, J. M. (1984). The effects of amphetamine and scopolamine on adjunctive drinking and wheel-running in rats. *Psychopharmacology, 82,* 360–367.

Wilcox, G. L. (1988). Pharmacological studies of grooming and scratching behavior elicited by spinal substance P and excitatory amino acids. In D. L. Colbern and W. H. Gispen (Eds.), *Neural mechanisms and biolgocial significance of grooming behavior* (pp. 228–236). New York: New York Academy of Science.

Winslow, J. T., DeBold, J. F., & Miczek, K. A. (1988). Alcohol effects on the aggressive behavior of squirrel monkeys and mice are modulated by testosterone. In B. Olivier, J. Mos, & P. F. Brain (Eds.), *Ethopharmacology of agonistic behavior in animals and humans.* Dordrecht, The Netherlands: Martinus Nijhoff.

Winslow, J. T., & Miczek, K. A. (1983). Habituation of aggression mice: Pharmacological evidence of catecholaminergic and serotonergic mediation. *Psychopharmacology, 81,* 286–291.

Zaidi, N. F., Agrawal, A. K., Anand, M., & Seth P. K. (1985). Neonatal endosulfan neurotoxicity: Behavioral and biochemical changes in rat pups. *Neurobehavioral Toxicology and Teratology, 7,* 439–442.

Zohar, J., & Insel, T. R. (1987). Drug treatment of obsessive-compulsive disorder. *Journal of Affective Disorders, 13,* 193–202.

11

Obsessive–Compulsive Disorder: Psychobiological Integration

Michael R. Liebowitz
Eric Hollander

The last decade has witnessed a surge of interest and knowledge concerning obsessive–compulsive disorder (OCD). Psychopharmacological studies with potent serotonin (5HT) reuptake blockers such as chlorimipramine (CMI) (Flament et al., 1985; Marks, Stern, Mawson, Cobb, & McDonald, 1980; Mavissakalian, Turner, Michelson, & Jacob, 1985; Montgomery, 1980; Thoren, Asberg, Cronholm, Jornestedt, & Traskman, 1980a) and behavioral treatment studies with exposure and response prevention (Rachman et al., 1979; Steketee et al., 1982) have raised therapeutic optimism and required updating of older neurologic (Schilder, 1938) and psychoanalytic models (Freud, 1958a, b). The therapeutic efficacy of CMI has generated interest in serotonin's role in OCD (Yaryura-Tobias, Turner, Michelson, & Jacob, 1976). This is further supported by recent acute challenge studies with 5HT agonists such as metachlorophenylpiperazine (mCPP) (Zohar, Mueller, Insel, & Zohar-Kadouch, 1987) and clinical trials with specific 5HT reuptake blockers such as fluoxetine (Fontaine & Chouinard, 1986; Turner, Jacob, Beidel, & Himmelhoch, 1985) and fluvoxamine (Perse, Greist, Jefferson, Rosenfeld, & Reuven, 1987; Price, Goodman, Charney, Rasmussen, & Heninger, 1987). Neuropsychological (Flor-Henry, 1983; Harvey, 1987; Gray, 1982) and brain imaging (Baxter et al., 1987a; Rapoport & Wise, 1988) approaches implicate specific frontal-cortical, limbic, and striatal systems. Newer epidemiological surveys find greater than anticipated prevalence (Myers et al., 1984) and family studies suggest intergenerational transmission of an OCD spectrum defined to include subclinical features (Carey & Gottesman, 1981).

These lines of investigation have been pursued separately, however, with little attempt at integration. We believe that it is now possible to develop psychobiological models of OCD that at least begin to integrate biochemical, neuropsychological, psychoanalytic, behavioral, and neuroanatomical findings. Such models of OCD should be consistent with all valid available data. They should help to resolve some of the uncertainies that still prevail, and also generate meaningful hypotheses for further study.

This chapter reviews and attempts to integrate both the recent advances and more classical observations in OCD. Ten sections focus on diagnostic criteria, psychopharmacology, behavior therapy, the serotonin model, neuropsychology and neuroanatomy, other pathophysiological models, relationship to associated conditions, epidemiology and family studies, integration of psychoanalytic and psychobiological perspectives, and directions for future research.

DEFINITION

Current diagnostic criteria for OCD are based on clinical consensus, unvalidated by biological markers, treatment outcome, or family studies. The criteria may encompass pathophysiologically heterogeneous subtypes, as suggested by variability in treatment and biochemical findings reviewed below. From the perspective of what is driving the distress, clinical experience suggests that OCD patients fall into three groups.

The most common type is characterized by an excessive fear of physical harm or danger to oneself or others, or property. Examples include the fear of getting AIDS from being in the same room as a high-risk person, which may lead to excessive washing, or the fear of having pushed someone off a subway platform, which can lead to excessive checking.

The second type involves a vague sense of unease rather than actual danger in the face of certain normal exposures, which patients cannot clarify. This may also lead to excessive washing, hoarding, or arranging of things.

The third type has its origin in a striving for perfection and symmetry, be it flawless religious observance (scrupulosity), absolute moral behavior, never having an angry thought or sexual impulse, or having everything absolutely neat and orderly. Repetitive washing (after masturbation), checking (so that nothing possibly useful is discarded in the trash), arranging (so that every edge is perfectly straight) or intense mental struggle to suppress unacceptable thoughts may ensue. However, while the compulsive behavior is a burden or the angry or sexual thoughts seen as ego-alien and intrusive, the underlying excessively perfectionistic standards are felt to be rational and good, albeit difficult to live with.

Conditions symptomatically similar to OCD are now excluded in the Diagnostic and Statistical Manual of Mental Disorders, Third ed., (DSM-III-R), such as recurrent thoughts that something is wrong with one's appearance (body dysmorphic disorder) and compulsive hair pulling (trichotillomania). Without empirical justification, DSM-III-R excludes compulsive acts that may be inherently pleasurable, such as repetitive masturbation, even if subjects describe them as ego dystonic and done to relieve tension.

OCD's boundary with overvalued ideas is also unclear. Overvalued ideas are isolated, preoccupying beliefs that come to dominate an individual's life but are neither obsessional or delusional (McKenna, 1984). Their mechanism(s) is (are) unknown. They differ from obsessions in not being seen as senseless by the sufferer; rather, the ideas are seen as natural rather than intrusive. In reality, however, some OCD patients, particularly the perfectionistic subtype, also do not see their underlying standards as senseless, although resultant compulsive behavior is usually regarded as excessive.

PSYCHOPHARMACOLOGY

Recent Advances

Associated depression, anxiety, or psychosis can often be helped by standard psychopharmacological agents, but these are frequently ineffective in treating core OCD symptoms. However, CMI, a tricyclic agent with potent 5HT reuptake blocking properties, is of significant benefit for a substantial proportion of OCD patients (Flament et al., 1985; Marks et al., 1980; Mavissakalian et al., 1985; Montgomery, 1980; Thoren et al., 1980a). First found to help obsessional symptoms in the late 1960s, CMI's approval for OCD in the U.S. has been delayed by an initial research focus on depression instead of OCD, early comparisons with imipramine in OCD that lacked a placebo control group, and studies in which low dosages and poor rating scales may have hampered efforts to demonstrate efficacy. A multicenter trial of CMI in OCD completed in the fall of 1987 will hopefully lead to marketing.

CMI is imipramine with a chlorine substitution on carbon three. Of the six published placebo-controlled trials of CMI in OCD (Flament et al., 1985; Maxissakalian et al., 1985; Rapoport & Michelson, 1980; Thoren et al., 1980b), five show significant CMI superiority to placebo. The average symptomatic improvement with CMI was 40% to 50%, as measured by OCD rating scales or proportion of patients considered responders. A majority of these studies had mean dosages under 150mg/day and were less than six weeks in duration; CMI appears more effective when given up to 250 mg/day for 10 to 12 weeks.

Significant accompanying depressive symptoms are not required for an OCD patient to benefit from CMI (Flament et al., 1985; Maxissakalian et al., 1985; Thoren et al., 1980a). Extensive placebo-controlled comparisons of standard antidepressants are lacking in OCD. However, CMI has proven more effective in OCD than the monoamine oxidase inhibitor (MAOI) clorgyline (Insel, Murphy et al., 1983), imipramine (Volovka, Neziroglu, Yaryura-Tobias, 1984), desipramine (Zohar & Insel, 1987) and zimelidine, a less potent 5HT reuptake blocker than CMI. CMI, but not amitriptyline (Ananth, Peckhold, Van Den Steen, & Engelsmann, 1981), was effective in one trial and CMI, but not nortriptyline was effective in another (Thoren et al., 1980a).

Early results with the highly selective 5HT reuptake blockers fluoxetine (Fontaine & Chouinard, 1986; Turner et al., 1985) and fluvoxamine (Perse et al., 1987; Price et al., 1987) are promising. Recently approved as an antidepressant, fluoxetine significantly benefited 5 of 10 (Turner et al., 1985), and 5 of 7 OCD (Fontaine & Chouinard, 1986) patients in two open trials. Fluvoxamine is still experimental. In a 6 to 8 week placebo-controlled trial, 9 of 21 OCD patients were much improved on active drug, compared to 0 of 21 assigned to placebo ($p = .001$, Fisher exact test) (Price et al., 1987). In a 20-week double blind crossover study, 9 of 16 (56%) were rated better ("substantial or complete loss of symptoms with pronounced improvement of social or role function") on fluvoxamine compared to 0% on placebo (Perse et al., 1987).

Lithium (Rasmussen, 1984), L-tryptophan (Rasmussen, 1984), and clonidine (Lipsedge & Prothero, 1987) reportedly augment the effects of CMI, but placebo comparisons are needed. Alprazolam (Tollefson, 1985), L-tryptophan (Yaryura-Tobia & Bhagavan, 1977), d-amphetamine (Insel, Hamilton, Guttmacher, & Murphy, 1983), trazadone (Prasad, 1985) and doxepin (Ananth, Solyom, & Sookm, 1975) have been reported of some benefit in open series. Zimelidine seemed useful in an open trial (Kahn & Jolles, 1984) and in comparison to imipramine in another (Prasad, 1984), but less useful than CMI in a third study (Insel, Mueller, Alterman, Linnoila, & Murphy, 1985). Phenelzine (Isberg, 1981) and tranylcypromine (Jenike, 1981) (in OCD with associated panic attacks), and antiandrogens (Casas et al., 1986) were useful in recent reports, but imipramine (Foa, Steketee, Kozak, & Dugger, 1987), oxytocin (Ansseau, et al., 1987), and carbamazepine (Joffe & Swinson, 1987) were not.

Continued Uncertainties

Clinical experience suggests relapse following CMI discontinuation after short-term treatment. In a placebo-controlled discontinuation study of OCD patients on CMI for 6 to 24 months, 16 of 18 relapsed within 7 weeks of stopping treatment (Pato, Zohar, & Murphy, 1988). There was no correlation between tendency to relapse and duration on CMI, suggesting indefinite maintenance treatment may be required. Whether additional behavior therapy or higher medication dosages helps prevent relapse is unclear.

Why are the response rates to 5HT reuptake blockers not higher in OCD? Sample sizes are small; the effects of comorbidity not well examined; studies brief; rating instruments still in development; and the criteria for response, dosage schedules, drugs, and duration of treatments not uniform or always well-defined. Nevertheless, the proportion of patients responding to 5 HT reuptake blockers tends to be 40% to 60% across a number of studies. If OCD has a uniform pathophysiology, nonresponders are not getting the proper dosage or duration of medication. If the disorder as now defined is pathophysiologically heterogeneous, nonresponders are not getting the proper treatment.

Plasma levels have been compared to treatment response only for CMI, with inconsistent results. Positive (Insel, Murphy et al., 1983), negative (Thoren et al., 1980a), inverse "u" shaped (best response in midrange levels) (Stern, Marks, Mawson, & Luscomb, 1980) and no correlations (Flament et al., 1985) between improvement and CMI plasma levels have been noted.

Results with intravenous CMI suggest that at least some oral CMI nonresponders may not be getting the necessary dosage. Several uncontrolled studies report efficacy for IV CMI up to 200 to 300mg/day in patients unresponsive to moderate oral CMI trials (150–200mg/day) (Rack, 1973, 1977; Warneke, 1984, 1985). The IV route avoids first pass hepatic metabolism, producing a higher plasma CMI to its metabolite desmethyl CMI (DCMI) ratio compared to the same oral dose. CMI has a selective 5HT reuptake inhibiting effect, while DCMI also blocks the reuptake of norepinephrine. CMI levels fluctuate more, peak levels are higher, and CNS accumulation more rapid with IV administration. Placebo-controlled studies are needed to assess the role of medical drama. Also, prior reports do not distinguish clearly beteeen those IV

CMI responders who failed to tolerate substantial oral CMI doses and those who failed to benefit.

Arguing for pathophysiological heterogeneity in OCD are findings suggesting that the subset of patients in whom 5HT abnormalities can be demonstrated at baseline respond best to 5HT reuptake blockers. Studies of cerebrospinal fluid (CSF), 5 hydroxyindolacetic acid (5-HIAA), the principal CNS 5HT metabolite, find OCD patients ranging from high (Zohar & Insel, 1987) to normal compared to controls (Thoren et al., 1980b), with the high 5-HIAA patients comprising the CMI-responsive subset. Similarly, in one study platelet 5HT levels in OCD patients range from high to normal compared to normal controls, with the high platelet 5HT patients showing better responses to CMI (Flament, Rapoport, Murphy, Berg, & Lake, 1987). These findings require replication in larger samples as well as with other indices of 5HT function and with other drugs beside CMI.

Few demographic or clinical predictors of 5HT reuptake blocker responsivity have been noted. Neuropsychiatric variables could be useful but have not been sufficiently compared to outcome. Jenike noted concomitant schizotypal features to be a poor prognostic feature for standard medications and behavior therapy, but 5HT reuptake blockers were not studied (Jenike, Baer, Minichiello, Schwartz, & Carey, 1986). Rasmussen found little difference in treatment outcome among different OCD subtypes, except that strong needs for symmetry were associated with a poor prognosis (Rasmussen & Tsuang, 1986).

The mechanisms of 5HT reuptake blocker efficacy in OCD are poorly understood. Thoren and colleagues found a significant positive correlation between decrease in CSF 5-HIAA and decrease in OCD symptoms following CMI treatment in an adult sample (Thoren et al., 1980b), as did Flament et al. comparing change in platelet 5HT CMI level and outcome in adolescents (Flament et al., 1987). Because responders had higher baseline levels than nonresponders and appeared high in comparison to the normal range, these findings provide preliminary evidence for normalization of 5HT function with successful treatment. Consistent with this, exacerbation of OCD symptoms following the 5HT agonist mCPP was seen at baseline but not after successful CMI treatment (Zohar, Insel, Zohar-Kadouch, Hill, & Murphy, 1988).

BEHAVIOR THERAPY

Marks argues that it is impossible to test whether compulsive rituals are learned or conditioned (Marks, 1981). He suggests that environmental conditions preceding a ritual should be called evoking stimuli and the ritual seen as an evoked rather than a conditioned response. One form of behavioral treatment for OCD is aimed at continuous exposure to the evoking stimulus until the evoked response subsides.

Current behavioral treatment of OCD involves the combination of three related procedures: "exposure" to feared objects or situations; "response prevention," in which compulsive rituals are avoided; and imaginal exposure, which may help fears of future catastrophes associated with obsessions (Marks, 1981; Steketee et al., 1982). Patients with contamination fears and compulsive handwashing would be exposed to feared dirt, feces, and so on, while not engaging in excessive cleaning or washing. They would also imagine themselves encountering feared substances and coping without ritualizing. The goal is to become convinced emotionally that no catastrophe ensues from normal exposures, so ritualistic behaviors can be abandoned. Although often done on a weekly outpatient basis, 3 weeks of daily (weekday) sessions, either on an inpatient or outpatient basis, may be more effective.

As summarized in several recent reviews (Marks, 1981; Steketee et al., 1982), uncontrolled studies report quite significant improvement in compulsive rituals after exposure treatment. However, while promising, behavior therapy for OCD cannot yet be regarded as having proven effectiveness, because large samples have not been compared with nonexposure control groups under conditions of blind evaluation.

Factors noted to limit success of OCD patients in behavior therapy include poor compliance, severe concomitant depression, strongly held beliefs that rituals are necessary to prevent catastrophe, high baseline anxiety, and associated schizotypal or borderline personality (Jenike et al., 1986; Marks, 1981; Steketee et al., 1982). Patients unable to engage in exposure and response prevention are considered noncompliant rather than nonresponsive, and not included in the final determination of response rate, thus inflating positive outcome. In some studies, checkers did less well than washers. A small minority of patients are reported fully compliant with treatment but fail to habituate during exposure (Marks, 1981). Patients with only obsessions respond poorly to behavior therapy because there is no target for exposure, and thought stopping is generally not helpful.

In patients with both obsessions and compulsions, behavior therapy is generally more helpful for the compulsive rituals. The degree to which obsessions also improve, as opposed to being better tolerated without eliciting rituals, is unclear.

We hypothesize that 5HT dysfunction in OCD patients is linked primarily to obsessive thoughts, not to compulsive rituals. Biochemical study before and after behavior therapy would reveal whether OCD patients with baseline abnormalities in 5HT status respond, and whether such abnormalities are normalized or continue but are handled more adaptively. In principle, deconditioning could result in 5HT normalization, analagous in reverse to the presynaptic 5HT facilitation that accompanied conditioned "anxiety" in aplysia (Kandel, 1983).

Behavioral treatment is also reported to result in lasting gains in a high proportion of OCD patients (Marks, 1981), but blind controlled evaluations are lacking. While drug and behavioral therapies might be synergistic for OCD, only one reported study with a limited sample size has examined this, finding both CMI and behavior therapy effective but without significant additive effects (Marks et al., 1980). Additional behavior therapy-pharmacotherapy studies are needed for OCD to compare the spectra of patients responding to each.

SEROTONIN MODELS

Serotonin dysregulation in OCD was originally suggested by the substantial efficacy of CMI. CMI's desmethyl metabolite potently blocks norepinephrine reuptake, however. Recent reports of significant anti-OCD activity of the more specific 5HT reuptake blockers fluoxetine and fluvoxamine strengthen the case for 5HT involvement in at least the large subset of OCD patients who respond to one or more of these drugs.

Our understanding of 5HT involvement in OCD has grown increasingly complex, and is still evolving. In contrast to the earlier belief in a straightforward 5HT deficiency (Thoren et al., 1980b; Yarayura Tobias et al., 1976), evidence is now accumulating that increased rather than decreased 5HT activity and sensitivity of some CNS systems may play a mediating role in OCD. Elevated CSF 5-HIAA levels might indicate greater presynaptic firing, 5HT release, and 5HT metabolism. While this could occur in compensation for postsynaptic receptor or downstream subsensitivity, it could also occur as a primary abnormality. One CSF study found greater 5-HIAA activity in OCD compared to normal controls, with the patients responding well to CMI (Zohar & Insel, 1987). Another found no significant difference (Thoren et al., 1980b). However, in this study also patients with higher CSF 5-HIAA responded better to CMI, as did adolescents with high platelet 5HT levels in a third trial (Flament et al., 1987).

In addition, acutely increasing postsynaptic 5HT activity appears to worsen OCD. Three studies have examined behavioral responses to mCPP, a 5-HT1B postsynaptic agonist (Charney et al., 1988; Hollander, Fay, & Liebowitz, 1988; Zohar et al., 1987). Zohar et al. found that 10 of 12 OCD patients, but 0 of 12 controls showed transient increases in obsessions and compulsive urges following 0.5 mg/kg oral mCPP challenge (Zohar et al., 1987). Six of 12 patients developed new obsessions or reactivated dormant ones during the challenge. In a different investigation, no specific worsening of OCD was seen with 0.1 mg/kg IV mCPP challenge, possibly due to the lower dosage (there were no mCPP blood levels in the IV study) and/or more transient symptom production with intravenous medication (Charney et al., 1988). We have reported worsening of obsessive–compulsive features in 6 of 8 OCD patients blindly challenged with 0.5 mg/kg oral mCPP (Hollander et al., 1988), replicating Zohar et al.'s finding.

All 5HT agents do not worsen OCD, as demonstrated by negative findings with the 5HT precursor tryptophan (Charney et al., 1988) and the 5HT releaser fenfluramine (Hollander et al., 1988). These less specific challenges stimulate a variety of 5HT receptors, including 5HT1A, 5-HT1B and 5-HT2, whose separate behavioral effects could nullify each other. OCD patients also become more anxious than controls with oral mCPP (Zohar et al., 1987); OCD exacerbation could be secondary to anxiety increase. Reports that caffeine (Zohar et al., unpublished data) and yohimbine (Rasmussen, Goodman, Woods, Heninger, & Charney, 1987) increase anxiety in OCD patients without simultaneously worsening obsessions, however, suggest that worsening with mCPP is a specific obsessional effect, not merely secondary to an increase in anxiety.

Zohar et al. found blunted cortisol rise but normal prolactin increase as well as symptomatic exacerbation with oral mCPP in OCD patients (Zohar et al., 1987), while both the intravenous mCPP and tryptophan (Charney et al., 1988) studies found evidence of blunted prolactin increase but normal cortisol and behavioral responses. This suggests blunted postsynaptic receptor sensitivity in neuroendocrine systems, divergent from the behavioral response, but possibly compensatory for heightened presynaptic 5HT activity. Prolactin and behavioral or cortisol abnormalities may be mediated differently.

Platelet imipramine binding is considered closely related to platelet 5HT reuptake, although the utility of the platelet as a model for CNS neuronal function is debated. One study found decreased platelet imipramine binding (Bmax) in OCD patients (Weizman et al., 1986); another found no difference from normals (Zohar & Insel, 1987). The significance of this is uncertain. Similar findings have been noted in a variety of other clinical states including depression (Weizman et al., 1986). While current affective state has been controlled for in studying OCD, low imipramine binding may be a trait marker for some affectively ill patients, reduced even when they are euthymic (Baron et al., 1986). Future studies in OCD should control for affective history as well.

Excessive 5HT activity could produce OCD by its influence on neuropsychological functioning. In rodents, increases in 5HT inputs from raphe nuclei bias the septo–hippocampal behavioral inhibition system to regard more incoming stimuli as potentially aversive, and to check more closely for the match between actual and predicted phenomena (Gray, 1982). If this model is applicable to man, supression of 5HT inputs in patients with high baseline limbic 5HT activity should ameliorate OCD. Chronic administration of CMI decreases CSF 5-HIAA (Thoren et al., 1980b), perhaps through increased synaptic 5HT levels stimulating inhibitory presynaptic autoreceptors. Chronic CMI treatment also appears to down-regulate certain 5HT receptors, since following successful CMI treatment (while still on medication), OCD patients became less sensitive to the behavioral and hyperthermic effects of mCPP (Zohar et al., 1988). The chronic effects of 5HT reuptake blockers appear different from their acute effects, which are to increase synaptic 5HT levels. Amelioration of OCD with 5HT reuptake blockers usually requires at least 8 to 12 weeks of therapy, consistent with receptor down-regulation. Acute 5HT reuptake blockade has been found at times to transiently worsen OCD.

If elevated 5HT inputs in man contribute to an exaggerated concern with harm to people or property and difficulty in feeling certain, low 5HT status should have the opposite effect. Several studies do in fact support the association of low CNS 5HT status with diminished concern over the consequences of one's actions, as manifested in impulsivity, aggression, and proneness toward violent suicide attempts (Brown et al., 1982; Virkkunen, Nuutila, Goodwin, & Linnoila, 1987). Cloninger has proposed that the personality dimension of "harm avoidance" is mediated by some aspect of CNS 5HT activity (Cloninger, 1987). OCD patients, high in harm avoidance and 5HT activity, would lie at one extreme, with impulsive sociopaths at the other extreme biochemically and behaviorally.

NEUROANATOMIC AND NEUROPSYCHOLOGICAL FINDINGS

Neuroanatomical Localization

The onset of OCD following head trauma (McKeon, McGuffin, & Robinson, 1984), epilepsy (Kettl & Marks, 1986), and von Economo's encephalitis (Schilder, 1938), as well as its association with neurological abnormalities (Grimshaw, 1964), point to neurological damage as a cause of OCD in some patients.

Rapoport has recently found smaller caudates in OCD adolescents and children vs normal controls as measured by volumetric CAT scan (Rapoport & Wise, 1988). Baxter et al., using fluorodeoxyglucose and PET scanning, compared adult OCD patients with unipolar depressives and normal controls (Baxter, Phelps, et al., 1987). In the OCD group metabolic rates were significantly increased bilaterally in the orbital gyri and caudate nuclei in relation to both comparison groups. Ten OCD patients were then treated with trazadone with or without an MAOI (Baxter, Thompson et al., 1987). The 8 responders, but not the two nonresponders, showed a relative increase in glucose metabolism in the heads of the caudate nuclei compared with the metabolic rate in the ipsilateral hemisphere as a whole.

Both the CAT and PET data point to caudate abnormalities in OCD. Baxter has hypothesized that the functional activity of the orbital pre-frontal cortex in OCD has increased beyond the capacity of the caudate to integrate it (Baxter, Thompson et al., 1987). This presumably leads to mental symptoms analogous to spill over motor symptoms seen in other basal ganglia movement disorders.

Rapoport has developed a model assuming the basal ganglia function as a repository of innate motor programs as well as a gating mechanism for sensory input (Rapoport & Wise, 1988). She hypothesizes an innate releasing mechanism in the basal ganglia, consisting of a neural mechanism for recognizing specific aspects of stimuli and releasing fixed action patterns. The system includes inputs from both anterior cingulate cortex (to an internal motivation detector) and cortical association areas that converge on the ventromedial caudate. Striatal activity inhibits a tonically discharging pallidal circuit, thereby releasing thalamic neuronal firing and fixed-action patterns. Hyperactivity of the cingulate cortex or its striatal target cells could in this model generate a repetitive behavior such as compulsive hand washing in the absence of external cues of dirtiness. In a review of 198 psychiatrically disabled patients treated with stereotactic cingulotomy, however, patients with depressive disorders had the best outcome, with OCD results much less positive.

In addition to the CAT and PET findings, OCD's association with Tourette's syndrome (Cummings & Frankel, 1985; Frankel et al., 1986; Pauls, Towbin, Leckman, Zahner, & Cohen, 1986), Von Economo's encephalitis (Schilder, 1938), Meige's syndrome and perhaps Sydenham's chorea (Rapoport & Wise, 1988) are all consistent with basal ganglia involvement. The reported benefit in OCD from psychosurgical procedures is also consistent with basal ganglia–prefrontal cortex involvement (Mindus et al., 1986), as is the recent popular media report of a patient whose intractable OCD was alleviated when a bullet hit the left frontal lobe in a failed suicide attempt. Certain kinds of frontal-lobe damage leave individuals so impetuous that they seem to choose their actions without consideration of outcome, which is the opposite of OCD. Lack of association with disorders such as Huntington's and Parkinson's, however, does not support basal ganglia involvement in OCD.

Another model for OCD involves dysregulation of frontal cortical–limbic systems. Favorable outcome in intractable OCD is still being reported with capsulotomy, which lesions the anterior limb of the internal capsule to interrupt fronto–limbic connections (Mindus et al., 1986). In one study 3 patients with intractable OCD were psychosurgically treated with capsulotomy, and 2 significantly improved, as did one patient with generalized anxiety disorder and one with a phobic disorder (Mindus et al., 1986). PET scanning pre- and postoperatively showed a statistically significant reduction in glucose utilization in the orbitomedial frontal cortex following surgery. This was also true regardless of diagnosis, however, suggesting a lack of specificity of both the procedure and the PET findings for OCD.

Studying the anxiolytic effects of benzodiazepines in animals, Gray (1982) has proposed that the septo–hippocampal system, together with the 'subicular loops' (Papez' circuit) and neocortical inputs from the entorhinal area and prefrontal cortex, function as a "behavioral inhibition system." According to Gray, this system has the task of predicting the next sensory event and checking whether it actually does occur; of operating the outputs of the behavioral inhibition system if there is a mismatch between actual and predicted events (novelty) or if the predicted event is aversive (punishment or nonreward). Independent of OCD, Gray has concluded that the role of ascending serotonergic projections to the septo–hippocampal system from dorsal and medial raphe nuclei is to add information that a stimulus is associated with punishment and "to bias the operation of the septohippocampal system more strongly toward inhibition of motor behavior." In this model excessive 5HT inputs into the behavioral inhibition system would create greater expectations of danger, resulting in disruption of routine functioning as increased attention was focused on potential harm. While compulsive behavior may seem like behavioral disinhibition rather than inhibition, Gray, and we, view obsessive thoughts and rituals, including washing, as forms of excessive checking or scanning for danger, while normal functioning is inhibited. 5HT reuptake blockers could ameliorate OCD by reducing serotonergic inputs into the septo–hippocampal system.

Gray's model fits with the psychopharmacological, neuropsychological (discussed later) and biochemical data for OCD. It could also help explain instances of OCD nonresponse to 5HT reuptake blockers. To the degree that excessive needs for orderliness, symmetry, perfectionism, and so on, do not involve exaggerated perceptions of danger, they may not reflect pathological serotonergic inputs into the behavioral–inhibition system, which could account for what may prove to be their poorer response to 5HT reuptake blockers. A test of this model would be that the exacerbation of OCD symptoms seen with acute 5HT agonist challenge should involve symptoms related to harm or danger, not orderliness, perfectionism, or symmetry.

Gray's model was developed to explain benzodiazepine effects on anxiety in rats, and best fits benzodiazepine-responsive human anxiety states, of which OCD does not figure prominently. Limbic involvement may be nonspecific for anxiety in general; the finding (Reiman et al., 1986) of parahippocampal assymetry of blood flow on PET scan in panic patients who subsequently panic with lactate is consistent with this. Basal ganglia, or at least caudate involvement may be more specific for OCD, although CAT and PET studies including controls with other anxiety disorders are needed to test this. Pitman (1987) suggests that limbic and basal ganglia systems together constitute a behavioral control system, the limbic system performing a comparator function and transmitting error signals to the basal ganglia, where they are translated into behavioral output.

Neuropsychological Findings

The PET data are consistent with Flor Henry's (1983) neuropsychological test finding of bilateral (left greater than right) frontal hemisphere dysfunction in OCD. Insel and colleagues, however, found no evidence to support frontal lobe involvement; instead they noted possible difficulty in visuospatial orientation (Insel, Donnelly, Lalakea, Alterman, & Murphy, 1983). Widespread organic deficits were noted in a small portion of Insel's sample and a larger segment of Flor Henry's. Harvey notes greater perseverative difficulty on Wisconsin Card Sort in obsessionals than in patients with gross frontal lobe damage, and recommends detailed frontal lobe assessment in OCD (Harvey, 1987). We have noted occasional OCD patients with diffuse cognitive impairment as indicated by low IQ, memory and discrimination problems, and right–left confusion. More typical are those with selective neuropsychological deficits. A few show verbal learning problems or difficulty suppressing responses to irrelevant information. OCD patients tend to either take a long time to make a decision on a visual discrimination task and be accurate, or respond quickly and inaccurately, although a few are both slow and inaccurate. If decision making is the problem, then increasing the difficulty of the task should not affect response time as much as if a primary cognitive defect is present, so future studies should vary task difficulty. Further studies of frontal lobe and basal ganglia–limbic function in conjunction with imaging, biochemistry, and treatment, are needed.

Decision-making and memory studies offer some support for abnormal neuropsychological functioning in OCD. Carr (1974) found that in all situations, OCD patients had an abnormally high subjective estimate of the probability of occurrence of unfavorable outcome. In a separate risk-taking study, compulsive patients were found to be the most cautious of all psychiatric groups (Carr, 1974). Because OCD patients consider certain undesired outcomes extremely likely, situations that have a potentially harmful outcome (germs, unlocked doors, etc.), no matter how unlikely, will be seen as potentially dangerous.

Overconcern about possible danger does not distinguish OCD from generalized anxiety. OCD patients are usually particularly focused, however, on one or more forms of possible harm to themselves or others or to property. This could be fundamental, or secondary to another unique feature of OCD, the inability to feel certain about things (Are my hands clean?, Is the gas fully turned off?, Did I push that person off the train platform?). Gray (1982), Klein (personal communication, 1987), and Pitman (1987) have independently hypothesized that OCD patients suffer dysfunction in brain match–mismatch mechanisms. Klein speculates that OCD patients require such a high level of concordance for a data–hypothesis fit that they are constantly plagued by doubt. Gray suggests that the septo–hippocampal system also functions to detect a mismatch between the intended outcome of a motor program and its actual outcome. In cybernetic terms, Pitman suggests that the core problem in OCD is the persistence of high error signals, or mismatch, that cannot be reduced to zero through behavioral output. Possible causes include conflict, intrinsic comparator defect, and attentional disturbance. Pitman's model offers a common explanation for features of OCD, obsessive–compulsive personality (OCP) and tics, while other data suggest pathophysiological discontinuities.

Taken together, the biochemical, neuroanatomic, and neuropsychological findings in OCD suggest the following schematic model. A key feature of OCD, as recognized by Aubrey Lewis (1935), was the feeling of subjective compulsion, of being forced to think or do something against one's desire or will. Current thinking is that subcortical systems in the limbic system and basal ganglia, together with frontal and inferior temporal association areas, function as an emotional modulator for the neocortex, endowing thoughts with varying degrees of anxiety. Thoughts and perceptions are run through subcortical processing via frontal and inferior temporal association areas (Nauta & Feirtag, 1986). Heightened serotonergic imputs to limbic (?septo-hippocampal), basal ganglia (?caudate) and/or frontal association cortex (?medial orbital frontal gyrus) may lower the threshold for alarm reactions to neocortical inputs. Increased serotonergic inputs could result from decreased inhibitory autoreceptor activity, increased noradrenergic input, or increased 5HT precursor availability to medial and dorsal raphe 5HT neurons, which project via the median forebrain bundle to limibic, basal ganglia, and neocortical (especially medial orbital frontal) structures (Aghajanian & Rasmussen, 1987). The net result is that feedback to the neocortex from limbic and basal ganglia alarm systems is at odds with the cortex's own nonthreatening cognitive appraisal of the situation. This mismatch activates frontal motor circuits to scan again (check, wash, etc.) for possible danger. The neocortex again perceives no threat, only to get an alarm reaction once more from the pathologically activated subcortical system or via the pathologically activated frontal association area. By normalizing 5HT activity and alarm functions in subcortical structures and/or in frontal association areas, 5HT reuptake blockers help OCD. A limitation of the model is that it does not explain the particular symptom selectivity of OCD in general or for any given patient.

OTHER PATHOPHYSIOLOGICAL MODELS

Noradrenergic abnormalities may also occur in OCD. Siever et al. (1983) found a blunted growth hormone (GH) response to the alpha 2 adrenergic agonist clonidine. The OCD patients also had increased baseline free 3-methoxy-4-hydroxyphenylglycol (MHPG) and norepinephrine (NE) compared to controls, suggesting increased presynaptic NE activity and compensatory decrease in postsynaptic alpha 2 adrenergic sensitivity, although the reverse causal sequence could also apply. Their findings were independent of associated depressive features. OCD patients have also been found to have greater CSF MHPG variability at baseline (Thoren et al., 1980b). Case studies report OCD amelioration with oral clonidine, alone or in combination with CMI (Lipsedge & Prothero, 1987). Transient amelioration of OCD following single dose intravenous clonidine has been observed in our laboratory (Hollander et al., 1988). While most closely linked to the noradrenergic system, clonidine may indirectly reduce 5HT turnover. Central noradrenergic inputs into the rat septohippocampal system are thought to tag stimuli as sufficiently important to require careful checking (Gray, 1982). Decreasing noradrenergic input also causes decreased firing of 5HT raphe neurons projecting to cortical and subcortical structures (Aghajanian, Sprouse, & Rasmussen, 1987).

The overlap of OCD and neuroleptic responsive Tourette's syndrome (discussed later) (Cummings & Frankel, 1985; Frankel et al., 1986; Pauls et al., 1986), occasional benefit in OCD with amphetamine (Insel, Hamilton et al., 1983b) or monoamine oxidase inhibitors (Isberg, 1981; Jenike, 1981), dopaminergic sensitivity of ritualistic animal displacement behavior, and the occurrence of stereotypic behavior with amphetamine toxicity, have suggested dopaminergic involvement in OCD. Weighing against this are the lack of neuroleptic efficacy in OCD, and the lack of a subjective sense of compulsion in amphetamine-induced perseverative behavior. Amphetamine benefit in OCD also tends to be transient.

Dopaminergic neural activity in OCD could mediate particular compulsive behaviors such as touching or symmetry, which seem to occur more frequently in OCD patients who also have schizophrenia (Fenton & McGlashan, 1986) or Tourette's syndrome (Pitman et al., 1987). It could also push OCD patients into frankly paranoid states, transform obsessions into overvalued ideas in which reality testing is marginal, or give rise to unrelated psychotic or schizotypal features. Several investigators suggest that OCD with psychotic features be diagnosed "obsessive psychosis," which they consider a distinct disorder with a worse prognosis than OCD (Solyom, DiNicola, Phil, Sookamn, & Luchins, 1985).

Neuroleptics have been found helpful for OCD with distinct paranoid features (Rivers-Bulkeldy & Hollander, 1982). Alternatively, OCD represents a psychopathological spectrum varying along a continuum of insight but with a common pathophysiology, as suggested by Insel and Akiskal (1986). They note that at times OCD patients with psychotic features improve with 5HT reuptake blockers. Lapses of otherwise typical OCD patients into psychosis could be mediated by stress-induced activation of the hypothalamic–pituitary–adrenal cortical axis, which in turn raises CNS dopamine levels, a mechanism suggested by Schatzberg to explain delusional forms of depression (Schatzberg, unpublished data, 1988). In this model, CMI could help OCD with psychotic features by treating the underlying 5HT disturbance.

In the two reported studies that examined dopamine metabolite levels in OCD, patients and normal controls did not differ significantly in CSF homovanillic acid (HVA) (Thoren et al., 1980b, Insel et al., 1985). However, prior to treatment, patients who went on to respond to CMI had higher HVA levels than nonresponders, paralleling the finding with 5-HIAA. While HVA and 5-HIAA were positively correlated prior to treatment, HVA went up while 5-HIAA went down with CMI. The data do not support separate 5HT and dopaminergically mediated patient subsets in the group studied, as the CMI nonresponders had baseline HVA levels quite similar to normals.

Animal displacement behaviors often involve grooming, checking, or nesting (?hoarding) activities under inappropriate conditions such as a territorial conflict. According to Holland (1974), displacement behaviors help animals cope with externally induced high arousal stemming from motivational conflict, frustration, or thwarting. Compulsive rituals are viewed as a human form of displacement behavior. Insel relates animal ritualistic behavior more specifically to threat from a member of the same species, viewing displacement behavior as helping to avoid conflict, channel aggression, and appease a more dominant individual (Winslow & Insel, 1988). If low 5HT levels predispose to aggressive responses, high 5HT individuals might be most prone to avoid aggressive encounters through displacement activities. However, high platelet 5HT levels have been associated with alpha male status in vervet monkeys (Raleigh, McGuire, Brammer, & Yuwiler, 1984).

OCD could represent an endogenous opiate deficit state. No reports of opiate treatment of OCD have been published, but acute challenge with the narcotic antagonist nalaxone exacerbated OCD in 2 patients (Insel & Pickar, 1983). Clonidine, which alleviates many symptoms of narcotic withdrawal, transiently alleviates OCD (Hollander et al., 1988). In dogs, both centrally injected 5HT and peripherally administered CMI pretreatment potentiate the effects of morphine and synthetic enkephalin (Sewell & Lee, 1980), a possible mechanism by which 5HT reuptake blockers help OCD.

ASSOCIATED CONDITIONS

The longitudinal and etiological relationships of OCD and OCP are unclear. One view is that a continuum exists from normal obsessional behavior to OCP to OCD, depending on the degree to which obsessional defenses dominate (Salzman & Thaler, 1981). OCD is seen as a decompensation of milder obsessional tendencies. OCD patients show preexisting poorly defined obsessive "traits" or "features" in 70% to 100% of cases, depending on the series (Rasmussen & Tsuang, 1986). In addition to being retrospective, however, these studies do not distinguish between subsyndromal OCD features and obsessional personality traits. The causal sequence could also be the reverse; that is, a diathesis toward OCD could manifest itself as OCP, and prospective studies are needed. While etiological thinking concerning OCP continues to focus on disturbed child–parent interactions (Pollack, 1987), biochemical and neuropsychiatric factors have received little attention. That individuals with OCP perceive relationships largely in terms of dominance and submission provides theoretical linkages with animal displacement behavior and 5HT activity.

OCD has some as yet unclear relationship to affective disorder. Depression is a frequent complication of OCD; in one recent series all 44 OCD patients had secondary or concurrent affective disorder (Rasmussen & Tsuang, 1986). While possibly a nonspecific reaction to the psychosocial disruption of the OCD, there is evidence for some overlap of mechanisms. Affective swings clearly tend to interact with OCD, depression usually exacerbating and hypomania or mania alleviating it. Secondary depression in OCD almost always takes an agitated form, possibly occurring when patients no longer feel able to cope with excessive fears. The ameliorative effects of hypomania could stem from reduction in these same fears. Biologically, OCD and depression have both been found to produce blunted growth hormone response to clonidone, reduced platelet imipramine binding (Weizman et al., 1986), and shortened REM latency (Insel et al., 1982).

A variety of evidence argues for the distinctness of OCD and affective disorder, including earlier age of onset and greater male to female ratio in OCD (Insel & Zohar, 1987). OCD patients had more stage 1 and 3 sleep and less rapid eye movement (REM) density early in the night than unipolar depressives (Insel et al., 1982). A retrospective followup study of hospitalized OCD and unipolar depressive patients found the OCD group to be less likely to have a family history of affective disorder, a remission during followup, or to die of unnatural causes such as suicide (Coryell, 1981). Other than the 5HT reuptake blockers, otherwise effective antidepressants and ECT do not appear very helpful for OCD. Also, with those drugs useful in both conditions, OCD often requires an 8 to 12 rather than the usual 4 to 6 week trial. Recent instances of imipramine (Foa et al., 1987) helping depression but not OCD in patients with both conditions also argue for pathophysiological dissimilarity.

The relationship between OCD and Tourette's syndrome is also puzzling. The two conditions occur together more frequently than expected by chance (Cummings & Frankel, 1985; Frankel et al., 1986; Pauls et al., 1986). Tourette's patients have a higher then expected incidence of first degree relatives with OCD, irrespective of whether the Tourette proband has OCD (Pauls et al., 1986). Some of the Tourette's patients' relatives had OCD exhibited only motor or vocal tics, or neither, leading to the hypothesis that a subtype of OCD may be due to partial expression of the gene for Tourette's syndrome (Comings & Comings, 1987). Clinical similarities between Tourette's and OCD, their familial association, and the fact that both were observed as symptoms of known basal ganglia disturbances (i.e., post encephalitic states), led Cummings and Frankel to hypothesize, prior to recent OCD CAT and PET findings, that Tourette's and OCD were due to related basal ganglia disturbances (Cummings & Frankel, 1985). Recent findings of CAT and PET caudate abnormalities in OCD are consistent with this.

Unlike OCD, Tourette's syndrome appears predominantly dopaminergically mediated. Elevated CSF HVA levels have been demonstrated. Tourette's patients respond to haloperidol, but inconsistently to 5HT reuptake blockers. Clonidine, however, may be helpful for some Tourette and OCD patients. While Tourette's syndrome involves repetitive purposeless involuntary movements that relieve tension, and OCD involves repetitive purposeful voluntary behavior, OCD patients cannot always explain why they perform a compulsive act. Certain kinds of compulsive behaviors such as touching and symmetry occur more often in Tourette's disorder than in OCD (Pitman et al., 1987). They are also common in the relatives of Tourette's patients, although checking and contamination fears are also seen. In a schizophrenic sample with concomitant OCD, washing and contamination fears were as prevalent as usual in OCD, but various rituals interfering with locomotion (stepping on cracks, rituals before entering doorways, touching, hopping) appeared more frequent (Fenton & McGlashan, 1986). OCD involving symmetry usually occurs in males, has an earlier age of onset, and responds less well to 5HT reuptake blockers (Rasmussen & Tsuang, 1986). Symmetry and/or touching could be dopaminergically rather than serotonergically mediated.

EPIDEMIOLOGICAL AND FAMILIAL FEATURES OF OCD

OCD used to be considered an uncommon condition affecting no more than 0.05% of the population. However, an epidemiological survey of 6,000 New Jersey teenagers, in which possible cases were followed up with clinical interviews, found 18 OCD cases, for a prevalence rate of 0.3% (Leonard, 1987). Data from the Epidemiological Catchment Area (ECA) study suggest a 6-month prevalence of 1% to 2% of the adult U.S. population, much higher than previously thought (Myers et al., 1984). ECA criteria, however, lack standards for symptom severity, and undoubtedly give inflated estimates of clinical illness by including subclinical cases who are not functionally impaired or severely distressed. Conservatively assuming that 10% of the ECA cases would meet OCD criteria on clinical exam, 100,000 to 200,000 Americans may be affected at any one time.

Existing twin studies of obsessional probands and limited family studies of OCD patients suggest heritability of an OCD spectrum defined to include subsyndromal OCD symptoms or OCP features (Carey & Gottesman, 1981). These include heightened concern about cleanliness or perfectionism that are not ego dystonic or resisted, and not a great source of interference to the affected individual. Distinctions between subsyndromal OCD features and OCP traits are not clearly drawn. OCD, strictly defined, has not been found to significant excess in the first-degree relatives of OCD patients compared to controls. Interpretation of existing family studies in OCD is limited by the absence of control groups in some studies, failure to use and/or publish operational diagnostic criteria, and inclusion of probands with additional or different disorders. None of the existing studies examined relatives blind to proband diagnosis. Lack of clarity concerning the "unit" of transmission, the possible influence of proband comorbidity, and the possibility of etiological heterogeneity within the OCD category, also complicate OCD family studies. Hyoptheses about disturbed familial interactions contributing to OCD have been offered (Hoover & Insel, 1984), but not studied in a controlled fashion.

INTEGRATING PSYCHOANALYTIC AND PSYCHOBIOLOGICAL PERSPECTIVES

Briefly summarizing psychoanalytic thinking on OCD, obsessive–compulsive patients are thought to be unable to cope with the instinctual conflicts of the Oedipal stage, and to have regressed to the preOedipal anal erotic phase of psychosexual development. Hostile and sexual impulses, initially toward the parents, and later others, are handled primarily via the defense mechanisms of isolation, displacement, reaction formation, and undoing, which are thought to generate the obsessive–compulsive symptoms.

There are a number of problems with the psychoanalytic model of OCD. Most important, highly interpretive, psychodynamically based treatment efforts have not generally been successful for the chronic OCD patient (Salzman & Thaler, 1981; Nemiah, 1984). Psychoanalytic investigators such as Salzman now suggest more limited psychodynamic techniques for long-term psychotherapy of OCD, such as exploration of excessive feelings of insecurity that make the patient require absolute guarantees before action is pursued. Therapists should also demonstrate by both interpretation and encouragement to action that such guarantees are a hindrance, not a necessity. This treatment approach is compatible with biological models of OCD. Acute OCD reactions and OCP are still viewed more optimistically by psychoanalytically oriented practitioners, though here too controlled studies are lacking.

The frequent failure of an exclusively psychodynamic approach to OCD lies, we believe, in its addressing symptoms rather than pathophysiologically mediating factors. In his classic description of the Rat Man, Freud described the analysis of a case of obsessional neurosis (Freud, 1958a). In brief, the patient, a young military officer, had become tormented by the thought that if he repaid a certain debt, a woman he loved, or his father (several years deceased), might undergo great harm, including having a rat eat through his or her anus. Freud linked the obsessional thoughts to unconscious psychic conflicts, especially repressed hostile impulses toward the father. Analytic therapy of less than a year's duration reportedly resulted in symptom remission. Longterm followup was impossible as the patient was killed in the First World War.

Freud noted that while repressed murderous feelings toward the father stemming from childhood were likely to result in neurosis, there was nothing in the nature of these psychosexual conflicts per se to produce obsessive–compulsive neurosis. Rather, some other "dispositional" factor also had to be present to specifically produce OCD. Freud later hyopthesized this to be a developmental fixation at the pregenital psychosexual stage of anal eroticism or sadism (Freud, 1958b). Freud also noted, however, that delineation of what factors actually brought about such disturbance of development would be left to biological research. Freud speculated that in the case of the Rat Man, the sadistic components of love had, from constitutional causes, been exceptionally strongly developed, and had consequently undergone a premature suppression.

Implicit in the early psychoanalytic formulation of OCD was the idea that biological abnormalities of some kind might skew the developmental process, forcing individuals into patterns of maladaptive coping with internal as well as external forces. Over time, however, the biological half of Freud's original equation, that underlying constitutional abnormalities shaped the "choice" of OCD as a neurosis, received increasingly less attention in psychoanalytic formulations of OCD.

The ramifications for psychosexual development of the neuropsychological deficits proposed for OCD would be profound. Occasional hostile or sexual impulses toward a parent, almost certainly ubiquitous in children, become much more frightening because of the heightened concern that they might occur, or even that they did occur. This would give rise to greater feelings of danger associated with normal psychosexual impulses. Magical thinking, which most adults turn to in the form of prayer and/or superstition to help them cope with danger or uncertainty, would also make sense in this context. For the Rat Man, the key feature is that once he had the terrifying thought that the rat torture could happen to a loved one, which in itself may not be abnormal, it became a cause of great alarm because he began to worry that it might really happen. This led to the use of magical thinking—if he did not repay a debt directly to the person to whom he owed it, his loved ones would suffer no harm. But then he became obsessed with how to indirectly repay the debt.

DIRECTIONS FOR FUTURE RESEARCH

The mechanisms of OCD and its treatment need to be further elucidated through integrated biochemical, challenge, imaging, and neuropsychological studies before and after drug and psychosocial treatment. The degree to which biochemical and neuropsychiatric abnormalities overlap or occur in distinct OCD subsets can be determined by simultaneous investigation of both areas. OCD subtypes may be elucidated by comparison of responders and nonresponders to different treatments. Family studies complemented by psychobiological investigations may be particularly useful in OCD, given the suggestions of pathophysiological heterogeneity. If familial transmission can be established, studies with DNA markers may be feasible.

The degree to which OCD is pathophysiologically distinct from the other anxiety disorders, as is now suggested by differences in pharmacological responsivity, will require further comparison with panic, generalized anxiety disorder (GAD), social phobia, and so on. The same applies to OCD vs affective and psychotic disorders, Tourette's body dysmorphic disorder, trichotillomania, etc. Further studies of 5HT function in a variety of psychiatric states is needed to clarify the notion of harm avoidance as 5HT mediated.

Reasons for clinical nonresponse need to be further understood by intensive study of treatment failures. Whether the different 5HT reuptake blockers have the same spectrum is unclear, and head-to-head comparisons or crossover studies may be needed. For example, we have the impression that CMI is more effective than fluoxetine for OCD complicated by agitated depression. The relative indications for drug or behavior therapy or the combination are also unclear, as is the utility of intravenous CMI. No or few studies have as yet been reported with other serotonergic agents such as the 5HT reuptake blocker sertraline, 5-HT1A receptor agonists such as buspirone or gepirone, 5-HT1B agonists such as mCPP administered chronically, 5HT receptor antagonists such as metergoline or ritansarin, 5HT releasers such as fenfluramine or 5HT synthesis inhibitors such as parachlorophenylalanine (PCPA).

After a period of relative neglect, the knowledge base in OCD is advancing as fast as that of any psychiatric disorder. Also as with other psychiatric disorders, much remains to be done.

REFERENCES

Aghajanian, G. K., Sprouse, J. S., & Rasmussen, K. (1987). Physiology of the midbrain serotonin system. In H. Y. Meltzer (Ed.), *Psychopharmacology, the third generation of progress* (pp. 141–149). New York: Raven Press.

American Psychological Association. (1987). *Diagnostical and statistical manual of mental disorders, third edition, revised.* Washington, DC: Author.

Ananth, J., Pecknold, J., Van Den Steen, N., & Engelsmann, F. (1981). Double-blind comparative study of clomipramine and amitriptyline in obsessive neurosis. *Progress in Neuro-Psychopharmacology and Biological Psychiatry, 5,* 257–262.

Ananth, J., Solyom, L., & Sookm, D. (1975). Doxepin in the treatment of obsessive compulsive neurosis. *Psychomatics, XVI,* 185–187.

Annsseau, M., Legros, J., Mormont, C., Cerfontaine, J., Papart, P., Geenen, V., Adam, F., & Franck, G. (1987). Intranasal oxytocin in obsessive–compulsive disorder. *Psychoneuroendocrinology, 12,* 231–236.

Baron, M., Barkai, A., Gruen, R., Peselow, E., Fieve, R. R., & Quitkin, F. (1986). Platelet imipramine binding in affective disorders: Trait versus state characteristics. *American Journal of Psychiatry, 143,* 711–717.

Baxter, L., Phelps, M., Mazziotta, J., Guze, B., Schwartz, J., & Seline, C. (1987). Local cerebral glucose metabolic rates in obsessive–compulsive disorder: A comparison with rates in unipolar depression and in normal controls. *Archives of General Psychiatry, 44,* 211–218.

Baxter, L., Thompson, J., Schwartz, J., Guze, B., Phelps, M., Mazziotta, J., Selin, C., & Moss, L. (1987). Trazodone treatment response in obsessive–compulsive disorder-correlated with shifts in glucose metabolism in the caudate nuclei. *Psychopathology, 20,* 114–122.

Brown, G., Ebert, M., Goyer, P., Jimerson, D., Klein, W., Bunney, W., & Goodwin, F. (1982). Aggression, suicide, and serotonin: Relationships to CSF amine metabolites. *American Journal of Psychiatry, 139,* 741–746.

Carey, G., & Gottesman, II. (1981). Twin and family studies of anxiety, phobic, and obsessive disorders. In D. F. Klein & J. Rabkin (Eds.), *Anxiety: New research and changing concepts* (pp. 117–135). New York: Raven Press.

Carr, A. (1974). Compulsive neurosis: A review of the literature. *Psychological Bulletin, 81,* 311–318.

Casas, M., Alvarez, E., Duro, P., Garcia-Ribera, C., Udina, C., Velat, A., Abella, D., Rodriguez-Espinoza, J., Salva, P., & Jane, F. (1986). Antiandrogenic treatment of obsessive–compulsive neurosis. *Acta Psychiatrica Scandinavica, 73,* 221–222.

Charney, D., Goodman, W., Price, L., Woods, S., Rasmussen, S., & Heninger, G. (1988). Serotonin function in obsessive–compulsive disorder. *Archives of General Psychiatry, 45,* 177–185.

Cloninger, C. R. (1987). A unified biosocial theory of personality and its role in the development of anxiety states. *Psychiatric Development, 3,* 167–226.

Comings, D., & Comings, B. (1987). Hereditary agoraphobia and obsessive–compulsive behavior in relatives of patients with Gilles de la Tourette's syndrome. *British Journal of Psychiatry, 151,* 195–199.

Coryell, W. (1981). Obsessive–compulsive disorder and primary unipolar depression: Comparisons of background, family, history, course and mortality. *Journal of Nervous and Mental Disease, 169,* 220–224.

Cummings, J., & Frankel, M. (1985). Gilles de la Tourette syndrome and the neurological basis of obsessions and compulsions. *Biological Psychiatry, 20,* 1117–1126.

Fenton, W., & McGlashan, T. (1986). The prognostic significance of obsessive–compulsive symptoms in schizophrenia. *American Journal of Psychiatry, 143,* 437–441.

Falment, M., & Rapoport, J. (1989). Prospective followup study of adolescents. In J. Rapoport (Ed.), *Obsessive compulsive disorder in children and adolescents.* Washington, DC: APPI Press.

Falment, M., Rapoport, J., Berg, C., Sceery, W., Kilts, C., Mellstrom, B., & Linnoila, M. (1985). Clomipramine treatment of childhood obsessive–compulsive disorder: A double-blind controlled study. *Archives of General Psychiatry, 42,* 977–983.

Flament, M., Rapoport, J., Murphy, D., Berg, C., & Lake, R. (1987). Biochemical changes during clomipramine treatment of childhood obsessive–compulsive disorder. *Archives of General Psychiatry, 44,* 219–225.

Flor-Henry, P. (1983). The obsessive–compulsive syndrome. In J. Wright (Ed.), *Cerebral basis of psychopathology* (pp. 301–311). Boston: John Wright.

Foa, E., Steketee, G., Kozak, M., & Dugger, D. (1987). Effects of imipramine on depression and obsessive compulsive symptoms. *Psychiatric Research, 21,* 123–136.

Fontaine, R., & Chouinard, G. (1986). An open clinical trial of fluoxetine in the treatment of obsessive–compulsive disorder. *Journal of Clinical Psychopharmacology, 6,* 98–101.

Frankel, M., Cummings, J., Robertson, M., Trimble, M., Hill, M., & Benson, F. (1986). Obsessions and compulsions in Gilles de la Tourette's syndrome. *Neurology, 4336,* 1180–1182.

Freud, S. (1958a). Notes upon a case of obsessional neurosis (1909). In J. Strachey (Ed.), *The standard edition of the complete psychological works of Freud, X* (pp. 153–319). London: Hogarth Press.

Freud, S. (1958b). The disposition to obsessional neurosis (1913). In J. Strachey (Ed.), *The standard edition of the complete psychological works of Freud, XII* (pp. 153–319). London: Hogarth Press.

Gray, J. (1982). *The neuropsychology of anxiety.* New York: Oxford University Press.

Grimshaw, L. (1964). Obsessional disorder and neurological illness. *Journal of Neurology, Neurosurgery, and Psychiatry, 27,* 229–231.

Harvey, N. (1987). Neurological factors in obsessive–compulsive disorder. *British Journal of Psychiatry,* 567–568.

Hollander, E., Fay, M., & Liebowitz, M. (1988). Serotonergic and noradrenergic function in obsessive–compulsive disorder. *American Journal of Psychiatry, 145*, 1015–1017.

Holland, H. (1974). Displacement activity as a form of abnormal behaviour in animals. In H. Beech (Ed.), *Obsessional states.* London: Methuen.

Hoover, C., & Insel, T. (1984). Families of origin in obsessive compulsive disorder. *Journal of Nervous and Mental Disease, 172*, 207–215.

Insel, T., & Akiskal, H. (1986). Obsessive compulsive disorder with psychotic features: A phenomenologic analysis. *American Journal of Psychiatry, 143*, 1527–1533.

Insel, T., Donnelly, E., Lalakea, M., Alterman, I., & Murphy, D. (1983). Neurological and neuropsychological studies of patients with obsessive–compulsive disorder. *Biological Psychiatry, 18*, 741–751.

Insel, T., Gillin, C., Moore, A., Mendelson, W., Loewenstein, R., & Murphy D. (1982). The sleep of patients with obsessive–compulsive disorder. *Archives of General Psychiatry, 39*, 1372–1377.

Insel, T., Hamilton, J., Guttmacher, L., & Murphy, D. (1983). D-amphetamine in obsessive–compulsive disorder. *Psychopharmacology, 80*, 231–235.

Insel, T., Mueller, E., Alterman, I., Linnoila, M., & Murphy, D. (1985). Obsessive–compulsive disorder and serotonin: Is there a connection? *Biological Psychiatry, 20*, 1174–1188.

Insel, T., Murphy, D., Cohen, R., Alterman, I., Kilts, C., & Linnoila, M. (1983). Obsessive–compulsive disorder: a double-blind trial of clomipramine and clorgyline. *Archives of General Psychiatry, 40*, 605–612.

Insel, T., & Pickar, D. (1983). Naloxone administration in obsessive–compulsive disorder: Report of two cases. *American Journal of Psychiatry, 140*, 1219–1220.

Insel, T., & Zohar, J. (1987). Pharmacological approaches to obsessive compulsive disorder. In H. Y. Meltzer (Ed.), *Psychopharmacology, the third generation of progress.* New York: Raven Press.

Isberg, R. (1981). A comparison of phenelzine and imipramine in an obsessive–compulsive patient. *American Journal of Psychiatry, 138*, 1250–1251.

Jenike, M. (1981). MAOI for obsessive compulsive disorder. *American Journal of Psychiatry, 138*, 1249–1250.

Jenike, M., Baer, L., Minichiello, W., Schwartz, C., & Carey, R. (1986). Concomitant obsessive–compulsive disorder and schizotypal personality disorder. *American Journal of Psychiatry, 143*, 530–532.

Joffe, R., & Swinson, R. (1987). Carbamazepine in obsessive–compulsive disorder. *Biological Psychiatry, 22*, 1169–1171.

Kahn, R., & Jolles, J. (1984). Zimeldine treatment of obsessive–compulsive disorder: Biological and neuropsychological aspects. *Acta Psychiatrica Scandinavica, 69*, 259–261.

Kandel, E. (1983). From metapsychology to molecular biology: Explorations into the nature of anxiety. *American Journal of Psychiatry, 140*, 1277–1293.

Kettl, P., & Marks, I. (1986). Neurological factors in obsessive compulsive disorder. Two case reports and a review of the literature. *British Journal of Psychiatry, 149*, 315–319.

Leonard, H. (Oct. 8, 1987). *OCD and OC personality in childhood.* Presented at

Obsessions and Rituals: New Findings in Research and Treatment, Providence, RI.

Lewis, A. (1935). Problem of obsessional illness. *Proceedings of the Royal Society of Medicine, XXIX*, 325–336.

Lipsedge, M., & Prothero, M. (1987). Clonidine and clomipramine in obsessive–compulsive disorder. *American Journal of Psychiatry, 144*, 965–966.

Marks, I. (1981). Review of behavioral psychotherapy, I: Obsessive–compulsive disorders. *American Journal of Psychiatry, 138*, 584–592.

Marks, I., Stern, R., Mawson, S., Cobb, J., & McDonald, R. (1980). Clomipramine and exposure for obsessive–compulsive rituals. *British Journal of Psychiatry, 136*, 1–25.

Mavissakalian, M., Turner, S., Michelson, L., & Jacob, R. (1985). Tricyclic antidepressants in obsessive–compulsive disorder: Antiobsessional or antidepressant agents? *American Journal of Psychiatry, 142*, 572–576.

McKenna, P. (1984). Disorders with overvalued ideas. *British Journal of Psychiatry, 145*, 579–585.

McKeon, J., McGuffin, P., & Robinson, P. (1984). Obsessive–compulsive neurosis following head injury: A report of four cases. *British Journal of Psychiatry, 144*, 190–192.

Mindus, P., Ericson, K., Greitz, T., Meyerson, B., Nyman, H., & Sjogren, I. (1986). Regional cerebral glucose metabolism in anxiety disorders studied with positron emission tomography before and after psychosurgical intervention. *Acta Radiologica Supplementum, 369*, 444–448.

Montgomery, S. (1980). Clomipramine in obsessional neurosis: A placebo-controlled trial. *Pharmacological Medicine, 37*, 1281–1285.

Myers, J., Weissman, M., Tischler, G., Holzer, C., Leaf, P., Orvaschel, H., Anthony, J., Boyd, J., Burke, J., Kramer, M., & Stoltzman, R. (1984). Six-month prevalence of psychiatric disorders in three communities: 1980–1982. *Archives of General Psychiatry, 41*, 959–967.

Nauta, W., Feirtag, M. (1986). *Fundamental neuroanotomy*. New York: W. H. Freeman & Co.

Nemiah, J. (1984). Foreward. In T. R. Insel (Ed.) *Obsessive compulsive disorder.* Washington DC: APA Press, Inc.

Pato, M. Zohar-Kadouch, R., Zohar, J., Murphy, D. L. (1988). Return of symptoms after discontinuation of clomipramine in patients with obsessive–compulsive disorder. *American Journal of Psychiatry, 145*, 1521–1525.

Pauls, D., Towbin, K., Leckman, J., Zahner, G., & Cohen, D. (1986). Gilles de la Tourette's syndrome and obsessive–compulsive disorder: Evidence supporting a genetic relationship. *Archives of General Psychiatry, 43*, 1180–1182.

Perse, T., Greist, J., Jefferson, J., Rosenfeld, R., & Reuven, D. (1987). Fluvoxamine treatment of obsessive–compulsive disorder. *American Journal of Psychiatry, 144*, 1543–1548.

Pitman, R. (1987). A cybernetic model of obsessive–compulsive psychopathology. *Comprehensive Psychiatry, 28*, 334–343.

Pitman, R., Green, R., Jenike, M., & Mesulam, M. (1987). Clinical comparison of

Tourette's disorder and obsessive–compulsive disorder. *American Journal of Psychiatry, 144,* 1166–1171.

Pollack, J. (1987). Obsessive–compulsive personality: Theoretical and clinical perspectives and recent research findings. *Journal of Personality Disorders, 1,* 249–262.

Prasad, A. (1984). A double blind study of imipramine versus zimeldine in treatment obsessive compulsive neurosis. *Pharmacopsychiatry, 17,* 61–62.

Prasad, A. (1985). Efficacy of trazodone as an anti obsessional agent. *Pharmacology, Biochemistry and Behavior, 22,* 347–348.

Price, L., Goodman, W., Charney, D., Rasmussen, S., & Heninger, G. (1987). Treatment of severe obsessive–compulsive disorder with fluvoxamine. *American Journal of Psychiatry, 144,* 1059–1061.

Rachman, S., Cobb, J., Grey, S., McDonald, B., Mawson, D., Sartory, G., & Stern, R. (1979). The behavioural treatment of obsessional–compulsive disorders, with and without clomipramine. *Behaviour Research and Therapy, 17,* 467–478.

Rack, P. (1973). Clomipramine (Anafranil) in the treatment of obsessional states with special reference to the Leyton Obsessional Inventory. *Journal of International Medical Research, 1,* 397–402.

Rack, P. (1977). Clinical experience in the treatment of obsessional states (2). *Journal of International Medical Research, 5,* 81–90.

Raleigh, M., McGuire, M., Brammer, G., & Yuwiler, A. (1984). Social and environmental influences on blood serotonin concentrations in monkeys. *Archives of General Psychiatry, 41,* 405–410.

Rapoport, J., & Mikkelson, E. (1980). Clinical controlled trial of chlorimipramine in adolescents with obsessive–compulsive disorder. *Psychopharmacology Bulletin, 16,* 61–63.

Rapoport, J., & Wise, S. (1988). Obsessive–compulsive disorder: A basal ganglia disease? In J. Rapoport (Ed.), *Obsessive–compulsive disorder in children and adolescents* (pp. 327–344). Washington, DC: APPI Press.

Rasmussen, S. (1984). Lithium and tryptophan augmentation in clomipramine-resistant obsessive–compulsive disorder. *Am J Psychiat, 141,* 1283–1285.

Rasmussen, S., Goodman, W., Woods, S., Heninger, G., & Charney, D. (1987). Effects of yohimbine in obsessive conpulsive disorder. *Psychopharmacology, 93,* 308–313.

Rasmussen, S., & Tsuang, M. (1986). Clinical characteristics and family history in DSM III obsessive–compulsive disorder. *Am J Psychiat, 143,* 317–322.

Reiman, E., Raichle, M., Robins, E., Butler, F., Herscovitch, P., Fox, P., & Perlmutter, J. (1986). The application of positron emission tomography to the study of panic disorder. *American Journal of Psychiatry, 143,* 469–477.

Rivers-Bulkeldy, N., & Hollender, M. (1982). Successful treatment of obsessive-compulsive disorder with loxapine. *American Journal of Psychiatry, 139,* 1345–1347.

Salzman, L., & Thaler, F. (1981). Obsessive–compulsive disorders: A review of the literature. *American Journal of Psychiatry, 138,* 286–296.

Schilder, P. (1938). The organic background of obsessions and compulsions. *American Journal of Psychiatry, 94,* 1397–1416.

Sewell, R., & Lee, T. (1980). Opiate receptors, endorphins and drug therapy. *Postgraduate Medical Journal, 56,* 25–30.

Siever, L. J., Insel, T. R., Jimerson, D. C., Lake, C. R., Uhde, T. W., Aloi, J., & Murphy, D. L. (1983). Growth hormone response to clonidine in obsessive–compulsive patients. *British Journal of Psychiatry, 142,* 184–187.

Solyom, L., DiNicola, V., Phil, M., Sookamn, D., & Luchins, D. (1985). Is there an obsessive psychosis? Aetiological and prognostic factors of an atypical form of obsessive–compulsive neurosis. *Canadian Journal of Psychiatry, 30,* 372–380.

Steketee, G., Foa, E., & Grayson, J. (1982). Recent Advances in the behavioral treatment of obsessive–compulsives. *Archives of General Psychiatry, 39,* 1365–1371.

Stern, R., Marks, I., Mawson, D., & Luscombe, D. (1980). Clomipramine and exposure for compulsive rituals: II. Plasma levels, side effects and outcome. *British Journal of Psychiatry, 136,* 161–166.

Thoren, P., Asberg, M., Cronholm, B., Jornestedt, L., & Traskman, L. (1980a). Clomipramine treatment of obsessive–compulsive disorder. *Archives of General Psychiatry, 37,* 1281–1285.

Thoren, P., Asberg, M., Bertillson, L., Mellstrom, B., Pharm, M., Sjoqvist, F., & Traskman, L. (1980b). Clomipramine treatment of obsessive–compulsive disorder. II. Biochemical aspects. *Archives of General Psychiatry, 37,* 1289–1294.

Tollefson, G. (1985). Alprazolam in the treatment of obsessive symptoms. *Journal of Clinical Psychopharmacology, 5,* 39–42.

Turner, S., Jacob, R., Beidel, D., & Himmelhoch, J. (1985). Fluoxetine treatment of obsessive–compulsive disorder. *Journal of Clinical Psychopharmacology, 5,* 207–212.

Virkkunen, M., Nuutila, A., Goodwin, F., & Linnoila, M. (1987). Cerebrospinal fluid monomine metabolite levels in male arsonists. *Archives of General Psychiatry, 44,* 241–247.

Volavka, J., Neziroglu, F., & Yaryura-Tobias, J. (1984). Clomipramine and imipramine in obsessive–compulsive disorder. *Psychiatry Research, 14,* 83–91.

Warneke, L. (1984). The use of intravenous chlormipramine in the treatment of obsessive compulsive disorder. *Canadian Journal of Psychiatry, 46,* 135–141.

Warneke, L. (1985). Intravenous chlorimipramine in the treatment of obsessional disorder in adolescence: Case report. *Journal of Clinical Psychiatry, 46,* 100–103.

Weizman, A., Carmi, M., Hermesh, H., Shahar, A., Apter, A., Tyano, S., & Rehavi, M. (1986). High-affinity imipramine binding and serotonin uptake in platelets of eight adolescent and ten adult obsessive–compulsive patients. *American Journal of Psychiatry, 143,* 335–339.

Winslow, J. T., & Insel, T. Neuroethological models of obsessive–compulsive disorder. In J. Zohar, T. Insel, & S. Rasmussen (Eds.), *The psychobiology of obsessive–compulsive disorder* (pp.   ). New York: Springer Publishing Company.

Yaryura-Tobias, J., Turner, S., Michelson, L., & Jacob, R. (1976). Chlorimipramine for obsessive–compulsive neurosis: An organic approach. *Current Therapy Research, 20,* 541–548.

Yaryura-Tobias, J., & Bhagavan, H. (1977). L-tryptophan in obsessive–compulsive disorders. *American Journal of Psychiatry, 134,* 1298–1299.

Zohar, J., & Insel, T. (1987). Obsessive–compulsive disorder: Pychobiological approaches to diagnosis, treatment, and pathophysiology. *Biological Psychiatry, 22,* 667–687.

Zohar, J., Insel, T., Zohar-Kadouch, R., Hill, J., & Murphy, D. (1988). Serotonergic responsivity in obsessive–compulsive disorder. *Archives of General Psychiatry, 45,* 167–172.

Zohar, J., Mueller, E., Insel, T., Zohar-Kadouch, R., & Murphy, D. (1987). Sertonergic responsivity in obsessive–compulsive disorder. *Archives of General Psychiatry, 44,* 946–951.

Index